# LightWave 3D™
# Character Animation

**Timothy Albee**

Wordware Publishing, Inc.

**Library of Congress Cataloging-in-Publication Data**

Albee, Timothy.
  Lightwave 3D 7 character animation / by Timothy Albee.
    p. cm.
  Includes index.
  ISBN 1-55622-901-1
  1. Computer animation. 2. Computer graphics. 3. LightWave 3D. I.
Title.
  TR897.7 .A43 2002
  006.6'96--dc21                           2002001741

ISBN 1-55622-901-1

10 9 8 7 6 5 4 3 2 1
0203

All inquiries for volume purchases of this book should be addressed to Wordware Publishing, Inc., at the
above address. Telephone inquiries may be made by calling:

(972) 423-0090

# Contents

# Foreword

Perhaps you're one of those people who, as a kid, sat in a darkened movie theater watching a great animated movie and said to yourself: "I want to do that."

I know I was. At the time, all I could do was draw my own "flipbooks," as there was very little written about the technique of animation. The big breakthrough for me came when I discovered something called an "Animation Kit" at Disneyland some 45 years ago. It consisted of a simple light board, some model sheets of Disney characters, a booklet on "How to Animate," and some punched paper.

With this animation kit, I could finally create my own animation! After seeing my first pencil tests, I was hooked. My fate was sealed. I knew this was what I wanted to do with my life.

Of course, my first work was quite crude; so my next task was to find a way to learn the skills it took to become a real animator.

A generation or two ago, there were no schools teaching animation. About the only way to learn "the craft" was to serve an often lengthy apprenticeship with a journeyman animator. Slowly, under this apprenticeship, the secrets of animation would be revealed at a rate designed (no doubt for job security) by those who held the few positions there were as animators.

I was lucky in that I was able to study under the great master animator Art Babbit, who animated the queen in *Snow White* and Geppetto in *Pinocchio*. Art maintained that an animator should be something of a Renaissance man. He should be well-read and be well versed in the arts, including painting, drawing, music, dance, and films. In other words, in order to portray life, you needed to understand life. In 1980, Art disliked intensely the idea that computers might someday "take over" the animation business. He said if they did, the operator would have to be an animator. He was certainly right about that.

The art of animation was brought to one of its high points during the 1940s at the Disney studios by a group of animators known as "the nine old men." They were revered by their underlings as almost "god-like" and have since been accorded the greatest of respect by everyone in the industry. The performances they leave us today are among our greatest cultural treasures. Their work has served as an inspiration to countless young students of the craft. Any serious study of animation must include the works of these masters.

Animation has changed much in recent years. A great deal of this change is due to a resurgence of interest in it as a medium, and the introduction of the computer as an animator's tool. Although the work of the early computer animation pioneers was revolutionary and impressive, I believe it was not until experienced traditional and stop motion animators learned to use computers that the CG industry as we know it today was born. The responsibilities of the animator did not change when animators exchanged their pencils for mice and keyboards. Now they simply had a very powerful assistant that relieved them of the burden of drawing and could quickly generate perfect inbetweens. But it will always require someone with the skills of an animator to bring a character to life, no matter what the medium.

With all this activity, there is now a great demand for the knowledge that created the big CG hits of today. There are a few good schools that teach animation, but of course, the quality of instruction is only as good as the instructors themselves. And not all of them have hands-on experience in the field. There is nothing like learning from someone who has been in the trenches as the author of this book has been for many years. Until recently, there has been relatively little written about the actual hands-on, nuts-and-bolts process of creating an animated performance. The problem I find with most animation books today is they give you only part of the picture. Some books on animation have emphasized only the technical side. Other books talk only about acting. Still others concentrate on action analysis. This book represents one-stop shopping for the aspiring computer animator. Not only does it deal with all the technical mysteries of such things as Inverse Kinematics but it also reveals all of the time-honored principles of classical character animation.

In my career, I have met only a very small handful of individuals whose knowledge encompasses both the technical and the artistic aspects of animation. Such a person is a rare bird indeed, and Timothy Albee is one of these. Tim takes you step by step through all the stages you will need to bring your characters to life. You have here, distilled into one book, all the skills and knowledge you need to begin to create your own performances.

Now the rest is up to you.

Tom Roth
Animator, *Hercules* (Hades), *Dinosaur* (Yar), *Stuart Little*, *Shrek*, *All Dogs Go to Heaven*, *Scooby Doo*

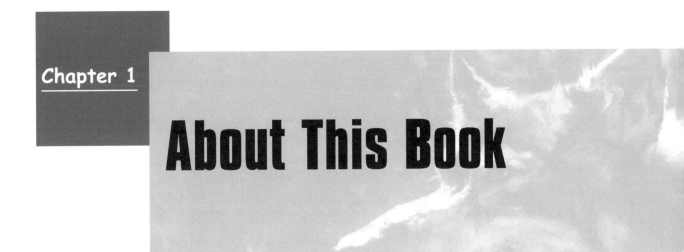

## Chapter 1

# About This Book

## 1.1 Who is This Book For?

This book is for anyone who has ever had a character in their heart that they've wanted to bring to life with as much fluidity, power, and grace as can be seen in the best animated feature films. This is a book for anyone who has wanted to become an animator but hasn't gone to Sheridan College in Toronto or CalArts in Valencia. This is a book for animators who have progressed as far as they can on their own and want to hone their skills to the level of feature-quality animation. This is a book for feature-quality animators skilled on other software platforms who have a project that requires them to use LightWave.

This is the book I wish had been available when I was starting out as a LightWave animator.

This is not just a book on how to set up and point weight characters. It is not yet another book that covers the same basics that nearly every other book on animation presents as "all-there-is-to-know." This book covers the complex animation mechanics that are locked inside every beautifully animated scene but that are difficult to understand until someone shows you how. It took many gifted people with careers in animation going back over 30 years to show me what I hadn't learned in school or in the books I'd read. I've taught many people who've worked for me on projects ranging from films to video games how to see, understand, and internalize these techniques and subtleties. It is my goal in this book to pass this information on to a much larger audience, and by doing so, raise the level of animators and the way others perceive animators all across the board.

Animation is an incredible art. It encompasses so much technical and artistic skills that in my experience, nothing else comes close to the impact it has on the artist or the viewer. We're moved by good animation in a way we can't explain. And there are those of us who are so touched by it that it consumes us and we have to make it a part of ourselves. We give our lives to it. And once we finally understand how to breathe life into these ideas and archetypes we have had deep within our own mind's eye, there is no better place to be than in the space that is created when you're animating.

When you're working on a piece, time drops away. And it's not like working on a painting where the characters never move. You're working on a "drawing" that lasts through time; you're drawing in four dimensions. Your characters evolve ever so slightly from the beginning to the end of your scene, and in that they begin to breathe life of their own. This only happens, however, when you know the simple and complex mechanics of animation so well that they become a part of you; you don't have to think about them and you can just let the scene flow out through you.

We, as computer animators, have a much bigger challenge than traditional animators. Sure, the computer takes care of perspective for us, and we don't need an army of inbetweeners and digital ink and painters to see our work in the smoothness of animating on "ones" (a new image on every frame) and the beauty of brilliant color. But we do have issues and problems that traditional artists have never had to think about. I don't think it's ever been on record that a pencil has frozen or crashed and erased a stack of drawings—a day's work—because the animator forgot to save. Traditional animators don't also have to be "technical directors" and understand how to build setups that let them be creative, rather than fighting the computer every step of the way. They don't have to figure out why even though their character's hand is still flat on the table, his arm is now sticking straight out behind him. More often than not, we as computer animators have had to learn how to cope with all of this on our own, even if we did go to school for it.

This book is here to give you the tools you need to stop fighting the computer. It is here to let you learn and internalize the things that make animation come to life so your evolution as an animator can really begin. This is only the first step, but it is a first step from the point of view of feature-quality animation, and that is what will make all the difference in the world.

Yes, this book focuses on LightWave, and the sections on character setup show step by step how to use LightWave's Inverse Kinematics (IK) to build strong, dependable setups you can use for any character you envision. But even if you are using another package, if it supports a strong, dependable IK engine, the information will help you all the same. The buttons may be different between packages, but IK is still IK. What separates 3D packages in terms of those that are good for character animation and those that aren't is the solidity of the package's IK engine. LightWave has one of the best—quietly and without hype. (If you are using another software package, I'd suggest trying LightWave; you might just be pleasantly surprised. I've used all the major packages on projects from feature films to video games, and I keep coming back to LightWave. I've amazed motion technical directors with how much more powerful the setups on LightWave can be than on packages costing many times more.)

Everything else in this book will be directly useful to you regardless of what 3D software you're using (even if you're animating on paper)! Whether you are a traditional animator or computer animator, you must first and foremost be a good animator. Understanding the mechanics of animation, both the simple and complex, should be your primary goal. The computer provides the tools; you provide the force that drives them.

## 1.2 How to Use This Book

This book is broken down into sections. Each section deals with a different aspect of the character setup and animation process. If you're like most folks out there, you want to learn as much as you can about all parts of this gig. That's great! This book will cover everything you need to know to take your model, set him up for animation, learn the controls that make him move, and get him moving like a character that should be on the big screen.

If you're only interested in one aspect of this process, that's OK too! In today's high-end studios people are highly specialized and often times an animator won't know anything about modeling and is happy to keep it that way. If your focus is on learning to become a better animator, and that's it, the latter sections will give you all you need to know. There are scenes you can load that have all your setups and props made for you and you can jump right into bettering your skills as an animator.

3

If you want to be a better technical director and you don't really see yourself as having to ever animate a scene, the sections you'll be most interested in are the ones close to the front of the book. Pre-bending, boning, IK, and point weighting are all covered there.

Then there are those who are already a master at one aspect but want to get a handle on the others. This is a really good idea because you understand the issues those on the "other side" have to deal with, and if you're a hot-shot animator, you're much more likely to treat a TD with understanding if you know what it takes to get that character setup the way it is, and vice versa. For you folks (and the people new to LightWave from another package), there are two things you'll want to keep your eyes open for.

## NEWBIE NOTE:

Newbie notes are short little blips that give bits of information that you might not be familiar with, things to watch out for, and the like.

## NEWBIE BLOCKS

These are longer sections that will help you to get up to speed if you know Modeler but not Layout, or the other way around, or if you're new to LightWave from another package. Those of you who know how to get around inside these modules can most likely skip right over these blocks. Newbie blocks are here so you don't have to break your flow of concentration by turning to the LightWave manuals. There's no way for me to cover everything in these blocks, just the basics. I'm just trying to eliminate a bit of the frustration I remember trying to make an origami model when the book left out some important step because "everyone" was supposed to know it already.

> **NOTE:**
>
> Notes, on the other hand, are things that everyone should watch for. Notes are things that might help you right away, or they may be things that you'll keep in the back of your mind for a time later on down the road. They're bits of information that I've picked up along the way that will probably help you too.

> **ADVANCED NOTE:**
>
> Advanced notes are for the hard-core group. These are for the guys (and gals) who like to pull things apart to find out how they work. These are for the folks who aren't satisfied with just using something that works; they want to know how it works, and how they can modify it to suit their needs. You know who you are and these notes are for you.

# 1.3 The Models

This book ships with a CD that has models and test scenes on it. You're welcome to use the models for your own work; that's why they're there! (Not everyone is a modeler, right?) But if you do use one or some of the models, please give credit to the guy who built them for ya. Doesn't have to be much, just a passing nod, that's all I ask.

So, there are a couple of human characters on the CD for you to start creating character interaction. There are also some cartoony characters for you to squash and stretch to your heart's content. (There's also a realistic animal, if you're feeling daring. I have to tell you, though, quadrupedal animation is enough for a book unto itself.) Use these and have fun! Create some wonderful animations that'll look fantastic on that demo reel of yours! The exercises in the book will show you how!

## 1.4 **The Exercises**

This book is full of exercises, from life drawing in 3D to analyzing animation. Please take the time to do every one. There may be things you've already encountered, especially in the chapter on the basics of animation, but treat each exercise as though it were a scene you've been assigned that will eventually be reviewed by a director (and his entourage). Never knowingly leave anything wrong with your scene. Even if it is something rudimentary, like having your character getting up out of a chair or swinging a baseball bat, give that scene feeling, let your character have a reason for being in that chair at that moment, and let that reason show through in the action. Like Degas, show a moment in time. Let it seem that your character existed before the scene began and will go on after the scene ends. In treating each scene like this, your animation will grow farther and faster than you ever thought possible.

It is my greatest wish that you'll use this information to become the animator you've always wished you could be. Though I cannot promise to respond to every e-mail, if you have a movie of a scene that you're particularly proud of, pack it up as small as possible (and still have it readable) and send it my way (TimothyA@ptiAlaska.net); I'd love to see it. If I can, I'll make comments on it and get them back to you. Hopefully, in the not-too-distant future, I'll be watching for your name in the credits of a cool animated piece!

## Chapter 2

# Inverse Kinematics: Its Strengths and Weaknesses

## 2.1 IK

Inverse Kinematics (IK) is probably the single most important innovation to computer character animation. More important than cloth or fur simulations, more helpful than subdivision surfaces, it is the one tool that lets us as animators stop fighting the limitations of the software and start becoming artists again.

IK isn't perfect, and when it first began to be implemented in software packages, it was very disappointing. The mathematical engines, the "solvers," that calculate the rotations required for a chain of objects to reach a desired point have gotten a lot faster and more stable, but IK is still misunderstood.

When rumors of this new system of calculating rotations began to surface back in the early '90s, I think every one of us who was struggling with Forward Kinematics (FK) to attempt computer character animation had grand ideas of what it was going to be able to do. It was rumored to be capable of figuring out rotations for all parts of a body. All we'd have to do is sit back like a director and position hands and feet, and the computer would do the rest. It didn't quite work out that way.

IK was, and still is, hard to set up. And if you managed to figure out how to use IK, there were all these problems with miscalculations—legs bending the wrong way, arms and elbows flipping. It was a nightmare. Most of us just put our heads together to figure out clever ways of setting up FK hierarchies that would keep our character's feet from slipping and still be relatively easy to use.

There were some hard-core people out there, most of whom are what they call "motion technical directors" in the industry, who kept tinkering with IK. They were putting together little bits of IK chains until they broke and finding out where things began to fall apart. Thanks to the research these guys were doing, a set of rules began to evolve. If you stayed within these rules, IK began to behave with relative predictability. Character setups began to evolve from these much smaller, much simpler IK chains—setups that worked, setups that were dependable. You could twist and turn and tie your character up in knots and the setups (mostly) held together. These setups began appearing in the film, television, and gaming industries, and what at one time took days could be done in hours. IK did revolutionize computer character animation—it just took a while.

> **NOTE:**
>
> I like to use the phrase "easy power." This is a guideline that I think applies to everything in animation. It means to keep within your limits when the result really matters. If you do something at the outside edge of your ability and falter even a little, people will notice (the people who matter in "the industry," that is). If you do something within your range of do-ability, and you do it so well that your viewer is left awestruck and with a feeling that you could do way more but that you choose not to, <u>that</u> is doing something with "easy power." This applies not just to our own abilities, but to the computer's as well. (Picture in your mind facing down a starship turning easily in space to angle its guns toward you, a starship so big, so powerful looking that you just say, "Nope, forget it, my mistake... Bye!" That turn may be the extent of its prowess, but in doing it so well, implying so much more, a point was made.)

## 2.2 **IK's Strengths**

Most IK systems in effect today are fast, powerful, and customizable. You can now have many IK systems calculating at once and not bring the computer to a standstill.

You can assign limits and stiffness to the joints to help keep parts from pointing in directions they shouldn't.

IK is great at solving for the rotation of one or two parts. This means that arms, legs, and necks can all be driven by IK.

LightWave now feeds the rotations generated by IK to (most) other plug-ins so you can now use IK for a broader range of timesaving tools.

LightWave's IK allows you to have varying strengths of how much the chain pulls toward the goal (though it would be even better for this to be animatable). This is helpful in fine-tuning the chains that control the different parts of your character.

## 2.3 **IK's Weaknesses**

IK is not dependable when used to calculate rotations for a chain of more than two parts; this throws too many variables into the mix for IK to calculate properly and it usually makes a mess of things.

IK is not dependable for calculating more than two axes on any given part; this tends to make the part spin unpredictably when you least expect it.

Having too many goal objects attached to parts of other IK chains has been known to cause the IK Solver to miscalculate, resulting in jittering movement rather than smoothly following the goals.

Some software packages (thankfully not LightWave) have abbreviated floating-point calculations, and when you have a character too large or too small, decimal places of the goal's position aren't correctly fed to the IK engine, which results in jittering movement. (These software packages usually behave when you have your chains sized around human proportions.)

Nesting an IK chain at the end of an IK chain at the end of an IK chain can cause miscalculations not only in the child IK systems, but also in the scaling and rotation of the FK children of these systems.

## LightWave-Specific IK Weaknesses (at the time of this writing)

The Match Goal Orientation option has been known to not properly feed scaling, rotation, and translation (SRT) data to items that are children of items with this active.

The Keep Goal Within Reach option does not create keys for the goal object based on where this limitation has positioned it, even with Auto Key active (you must manually create keys for the goal objects that have been constrained or moved before advancing).

Using limits to control rotations of parts more often than not causes them to come to an abrupt and unnatural stop. (Having the stiffness of this joint ramp up in a user-definable way as the part neared the limit would end this problem.)

## Flipping

"Flipping" is a problem you'll run into in all IK systems. Flipping basically happens when a goal object crosses into an invisible zone that radiates from the IK chain's root. In this "flipping zone," your chain may try to pull away from your goal object or invert itself entirely. There are many factors that figure into where these flipping zones occur, including the initial relationships of the chain's parts to each other, and the initial rotation of the chain itself. You can control these zones to a degree by rotating the object to which the chain is parented, thereby swinging the flipping zones slightly out of the way.

Many people have tried to solve the flipping puzzle. Some software packages attempt to show the flipping zone. Some people have attempted to write expressions that control the rotation of the IK chain's root. Some have tried to pull the chain in the proper direction by assigning an external goal object for the second item in the chain. (This solution can have undesirable effects—like pulling too hard on the chain and keeping it from making contact with its goal—and should therefore be used only as a last resort.) So far, no solution really solves all instances of flipping all of the time. One thing I have noticed, though, is that if you're working with a "realistic" character and you're having bad flipping problems, take a closer look at what you're trying to get that character to do. Often times, if the skeleton is fighting you, you might be trying to get it to do something that our own skeletons would balk at as well.

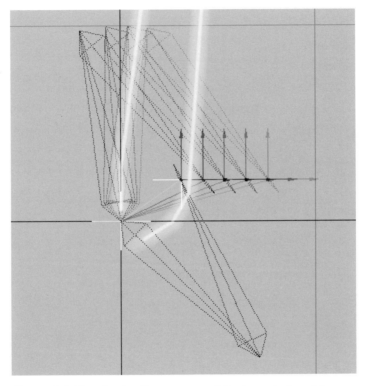

**Figure 2.1** The glowing lines represent the boundaries of the "flipping zone."

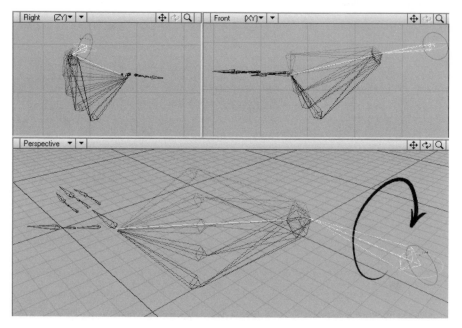

**Figure 2.2** Rotating an IK chain's parent along its bank axis to swing the "elbow" left and right.

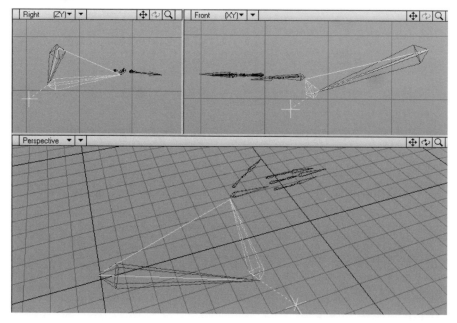

**Figure 2.3** Adding a goal object to help pull the elbow in the direction you want it to go. **CAUTION:** This does not always work and can cause more problems than it solves, but if used with care, it can be like an up-vector.

# 2.4 IK Setup Basics

The LightWave manuals do a good job of explaining all the ins and outs of using all of LightWave's IK settings. If you really want to learn how all of the settings in LightWave's IK controls work, there's nothing better than grabbing that tome and settling in for a nice light read. This section is here just to give a brief and rudimentary walk-through for those not familiar with how to set up IK in LightWave, and who want to feel like they've got a grasp of the concept. It also goes over some basic Layout interface information, so if you're new to Layout, follow along!

IK requires a chain of at least two items and a goal that this chain will strive to reach. In this exercise, we'll be using nulls and bones in LightWave Layout so we don't have to build anything in Modeler. You can't have bones without an object, so we'll first create a null object, and use it to create the bones for this exercise.

1. In Layout, make sure the Items tab is active, and click **Add**.

2. Select **Objects|Add Null....**

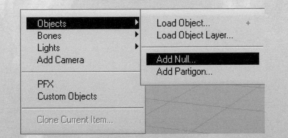

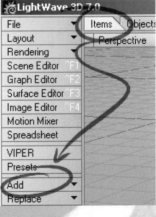

**Figure 2.5**

**Figure 2.4**

3. In the dialog box that appears, press **Enter** or click **OK** to accept the name "Null" for this object.

**Figure 2.6**

## NOTE:

I find it a lot easier to get a clear picture of where things are in 3D space if I set Layout to have more than one viewport. You can do this under **Display|Display Options|Viewport Layout**, or bring up the Display Options window by pressing **d**. (Note the "schematic" view in the illustration. It can make sorting through a complex scene or character setup a breeze! And of course, you can change each of the viewports to whatever you'd like by clicking on its name and choosing what kind of view you want for that window.)

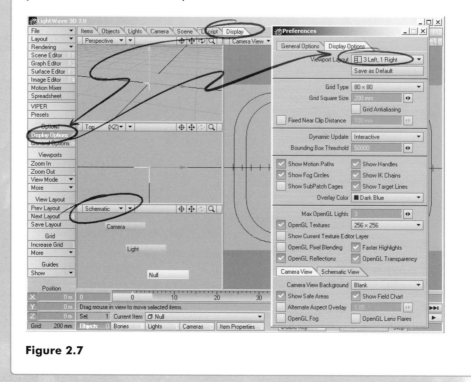

**Figure 2.7**

4. Add a bone to the null by clicking **Add**, and choosing **Bones|Add Bone**. Press **Enter** to accept the name "Bone."

**Figure 2.8**

5. Add a child bone to the one you just created by pressing =. (You can also do this by choosing **Bones|Add Child Bone =**.) Adding a bone this way makes the new bone a child of the bone you had selected. The new bone is the same length as its parent and positioned right at its parent's tip. Press **Enter** to accept the name "Bone." (LightWave will automatically append a revision number—(1), (2), (3)...—to objects with the same name so you can tell them apart easily.)

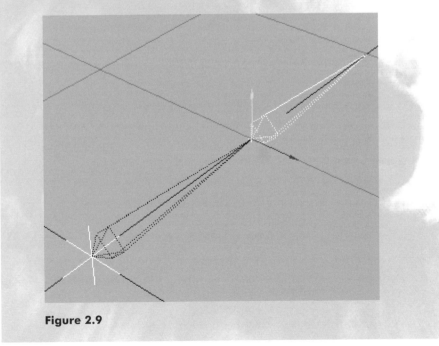

**Figure 2.9**

6. Add another child bone, accepting the default name of "Bone." This is the third bone in the chain and will be used to pull the other two bones toward the goal object we will be making shortly.

7. Set the Rest Length for Bone (3) to 0.100. With the Objects tab active, click on **Rest Length**, and enter **.1** in the numeric field. (I do this so this bone doesn't get in the way visually because it is just used to pull the other two toward the goal object we'll be creating in the next step.)

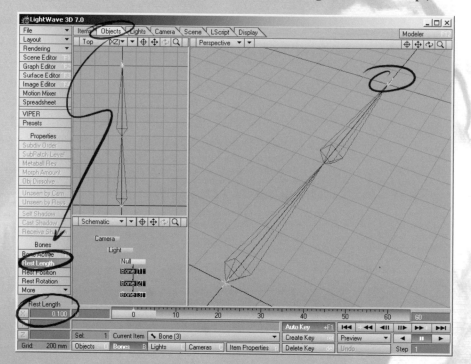

**Figure 2.10**

> **CAUTION:**
>
> When setting the size of a bone initially, you can't just use the Size or Stretch tool because LightWave uses a bone's changes in XYZ scale to warp the points associated with it. You <u>must</u> use Objects|Rest Length to set its initial "length."

8. Add another null object, and name this one "Goal." Position it at the tip of the second bone. (Because bones, by default, are 1 meter in length, you can move the null to the exact tip of the second bone by moving it 2 meters in the Z-axis. Typing this in numerically is a lot easier than eye-balling it.)

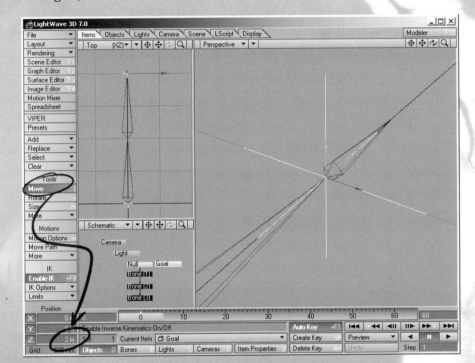

**Figure 2.11**

9. Create a keyframe for "Goal" at its new position if you are not using Auto Key. Pressing **Enter** once (or clicking on the **Create Key** button) brings up the Create Motion Key window. Press **Enter** to accept these settings.

## NOTE:

If you're not familiar with animating in LightWave, you can make your life a lot easier by having Layout automatically create keyframes for you whenever you move an object (or scale or rotate it). You do this by pressing o (Display|General Options) and setting Auto Key Create to Modified Channels or All Motion Channels. You must also have the Auto Key button active in order for LightWave to automatically record your changes (see illustration).

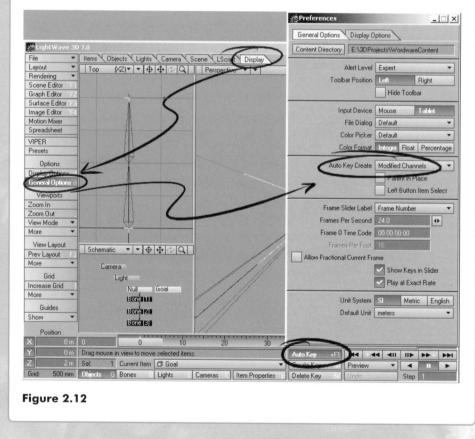

**Figure 2.12**

10. Set the rotational controls for the first bone you created (Bone (1)) to use IK to calculate for heading and pitch. With Bone (1) selected, click on **Motion Options** (or press **m**) to bring up the Motion Options window. On the Controllers and Limits tab, select **Inverse Kinematics** for both Heading Controller and Pitch Controller. This bone will be like a bicep, able to rotate forward and back, up and down.

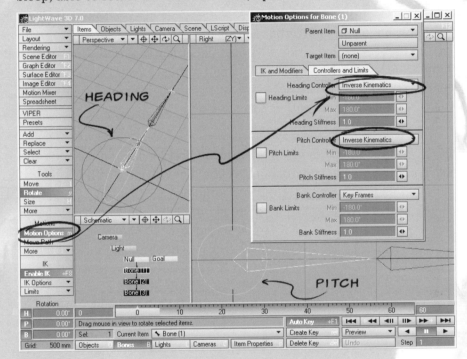

**Figure 2.13**

11. Set the rotational controls for the second bone you created (Bone (2)) to use IK to calculate for pitch only. This bone will be like a forearm, able to bend in only one direction.

12. Set your third bone (Bone (3)) to pull the chain toward the goal object. Select **Motion Options** for your third bone, and on the IK and Modifiers tab, set the Goal Object to **Goal** (the null we created in step 8). Click to check the box next to **Full-time IK**. Bone (3) now becomes an IK "puller" and will stretch the IK chain toward the goal object.

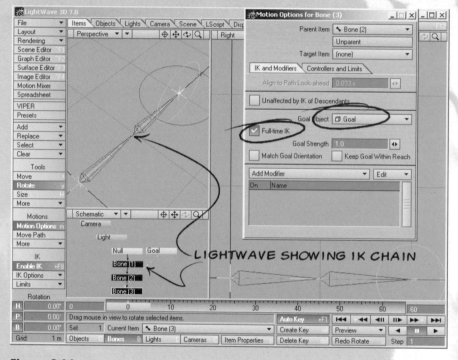

**Figure 2.14**

**CAUTION:**

An IK chain with a puller set to Full-time IK will use IK to figure the rotations for its parts on every single frame. Rotating a part manually on an axis controlled by IK will have no effect. A chain using part-time IK (a chain that doesn't have full-time IK checked on its puller) will seem to work just like a full-time chain when you move the goal object, but rotations are not stored for the chain's parts, _even if you have Auto Key active!_ You must select and create keys manually for each chain part whenever you reposition your goal object if you use part-time IK. (This may seem like a pain, but it can be helpful if you have a computer that is not powerful enough to handle many IK systems solving at once on every single frame.)

13. Move your goal object around and you'll see the chain bending to keep the base of the puller at the goal's center. You'll also notice that with the chain bent, as the goal crosses Y=0 it "pops" over to the other side. Pre-bending the chain in the direction you want it to favor can help this problem.

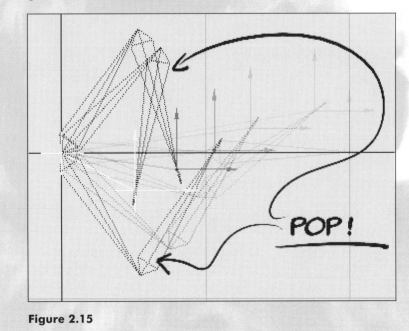

**Figure 2.15**

**NOTE:**

When you activate an IK chain, a light blue line will appear in your scene from the root of your IK chain to the chain's goal if you have Show IK Chains checked under Display|Display Options.

**CAUTION:**

If you're playing around with this scene and exploring (and I encourage you to do so), it may seem like a neat thing to use Match Goal Orientation to keep a hand oriented the same direction as the goal object, but don't. There is (at the time of this writing) some faulty calculation in this function that I haven't been able to figure out that causes severe scale and rotation problems for any object that is a child of an object that has Match Goal Orientation set.

# 2.5 IK Rules

Of course, you can do most anything with IK, and I encourage you to explore and push things past their limits, and find new ways to set up scenes and characters when you have time. But when you really need a setup you can depend on, here is a quick list of rules to follow:

▶ IK is only dependable for solving rotations for a maximum of two items.

▶ On any item controlled by IK, let IK solve for a maximum of two axes (heading and pitch, pitch and bank, or heading and bank).

▶ In a chain of two items, the child should only use IK to solve for one axis.

▶ Always give your IK chain a little "help" by angling the parts in the direction you want them to bend.

This may seem limiting, and it is. We have just restricted IK. We have limited what it could potentially botch and increased what you as an animator need to do. What it also does is put the realm of IK calculations into that range of "easy power" for the computer, giving you confidence that the solver is less likely to bugger things up when you're trying to meet a deadline. It is important to not only know your tools, but also to know that they are solid and will behave predictably. Following these rules in the creation of your own IK setups will result in something you can rely on in almost any situation.

## Chapter 3

# Prepping Your Character for Setup

You've got your character all ready to go, and you want to get started right away in making him (or her) move, act, emote; in general, you want to get him into that performance you've always known he (or she) could do. Before you can animate him, you've got to set him up. And before you can set him up, you've got to prep him for setup, and that means planning.

Planning your setup is probably the most crucial phase of CG animation (no, really). The setup you're going to create will dictate how easy it is to move your character into and out of poses. It will either follow your commands or frustrate the living daylights out of you by misbehaving just when you need the most precise control of your character.

If you build your characters with the same proportions, joints in the same places and whatnot, you'll be able to just plug this setup into your new character once you have him point weighted. Doing the proper planning and prep work makes not only this character work well, but any other character you'll use this setup for in the future.

> **NOTE:**
>
> There are very few "rules of thumb" when dealing with computers. If it isn't already, one of those rules should be: "The things you expect to take a long time on a computer often are the things that get done the quickest, while the things that you expect to breeze through often are the things that take all afternoon." I think one possible reason this is so is because we're paying more attention to the things we do when we think they're complicated. When we think something is easy, our mind isn't always fully there working on it. Keep focused, plan your attack, and know the result you want before you start.

## 3.1 **Where is He Going to Bend?**

Most people build their characters in a kind of "da Vinci-esque" spread-eagle pose. This is great for making sure all the proportions are correct, as you can tell at a glance if something is out of whack. All joints and appendages are out in the open, so to speak, for us to see and figure out where our skeleton's bones should be.

> **NOTE:**
>
> The exercises in this book will be tailored to using the ThinMan.lwo model, available on the companion CD. If you've got a character you're just dying to use, you may, but be aware that you might have to make nip-and-tuck alterations to the information to get it to fit your character. (This is especially so if your character has non-human proportions!)

I've made the character ThinMan.lwo especially for training with this book. His poly/patch count is 1506 polygons/patches. With him, even if you're running LightWave on a 366 MHz laptop, you'll still be able to get a good, workable real-time frame rate while you're animating. Though his lines are broad and caricaturistic, he is proportioned realistically so you'll be able to get a good range of action from him and not have either exaggerated or realistic action look odd on him.

**ADVANCED NOTE:**

To all those modelers out there: The frame rate an animator gets while he's animating your character plays a strong role in how well he can animate him. If you absolutely must have a character with an incredibly high pre-NURBed poly/patch count, also make a "stand-in" character for your animator to work with. This stand-in should have all the joints and bends in all the same places, but at a fraction of the poly/patch count, allowing the animator to animate with ease, then swap the stand-in with your work of art at the time of rendering. (This also allows animation and modeling to go on side by side. As soon as the animator gets the weighted, setup scene with the stand-in model; he can start working, letting modeling continue almost up to the time of the final render.)

1. Copy the 3D directory from the companion CD to a place on your hard drive you'll be able to work from.

2. Start Modeler and set your content directory to the 3D directory you just copied to your hard drive.

**NEWBIE NOTE:**

LightWave Modeler has two separate Options panels. One is for display options (discussed later) and the other is for general options and can be found here: **Modeler|Options |General Options** (or by pressing **o**). General Options has important things like the Content Directory (where LightWave looks for images, objects, scenes, and the like), how many levels of Undo you have, whether polygons will default to quadrangles (for NURBial patches) or triangles, and how smooth your NURBed models will look as you're working on them. (This smoothness is the result of patch division, where the higher the number, the smoother the model will look but the more computationally intensive it will be to draw in real time. I usually use a level of 4.)

3. Load in ThinMan.lwo from Objects\BaseChar\ThinMan.

4. Find the places in the model where the joints will be. Turn the model around in the perspective view. Press **Tab** to convert patches into polygons. Set the view for your perspective window to **Wireframe Shade**. Try to get an idea of what points will need to pull with what bones in order to bend his body in ways that'll look right. (Printing a screen capture of Modeler and sketching rough bone layout or pivot points can be helpful at this point.) Things to note here are the actual points from which the different parts of the body rotate. This isn't always where you might think it is, so move your own arm, fingers, neck, knees, and back and see where these movements correlate to your model.

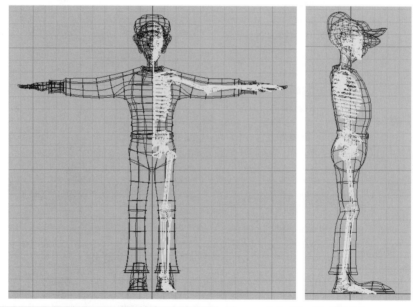

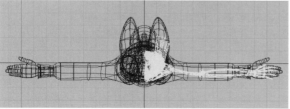

**Figure 3.1, Figure 3.2, Figure 3.3** Front, side, and top views of our character. A good knowledge of anatomy is important whether you are doing cartoonish or hyper-realistic characters. Things like scale, relationship, and rotation are stored deep in all our minds, though it isn't something that most of us are consciously aware of. Most people can't tell you exactly why something looks "right" or "wrong," but it is usually because of something being incorrectly proportioned or rotating from somewhere it shouldn't.

## 3.2 Pre-bending to Help IK

Since IK can only safely solve for a maximum of two parts, we need to look at our model and figure out what parts are going to be controlled with IK and which parts will be FK. Looking at Figures 3.1 through 3.3, the bicep and forearm will be one chain, and the thigh and calf will be another chain. I like having the neck as another chain so I can precisely control the position of the head at all times. That gives us five IK chains; the rest of the model will be FK.

IK needs all the help it can get, so we're going to modify our model a bit to give IK a hand. We're going to put in a much steeper bend at the knees so IK is more likely to bend correctly when our character is in an extreme pose. We're going to do the same for the arms, but with a bit of a twist.

Bones pull points along with them when they are moved or rotated. This is more like a magnet's pull than the way our skin slides over our muscles. This can cause problems in places like elbows, knees, and especially shoulders and under the arms. Things can pinch, bunch, and generally look wrong because it is so hard to get the points that control the model's skin to move like our skin does. A common but cumbersome solution is to build morph-targets that are controlled either manually or by expressions driven by the rotation of the offending bones. I prefer a much simpler strategy: Figure the range of normal movement for that part or set of parts, and have your base pose somewhere in the middle of that range.

Most people are more apt to move their arms forward than back. Most elbows don't like being bent beyond the point where they're straight out from the bicep. So the base pose for the arms should have the bicep angled forward somewhere around 45 degrees, and the forearm angled about 45 degrees from that. This gives us our pre-bend so IK knows that elbows don't bend backward and it also helps preserve the volumes of the elbow and shoulder when bones pull points around.

1. Pre-bend your model's arms so they match those in Figure 3.4. Pay close attention to the points in the underarm area. Make sure your model looks as if there is a body there under the shirt, and that the shirt hangs naturally from this frame.

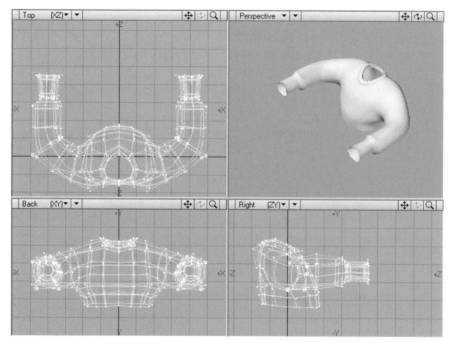

**Figure 3.4** Pre-bending the arms, preserving the volume of the bent elbow.

### NOTE:

When rotating selections of points for the arms, legs, or whatever, try to bear in mind where the joints would be in an actual skeleton (Figures 3.1 to 3.3). If you rotate your point selection from these joints, you'll have a much quicker time of point pulling to make your model look correct.

## NEWBIE NOTE:

Creating point selection sets (**Display|Grouping|Point Selection Sets...**) not only helps you know what points are what when you're pre-bending your model, it also makes things much easier when you're point weighting as well. (You add points to your selection from a selection set you've created by bringing up the Point Statistics window by pressing w with Points ^G active. You choose the point selection set you've created from the list, and click on the "+" symbol to its left. See Figure 3.5.)

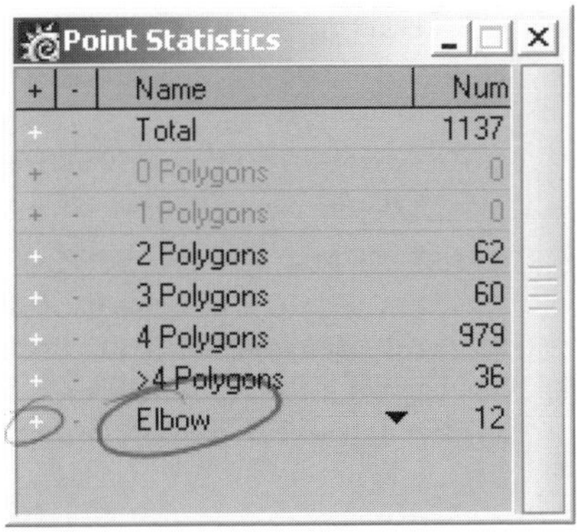

**Figure 3.5** Adding points from a selection set to your current selection.

## NEWBIE NOTE:

Make use of all the tools at your disposal when doing delicate point work. Press 0 (on the numeric keypad) to make windows go "full-screen" to get better views of tight areas. Hide and unhide parts of your model to get a clear shot at what you're trying to manipulate. Go back and forth between polygons and meta-NURBS to see how smoothly rings of points are laying. Alternate between Smooth Shade and Wireframe Shade in your Perspective window to see which points are causing bumps in your model. Activate and deactivate showing point selections, polygon selections, cages, guides, and whatnot in your Perspective window to eliminate clutter when you really need to see detail. (Press d to bring up the Display Options window. Choose the Viewports tab. Viewport 2 controls the upper-right window, the Perspective window by default. Click on Independent Visibility and you can enable and disable settings to make your modeling life easier.)

---

**CAUTION:**

Using Symmetry (**Modes|Symmetry On/Off**) can be a great help, but only if your model is <u>exactly</u> symmetrical before you start pulling points around. If a point is close but not exactly mirrored across the X-axis of your model, it won't be automatically selected when you select the point on the +x side of your model. You can get working on details and forget about this and have half of your model correct, and the other half misshapen. You can correct this by cutting your model down the center and mirroring. Mirroring, however, directly copies over all point weight information, so if you mirror your character's right side to become its left, both thighs (for example) will have exactly the same weight maps targeted at the RightThigh bone.

---

2. Pre-bend your character's legs to match those in Figure 3.6. Preserve the volume of the knee (see Figure 3.7) when bending points to make it look like there actually is a knee inside that tube of virtual fabric. Pay special attention to the pelvic area; you'll often see deep folds in the front of the pants when you swing the legs forward. You'll also have to watch the glutial area; it tends to get flat when legs are swung forward. Pull points to make this base pose look believable.

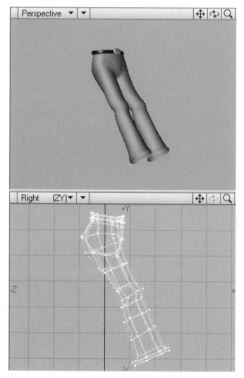

**Figure 3.6** Paying attention to the pelvic and glutial areas as the legs are swung forward to pre-bend for IK.

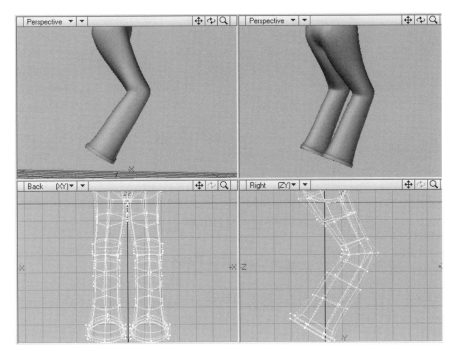

**Figure 3.7** Preserving the volume of the knees.

3. Lower the body and head to account for the height that was lost when we bent the knees. When you're doing this, tweak the points of the pant cuff to fall properly over the shoe. You'll also need to pull the top part of the shoe to be bent by the calf section angling toward the knee.

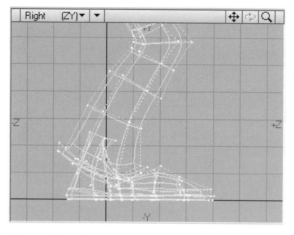

**Figure 3.8** Pulling the points of the pant cuff and shoe to make the bend of this area look believable.

4. Check the alignment and position the hands. Make sure they look natural within the shirt cuffs and the fingers point straight forward.

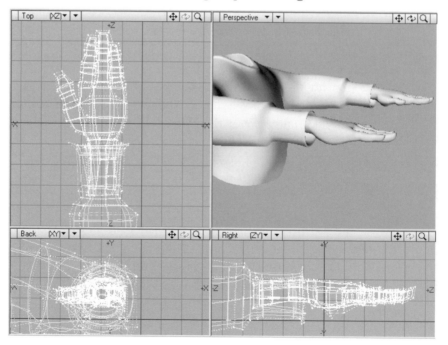

**Figure 3.9** Making sure the hands look right.

**NOTE:**

You may have noticed that our character only has four fingers. There's a convention in character design that says human characters have five fingers, animal characters have four. I break this convention in CG when I'm working with a cartoon human. This is just my personal preference, but it saves a lot of cumulative time in animation, and the clients I've dealt with would rather have better overall animation than an extra finger.

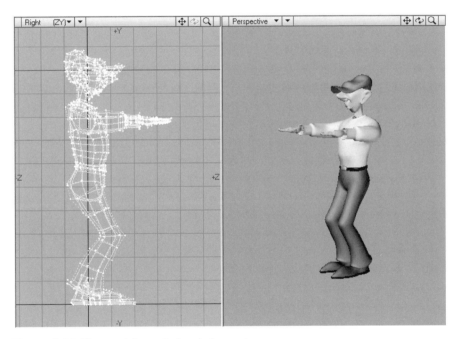

**Figure 3.10** The model, ready for skelegons!

## Chapter 4

# Boning Your Character

> **NOTE:**
>
> As you continue to work in CG, you'll notice that you "hit the groove." This is when things just flow. Whether you're animating or modeling, everything just falls right into place. Time seems to drop away, and you achieve as close to a Zen state as you can and still be using a computer. The problem is that this is usually the time when the computer crashes, the network freezes, or any number of other problems trash what you did since your last save. Oh, and when you're in that Zen state, you never seem to save. So you've lost your best work of the day. One would think that since you did it once, it would be easier the second time—not at all. The only remedy to this is to save often, and make a habit of it! Not just save, but save <u>revisions</u>. Crashes have happened in the middle of a save, and that corrupts what might be days or weeks worth of work (if that happens to your only version of the model or scene)! I often work revisions in pairs, saving first over "Blah_01.lwo," and then over "Blah_02.lwo." That way I've always got a backup that'll be safe (unless the drive head crashes or self-destructs in some other way). Also, always move on to a new set of revision numbers <u>any time you make a major change</u>! This may make for a whole lot of revisions in a directory, but it frees you to safely experiment knowing you can always go back (whether the decision is yours or your director's) to the way it was before.

# 4.1 Adding Bones to Your Character

We're ready to start adding bones to our character. Some of the bones will be used to pull the points of our character around. Others will be used to control the movements of these bones. We'll be using the skelegon tools in Modeler to put these bones in place. I find this saves time, lets you save the bone setup with the character, and gives you access to a whole slew of free Modeler plug-ins that make point weighting much easier.

---

**ADVANCED NOTE:**

If you are switching to LightWave from another package, be aware of the fact that all of our control objects <u>must</u> be bones. Other packages allow bones to exist as children of another object, taking all SRT (scaling, rotation, and translation) information from the parent object. This lets you have icons to represent the different controls that are quick and easy to distinguish from one another when your character is in a complex pose. LightWave 6.5 will not allow you to do this! Plug-ins such as LW Follower do not properly feed SRT information when working with the nested controls needed to overcome "gimbal lock" (the phenomenon of heading and bank becoming one and the same as pitch approaches 90° or –90°). LW Sock Monkey would theoretically work; however, neither I nor anyone I've talked with has been able to get reliable, reproducible results from it. If you are hooked on having the ease of instantly identifying a control object at a glance, you can work around this problem by selecting the desired parent item for the current bone in LightWave 6.0 under the object motion options. Save the scene, then reload it on your machine running 7. The "bug" of being able to parent bones to items outside of their parent object was fixed in 6.5, but when you load the saved scene, it works perfectly (and I have pressed this technique trying to see if it breaks, and in every scene I've used this trick it has worked perfectly. I cannot see any reason for this restriction).

---

1. Load the character you pre-bent for IK in the last chapter into Modeler. (If all you want to do is animate and you never see yourself modeling and you skipped the pre-bending, I've got a pre-bent model already made which you can find in Objects\chapters\ch_04.lwo.

2. Maximize the Right viewport and press **a** to Fit All.

3. Set your Foreground (Active) Layer to **Layer 2**, and your Background Layer to **Layer 1**.

## LightWave Modeler Layers

Clicking in the upper triangle makes that layer the foreground layer. You can view and modify items in this layer. Clicking in the lower triangle makes that layer the background layer. Items in this layer can be seen but not modified. (Holding down Shift while clicking adds or removes layers from your selected foreground or background layers.)

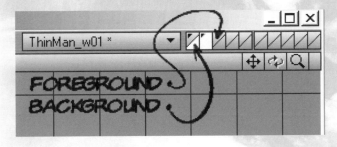

**Figure 4.1**

**NOTE:**

The order in which you create the skelegons in Modeler is the order in which they will become bones in Layout. I like to use the Up and Down Arrow keys when animating to select the next and previous bones, and have memorized how many presses it takes to get from one specific control to another. (For instance, with Spine1 selected, pressing the Down Arrow three times will select the Head control, one more press selects the RightHand_Trans control.) This lets me keep my eyes glued to my scene without breaking my concentration to go to a schematic view or to scroll visually through a list. This is why we'll be creating skelegons in a seemingly haphazard way; it actually makes animation much easier, for some, in the long run.

## 4.2 Spinal Controls

Spinal controls are the FK bones that will control the bending of your character's torso. These are the bones you will use first in posing your character to get a strong line of motion.

1. Create the skelegon that will be the bone that will be the root of your skeleton. Draw this bone as close to horizontal as you can and have its tip be where the spine connects with the pelvis. Remember that your spine is closer to your back than your front!

2. Create the skelegon that will be our character's pelvis as shown in Figure 4.2.

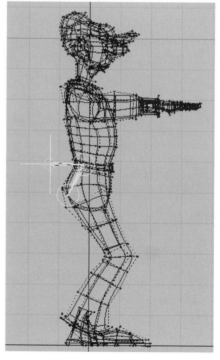

**Figure 4.2**  Angle the pelvis back, following the line of the tailbone.

> **NOTE:**
>
> Many people create skeletons with the buttocks as the base. I create mine with the lumbar area as the skeleton's base. This allows you to swing the hips without having to counter animate the spine. This makes animating everything from walks to slouches much faster and easier.

## Creating Skelegons

To create a skelegon, click on **Create| Skelegons**. Then, click and drag to create a skelegon.

While Create| Skelegons is active, clicking and dragging within either of the two circles at the base and head of the skelegon will drag that end to a new location. Clicking outside of those two circles will create another skelegon that is a child of the one you just created.

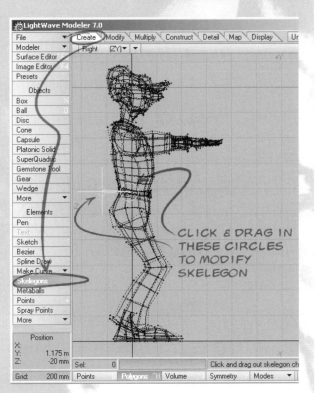

CLICK & DRAG IN THESE CIRCLES TO MODIFY SKELEGON

**Figure 4.3** This bone will be the root of your skeleton.

### NOTE:

Grid Snap can help or hinder you depending on what you're trying to do at that moment in Modeler. Activate Grid Snap, Display|View Options |Units|Grid Snap when you need to make things snap to an invisible grid (good for aligning items), and deactivate it when you need to make fine, delicate changes.

### NOTE:

Skelegons are considered polygons. You can select them with Polygons ^H active. Even though they look like they've got several polygons to them, LightWave treats each skelegon as a single polygon. Under the Polygon Statistics window (pressing w with Polygons ^H active) each skelegon is listed under its name in the Part drop-down list (the bottom line in the Polygon Statistics window).

3. Deactivate the Create|Skelegons tool by clicking on the **Polygons** ^H button.

4. Select the first skelegon we created.

5. Reactivate the Create|Skelegons tool.

6. Draw the skelegons that will be the first, second, and third spine bones. (Because we had our Root skelegon selected, the new skelegons are created as its children instead of children of the Pelvis, the last bone we created.)

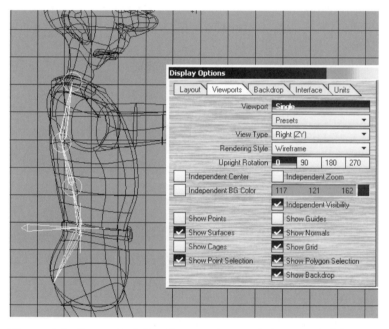

**Figure 4.4** Be sure to follow the curvature and placement of the spine in these skelegons. (I've turned off points, cages, and guides so I can more easily see what I'm doing.)

7. Deactivate the Create|Skelegons tool and select our Root skelegon again.

8. Name this skelegon **Root**.

## Naming Skelegons

Name skelegons by selecting them individually and choosing **Detail|Other| More|Rename Skelegon....** Naming a skelegon not only helps us tell skelegons apart, but also the bones and weight maps that will be generated automatically from these skelegons.

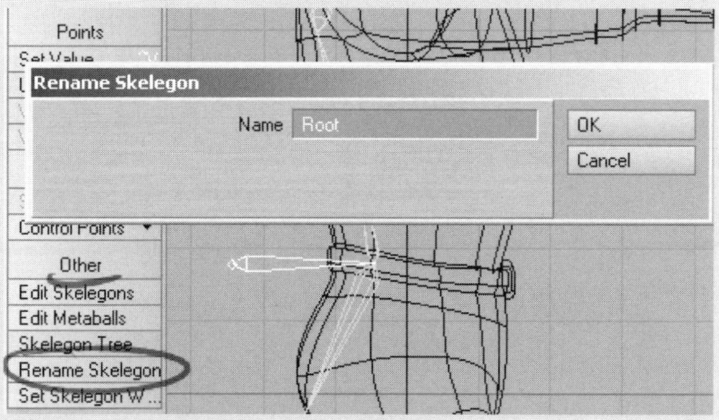

> Points
> Set Value
> **Rename Skelegon**
> Name  Root
> OK
> Cancel
>
> Control Points
> Other
> Edit Skelegons
> Edit Metaballs
> Skelegon Tree
> Rename Skelegon
> Set Skelegon W...

**Figure 4.5** Making it easier to know which skelegon is which.

9.  Rename the other skelegons **Pelvis**, **Spine1**, **Spine2**, and **Spine3** respectively (Spine1 being the most immediate child of Root).

10. Press **Ctrl+t** to activate Drag mode, and click-and-drag on the base (the stubby end, not the pointy end) of our Root skelegon. Drag this end close to where it meets with the Pelvis and Spine1 skelegons.

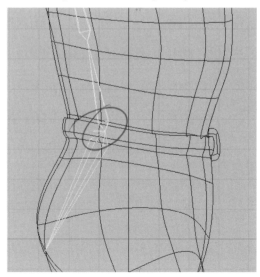

**Figure 4.6** Root will rotate from its base, and though it won't directly control any points in our model, it will control the bones that do. Having its rotation centered inside the body helps us much more than being able to see the bone from a distance.

11. Create another skelegon inside the character's head, making sure no other skelegons are selected before doing so. Name this bone **Head**.

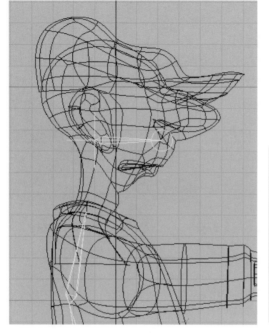

**NOTE:**

Sometimes, even with no skelegon selected, LightWave will draw new skelegons as children of a previously created skelegon. You can solve this problem by hiding all skelegons before drawing new ones.

**Figure 4.7** The base of this bone is at the juncture where the skull sits on the spinal column.

# 4.3 **Hand Controls**

Hand controls are used to move and rotate the hands. We'll also be building controls that will let us shrug the shoulders, expand or cave the chest, and rotate the elbow up or down.

1. Create and place another skelegon that reaches from the center of the wrist to the center of the middle finger's root knuckle. Name this bone **RightHand_Trans**.

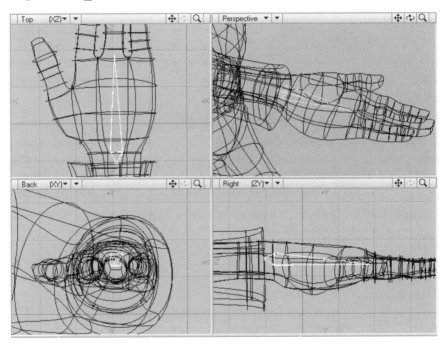

**Figure 4.8**  This bone will control the translation of the hand and its heading and bank.

2. Copy RightHand_Trans, then drag its tip (the pointy end) to somewhere around the middle of the palm.

3. Paste to create a new skelegon. Name this one **RightHand_Rot**.

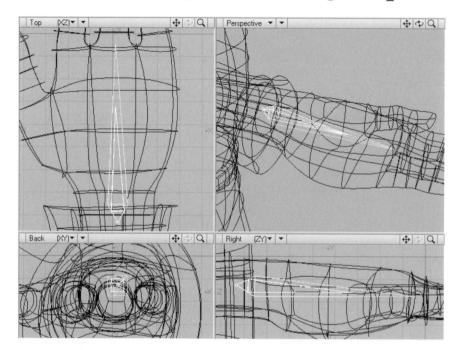

**Figure 4.9**  This bone will control the hand's pitch. Having these bones a different length makes them easer to select without using the Polygon Statistics window.

> ## NOTE:
>
> Now that LightWave has the ability to rotate objects in Layout based upon world coordinates, nesting controls as we are doing for the hand isn't technically necessary to control gimbal lock. Yes, it does mean that there is yet another control to consider during animation, but I find that I can more precisely control hand animation this way. So much acting comes from subtleties of the hands, and for me to be able to dictate exactly which way a wrist will unfold in a scene with complex acting is more important than eliminating a control.

4. Create a skelegon that follows the placement of the scapula. Place its tip where the shoulder joint will be. Name this skelegon **RightShoulder**.

5. With RightShoulder selected, create a tiny bone that points along the bicep toward the elbow. Name this skelegon **RightElbow**.

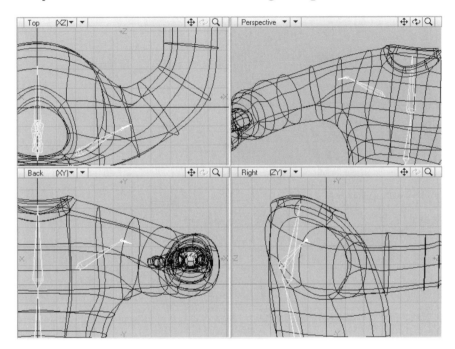

**Figure 4.10** RightShoulder and RightElbow.

6. Select **RightShoulder**, **RightElbow**, **RightHand_Trans**, and **RightHand_Rot**.

7.  Mirror them along the X-axis <u>without</u> merging points. Rename the new skelegons **LeftShoulder**, **LeftElbow**, **LeftHand_Trans**, and **LeftHand_Rot**, respectively.

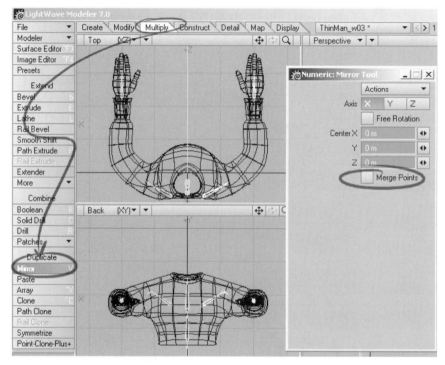

**Figure 4.11**   Mirroring the hand controls.

## Mirroring

1. With your skelegons selected, press **V** (case is sensitive with LightWave hotkeys) or select **Multiply|Mirror**.

2. Press **n** to open the Numeric input window.

3. Press **n** a second time to activate the controls. Make sure the X-axis is selected, and that the center is set to 0m along the X-, Y-, and Z-axes.

4. Deselect **Merge Points**. (This will automatically perform a **Merge Points|Automatic** after mirroring. This is handy in a lot of cases, but we want to know that any points on these skelegons that we don't merge on purpose stay that way; it can affect hierarchy.)

5. Close the Numeric window and press the **Spacebar** to drop the Mirror tool.

# 4.4 Foot Controls

Foot controls will control the placement of the foot and the bend of the toes. We'll also be creating the control for swinging the knee in and out.

**NOTE:**

If your character is digitigrade, meaning he walks on his toes, you'll need to use a different setup for his feet. You'll find this setup in Chapter 15, along with important notes on how to handle digitigrade and animal motion.

1. Create a skelegon for the right foot. Position its base in the center of the ankle, and its tip in the center of the ball of the foot.

2. Create a second skelegon (a child of the previous one) that stretches to the tip of the shoe. Name these two skelegons **RightFoot** and **RightToes** respectively.

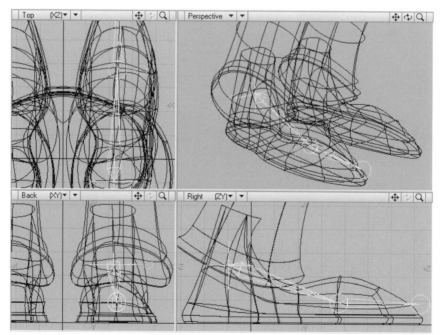

**Figure 4.12**   Positioning the foot and toe skelegons.

3. Make a small skelegon that has its tip at the center of the hip joint. (Use Figures 3.1 and 3.2 to help you.) Angle this bone so it lies along a path that points toward the knee. Name this skelegon **RightKnee**.

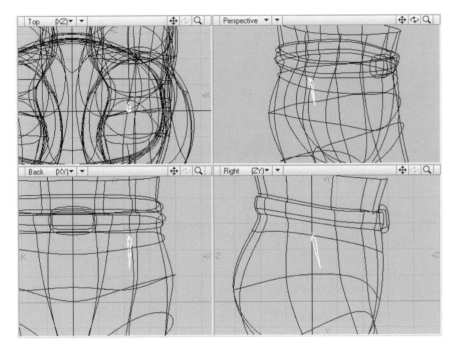

**Figure 4.13**   Positioning the RightKnee skelegon.

4. Mirror **RightKnee**, **RightFoot**, and **RightToes** along the X-axis. Rename the new bones accordingly.

49

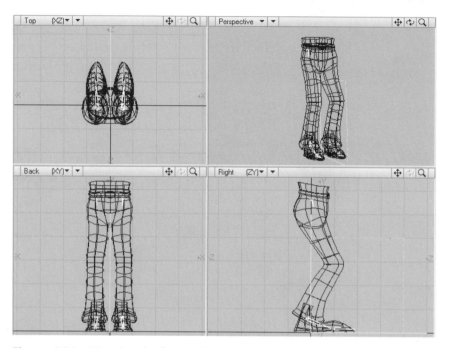

**Figure 4.14** Mirroring the foot and knee controls. All extraneous things are kept hidden to help preserve sanity.

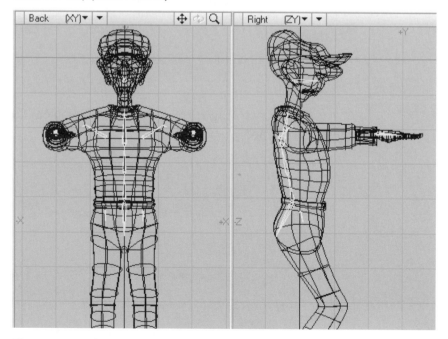

**Figure 4.15** The major controls for our character.

# 4.5 Fingers

Now that we've got the major controls that will drive the IK for our character, we'll put in the FK bones that will control the fingers. Because of my tendency to like to scroll up and down through things in Layout with the Up and Down Arrow keys, I like to build the fingers in a specific pattern. I like to start sculpting the hand position from the index finger, working my way to the middle finger, ring finger (if it's there), pinky finger, and finally the thumb. If you would rather start with the thumb or another finger, please feel free to modify this hand setup to suit your needs.

1. Create a chain of three skelegons along the right index finger. Name these **RightIndex_Base**, **RightIndex_Mid**, and **RightIndex_Tip** accordingly.

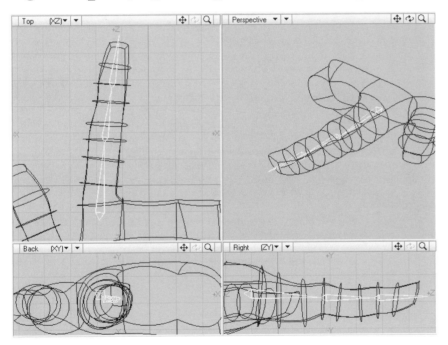

**Figure 4.16** I tend to place finger bones a bit higher than the center of the finger. This gives me the most realistic finger action in bends. Notice that while the connections between RightIndex_Tip and RightIndex_Mid and their parents fall on the isoparm (iso-parametric line, the lines that define NURBial patches) of their respective knuckle, the base of RightIndex_Base does not. The rotation point of this base knuckle is deeper inside the hand than what you might think. Bend your own fingers from this first knuckle, and see that the bend takes place not at the webbing, but deeper into your hand!

2. Create a chain of skelegons for the right middle finger. Name these **RightMiddle_Base**, **RightMiddle_Mid**, and **RightMiddle_Tip** accordingly.

3. Create a chain of skelegons for the right pinky finger. Name these **RightPinky_Base**, **RightPinky_Mid**, and **RightPinky_Tip** accordingly.

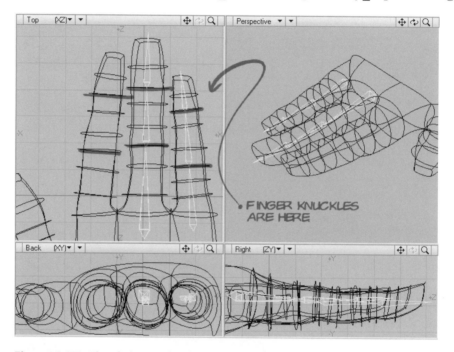

**Figure 4.17** The skelegons for the middle and pinky fingers. I've marked the knuckles with thick lines in this figure. I generally like to have a bend fall directly on an isoparm, and surround it with an isoparm on either side. It helps keep bulges in the right places while animating.

4. Create a chain of skelegons for the right thumb. Name these **RightThumb_Base**, **RightThumb_Mid**, and **RightThumb_Tip** accordingly.

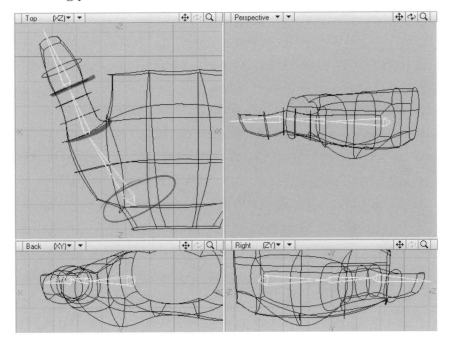

**Figure 4.18**  The skelegons of the thumb. Thumbs <u>do</u> have three parts of articulation, just like fingers! It's just that the base of our thumb is buried deep in our hand close to our wrist! Move your own thumb about, feeling for this base joint with the fingers of your other hand.

### ADVANCED NOTE:

There is actually another point of articulation in the hand that lets us fold our pinky and ring fingers over somewhat toward our thumb. So far, I haven't needed to build a setup that has this, but that doesn't mean that you won't be faced with a scene one day where you'll have to put this in. Just make a mental note that this rotation swings from the base of the palm, just on the other side of its center from where *Thumb_Base attaches.

5. Select and mirror the bones you have just created for the fingers (and thumb) across the X-axis (without merging points), and rename the new bones to reflect the fact that they're on the left.

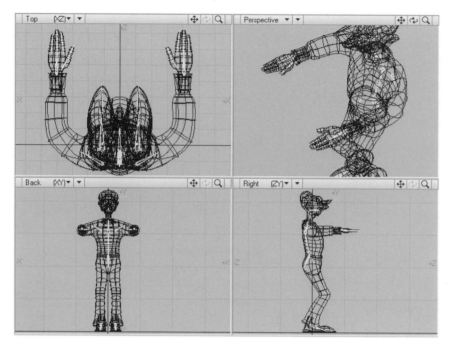

**Figure 4.19** All the IK and FK controllers have been created. All that remains for this part of the setup is to create the skelegons for the IK systems.

# 4.6 IK System Skelegons

IK system skelegons are the skelegons/bones that will be controlled by IK. Accuracy is a very big factor here, so we'll be using a few tricks that speed up precision placement. Some of the steps may seem a little odd, but they really are the fastest, most reliable ways I've found to do things.

1. Hide all the skelegons except for Spine3 (the top spinal skelegon) and Head.

2. With Spine3 selected, create a skelegon. Name this skelegon **Neck**.

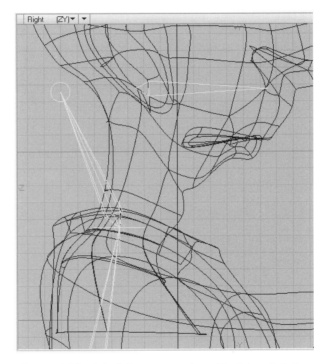

**Figure 4.20** It isn't important where Neck is pointed. We'll position it in a moment.

3. Change your selection mode to **Points** ^ **G**, and select first the point at the tip of Neck, then the point at the root of Head.

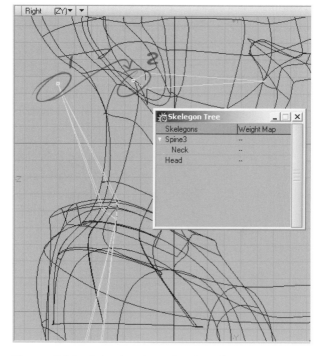

**Figure 4.21**   Selecting the points in order.

4. Press **Ctrl+w** to weld these two points together.

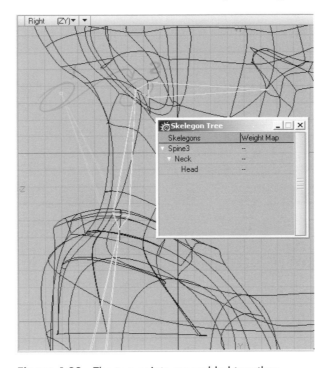

**Figure 4.22** The two points are welded together, forcing the tip of Neck to the exact position of Head. This also makes Head a child of Neck as seen in the Skelegon Tree window (Detail|Other|Skelegon Tree).

**NEWBIE NOTE:**

The order in which the points to be welded are selected is important. All selected points will be welded to the <u>last</u> point selected.

5. Select the single point that is now the tip of Neck and the base of Head. Press **Ctrl+u** to "unweld" this point into two points (a point for each skelegon it belonged to).

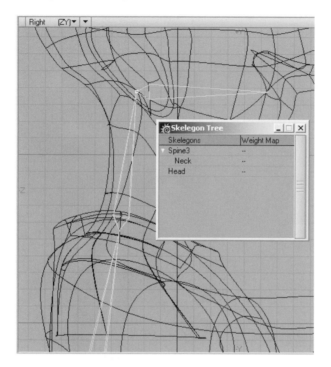

**Figure 4.23** Head is now no longer a child of Neck.

6. With Neck selected, create a small skelegon at its tip. Name this skelegon **Neck_Puller**.

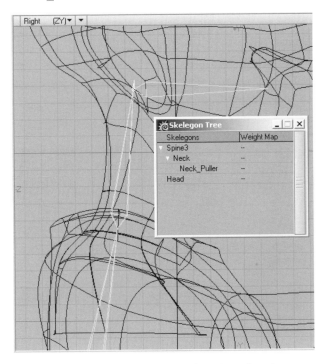

**Figure 4.24** With the addition of Neck_Puller, the hierarchy of the neck is now complete.

7. With RightElbow selected, create two more skelegons that lie along the arm. Name these two skelegons **RightBicep** and **RightForearm**, respectively.

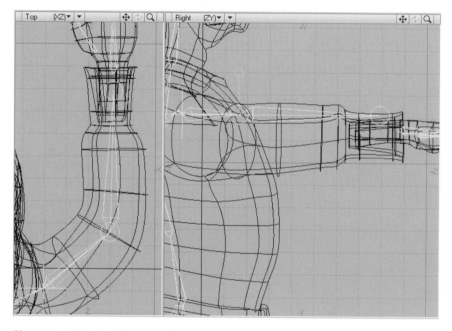

**Figure 4.25** RightBicep and RightForearm, newly created and ready to be positioned within the arm.

8. Position the right elbow joint, the meeting of RightBicep and RightForearm. It should be in the center of the arm along the Y-axis, but closer to the back of the arm on the X- and Z-axes.

9. Select the point at the tip of RightForearm. Then, add to your selection the points that are at the base of RightHand_Trans and RightHand_Rot (they should be right on top of one another).

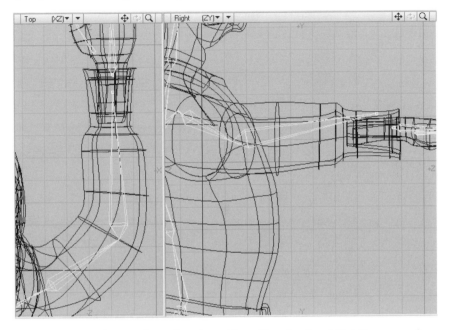

**Figure 4.26** Selecting the points that will position the tip of RightForearm after having positioned the elbow joint.

10. Press **Ctrl+w** to weld these points, moving the tip of RightForearm to the exact position of the base of the hand controls.

11. Select this newly welded point and press **Ctrl+u** to unweld it from the original three points, unparenting the hand controls from RightForearm.

12. With the RightForearm skelegon selected, create a small skelegon at its tip. Name this new skelegon **RightArm_Puller**.

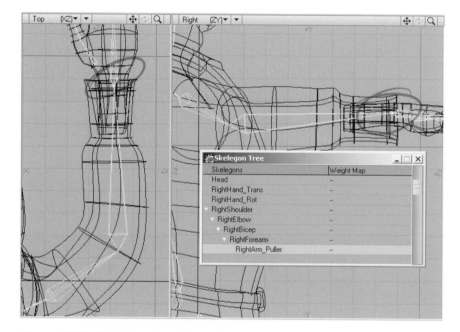

**Figure 4.27** The hierarchy of the right arm is complete!

13. Select **RightArm_Puller**, **RightForearm**, and **RightBicep**. Mirror these skelegons across the X-axis (without merging points). Rename the new skelegons appropriately.

14. Select the points that are the base of the LeftBicep and the tip of the LeftElbow (they should be right on top of one another). Press **Ctrl+w** to weld them together, making LeftBicep a child of LeftElbow.

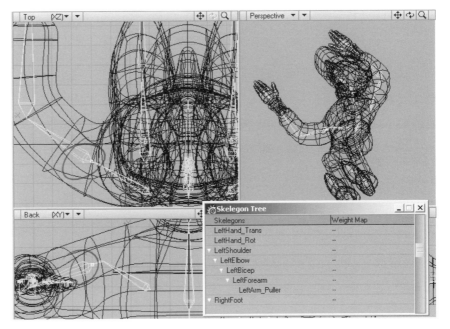

**Figure 4.28** Welding the mirrored skelegon chain of LeftBicep, LeftForearm, and LeftArm_Puller to the tip of LeftElbow.

15. Hide all skelegons except for RightKnee and RightFoot.

16. With RightKnee selected, create two skelegons that follow the line of the leg. Name them **RightThigh** and **RightCalf** accordingly.

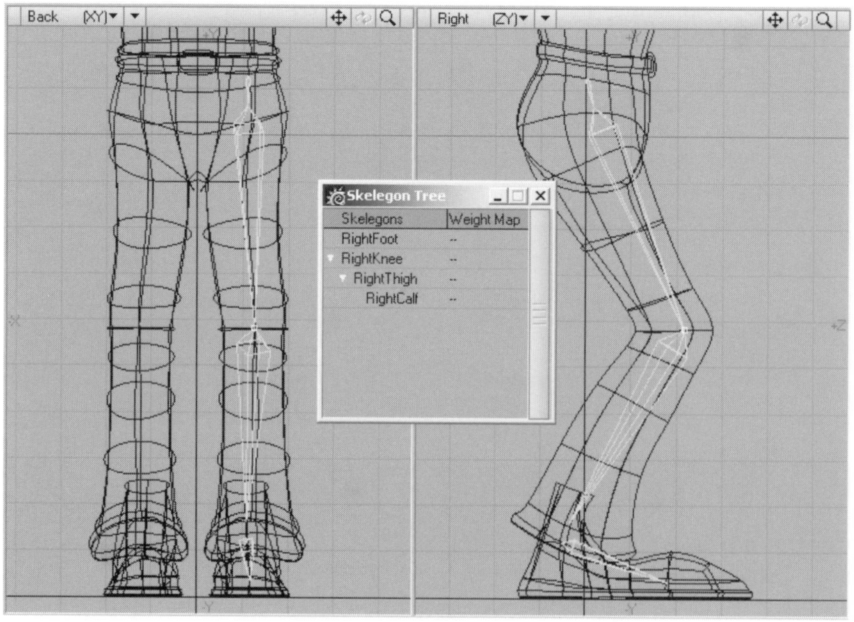

**Figure 4.29**  Position the knee joint slightly forward of the center of the model's knee.

17. Weld the point at the tip of RightCalf to the point at the base of RightFoot (just like we did before).

18. Select this newly welded point and unweld it.

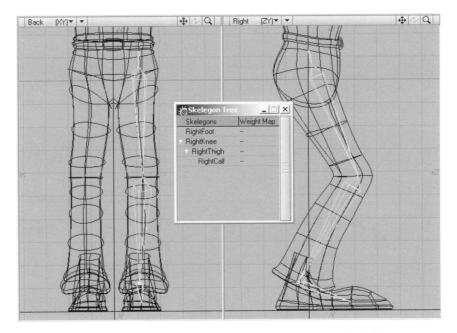

**Figure 4.30**  Welding and unwelding to position the tip of RightCalf.

19. With the RightCalf selected, add a tiny skelegon and name it
**RightLeg_Puller.**

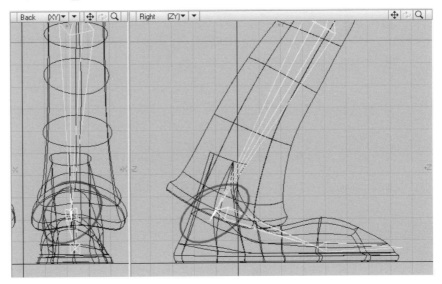

**Figure 4.31**  With the addition of RightLeg_Puller, the hierarchy of the right leg
is complete!

20. Mirror **RightLeg_Puller**, **RightCalf**, and **RightThigh** across the X-axis, again making sure to not automatically merge points. Rename these bones accordingly.

21. Unhide everything and weld the point at the tip of LeftKnee to the point at the base of LeftThigh.

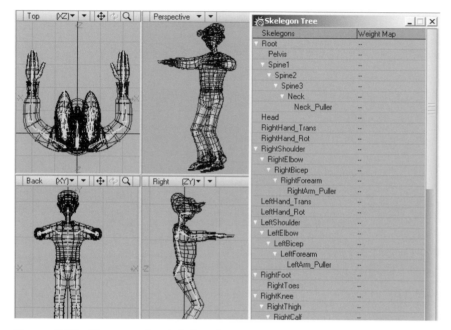

**Figure 4.32**　Your completed skeleton!

22. Select all your skelegons and cut them, leaving Layer2 empty.

23. Set Layer1 as your active layer and paste the skelegons into the same layer as your mesh.

24. Select **Map|Weight & Color|More|Bone Weights**.

25. Enter **0 m** for Threshold Value, and set Use Threshold to **Clip**. Click **OK**.

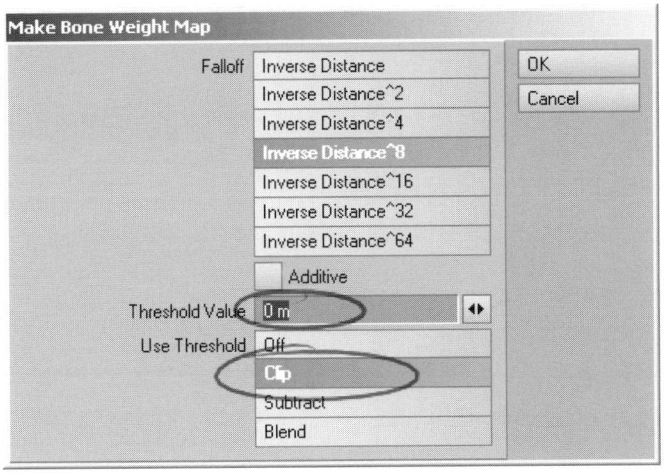

**Make Bone Weight Map**

| Falloff | Inverse Distance | OK |
| | Inverse Distance^2 | Cancel |
| | Inverse Distance^4 | |
| | **Inverse Distance^8** | |
| | Inverse Distance^16 | |
| | Inverse Distance^32 | |
| | Inverse Distance^64 | |
| | Additive | |
| Threshold Value | 0 m | |
| Use Threshold | Off | |
| | **Clip** | |
| | Subtract | |
| | Blend | |

**Figure 4.33** Using these settings creates weight maps for every skelegon with the values on every point being 0%.

26. Save a backup copy of your model, and then save the model itself. When you're ready, go on to Chapter 5.

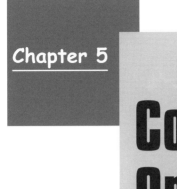

# Converting, Organizing, and Aligning

The skelegons you created in Modeler are placeholders for the bones that Layout will use to deform the mesh. So now, for the moment, we can leave Modeler behind and open up Layout.

## 5.1 Converting Skelegons to Bones

1.  Load your model from Chapter 4 into Layout.

> **NEWBIE NOTE:**
>
> If you just couldn't bring yourself to make the skelegons in the last chapter, there is a model that already has them created for you. As always, I strongly encourage you to go through all the steps so you have an understanding of how each part was created, and how to modify them should you ever need to. If you need the pre-skelegoned model, you will find it on the companion CD as Objects\chapters\ch_04.lwo.

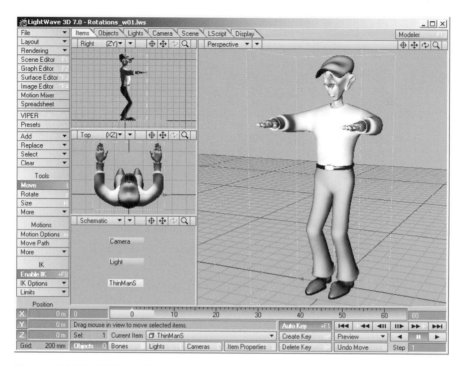

**Figure 5.1** I find it helpful to use multiple views in Layout. You have a better feel for where something is in 3D space, and the Schematic window can be invaluable for finding a specific character control at a glance (more on this in a bit)! You activate multiple views under Display|Display Options|Viewport Layout.

2.  In the Object Properties window (with **Objects** ^O active, choose **Item Properties**) set the Subdivision Order of your model to **Last**, and the Display SubPatch Level to **2**.

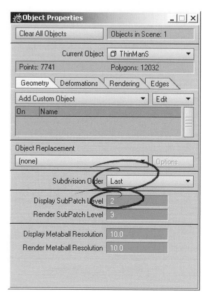

**Figure 5.2** The Object Properties window.

**NEWBIE NOTE:**

Because "ch_04" is a meta-NURB (sub-division surface) mesh, it will come in with a default Display SubPatch Level of 3. If you have a fast computer and a GL-accelerated graphics card, this level of detail will be fine. If you are on a slower computer or don't have the real-time rendering power of a full GL graphics card, you can reduce this level of detail and drastically increase performance. These settings let you animate at a level of detail where you can get the quickest response possible, and yet render at a complex level.

**NOTE:**

It is important to have the Subdivision Order set to Last with characters. (This is especially important if you are planning on having more than one character in a scene.) Bone influences are calculated for every point in a mesh, and when you have a mesh subdivided, that point count goes up exponentially. Updates can slow to a point where a scene becomes almost unworkable.

3. With your model selected, choose **Items|Add| Bones|Convert Skelegons into Bones**.

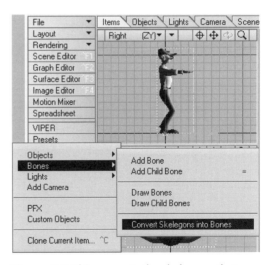

**Figure 5.3** This converts the skelegons that Modeler understands into bones that Layout understands.

4. With your model still selected, under **Scene Editor|Visibility**, choose **Hide Selected Items**. This will make the model invisible when it isn't selected (when a hidden item is selected, it will be visible as a wireframe in version 6.5 and earlier and as points in version 7) so it won't get in the way visually while we're setting up bones.

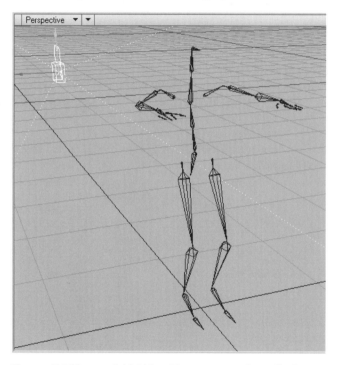

**Figure 5.4** The model hidden (the camera selected), these are the bones you've just created from skelegons.

# 5.2 **Organizing the Schematic into Something Helpful**

Everything you can do in preparation that keeps you from having to break concentration while animating is a good thing. A schematic laid out in a way that makes sense to you can be one of the greatest tools you'll encounter in 3D animation!

1.  Open the Scene Editor and select the following bones: **Neck, Neck_Puller, RightArm_Puller, LeftArm_Puller, RightLeg_Puller, LeftLeg_Puller.** We'll be hiding these bones; they are used only in IK calculations and we won't need to affect them directly.

2.  From within the Scene Editor, select **Visibility|Hide Selected Items.** With these bones hidden, they can't be accidentally selected by clicking on them in a non-schematic viewport when you're trying to select another control. (Layout isn't quite as good as Modeler for knowing what you're clicking on.)

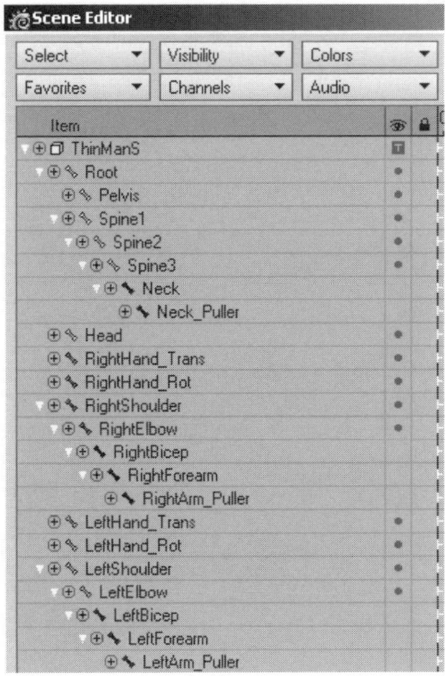

**Figure 5.5** In addition to hiding the bones that are driven by IK, I like to color code all the bones to help in at-a-glance identification of them when animating gets intense. My own preference is to have red for bones on the right, green for bones on the left, and cyan for centered bones such as the spine and head. I use darker colors for the bones only IK needs to know about once we get animating.

3. In a full-screen schematic view, organize your character into an iconic representation of a human. As in Figure 5.6, I lean toward a classic da Vinci layout, giving the rough impression of the character standing spread eagle, palms up.

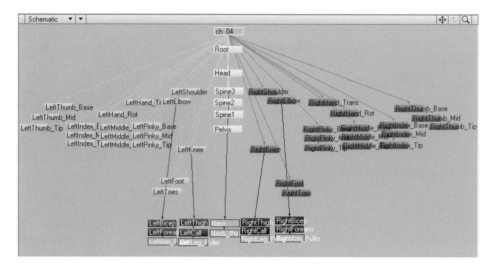

**Figure 5.6** Animation can be pretty hectic. Every bit of organization you can do beforehand helps. With the controls for your character laid out like this, you can quickly choose the control you need without having to scroll through a list. (This illustration is only a suggestion; it is what works best for me. Feel free to innovate and find what works best for you!)

## 5.3 Aligning the Spine, Pelvis, and Feet

NOTE:

Section 5.3 is for those of you who want to make your setup as intuitive as possible. It isn't imperative that you go through this step; your setup will work just fine if you choose not to but you will probably have some bones with their heading and pitch axes reversed. This is due to the "axis handle" that protrudes from the root of a skelegon while it's being drawn in Modeler (the alignment of which controls the bank rotation of the skelegon—see Figure 5.7). This is not a huge issue, but it can cause frustration during animation. This section realigns these "problem bones." Because your bones were created from skelegons that were "eyeballed" in Modeler, your rotations won't match exactly with my rotations. (Perhaps some bones I'm addressing here might be fine in your scene. It is a good idea to check <u>all</u> your bones to make sure their alignment is satisfactory for your preference of animation.) This section is not a section of absolutes; you'll have to use your own best judgment. This is good practice for the sections on animation, where there are no "rights" or "wrongs." Just bear in mind that if this section makes your head hurt, it isn't the end of the world if you choose to skip it. (Bear in mind as well that possibly some of the bones I'll be working on in this section might be properly aligned in your scene. If they are, just do a happy dance and move on to the next bone; LightWave works in mysterious ways—sometimes.)

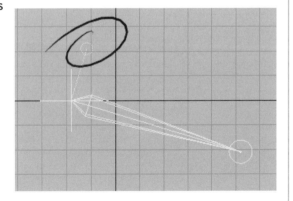

**Figure 5.7** The axis handle that controls the bank axis of skelegons in Modeler. (See the LightWave manuals for a full description of how to work this thingamajig.)

When we work with skelegons to craft our character's bone structure, we're at the mercy of what LightWave thinks is the correct rotation for each bone. Modeler uses a kind of IK to figure out how the skelegons should be rotated to get them positioned. Things look good at a glance...but are they?

**ADVANCED NOTE:**

Is this something that could have been bypassed by addressing the issue of skelegon axis handles in Chapter 4? Yes. However, varying the rotations of bones within chains is something that you will probably come across sometime in your career, and so I thought it best to address the issue.

1.  Select the **Root** bone.

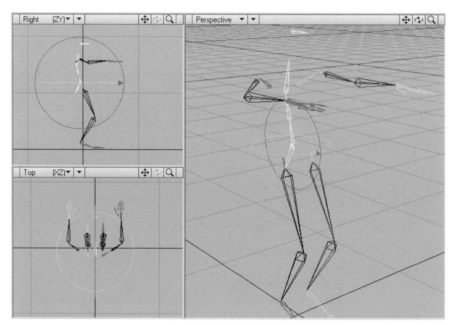

**Figure 5.8** Pitch is what we would normally think of in LightWave as the axis to rotate an item forward and backward (around its X-axis). With the way Root is currently oriented, to bend the character forward and backward, we would have to use Heading (represented by the red circle on your screen).

Sometimes bones created with skelegons have an odd +/−90 degree bank rotation to them (due to a kind of IK flipping). This flops what we would think of as heading and bank for the bone, its children, or both! This isn't a huge problem, and we could easily work around it. But when we're deeply engrossed in a scene, and the familiar left-right mouse movement that usually means "I'm rotating in heading" instead rotates these few bones in pitch, it can feel like an unnecessary speed bump in the roadway of production. So, here's how we're going to fix it.

2. Select your character's mesh (object).

3. Choose **Items│Add│Clone Current Item** ^C and enter **1** for the number of clones. (See Figure 5.9.)

4. In a schematic window, move this new object to a place where it won't interfere visually with the original model and its hierarchy.

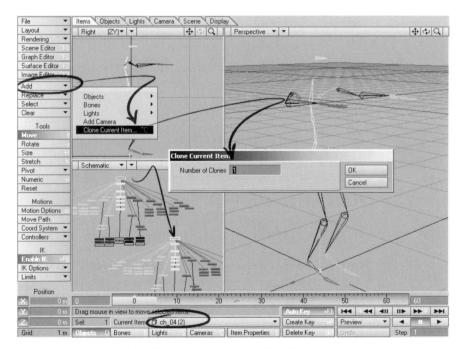

**Figure 5.9** Your model will be cloned, along with all its bone structure.

5.  With the clone of your model still selected, open the Scene Editor and select **Select|Select All Bones of Current Object**.

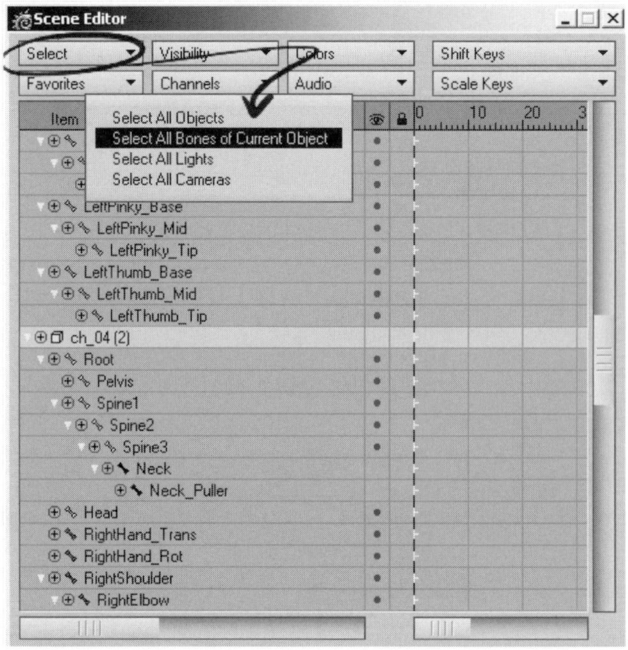

**Figure 5.10** All the bones of the cloned model will be selected.

6.  With all the bones of the cloned model selected, within the Scene Editor select **Colors|Color Selected Items|Orange**.

> **NOTE:**
>
> The orange bones will be our guides for us to match as we rotate our model back into alignment. If you notice in the Current Item field that you've got an orange bone selected, stop! LightWave only has <u>one</u> level of undo in Layout. Make sure you have the right bone selected before making changes.

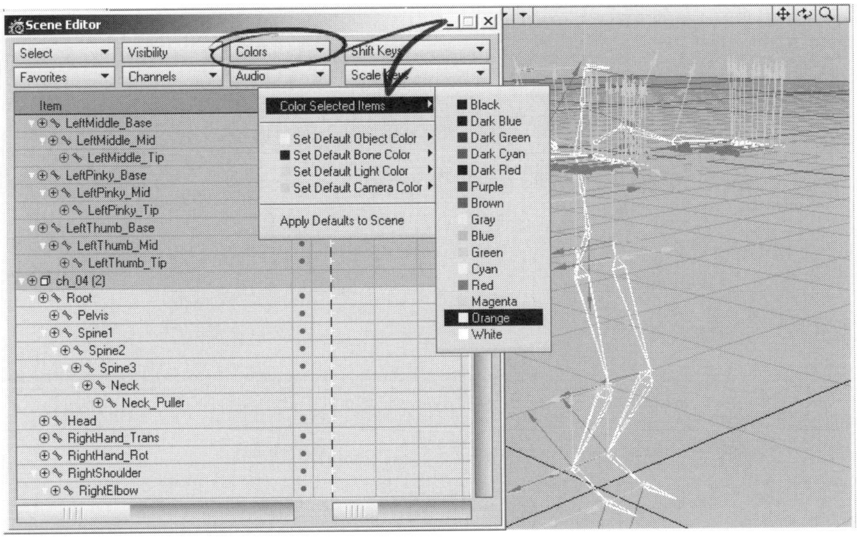

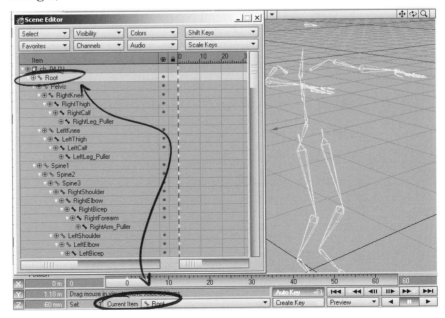

**Figure 5.11** All the bones you have selected will be colored orange.

7. Select the **Root** bone of your original mesh. (It should be cyan, not orange.)

**Figure 5.12** Just making sure that the right bone is selected.

8. Change your tool (what LightWave does when you move the mouse) to **Rotate (Items|Tools|Rotate)**.

9. In the numeric input field, change the entry for bank to **0**.

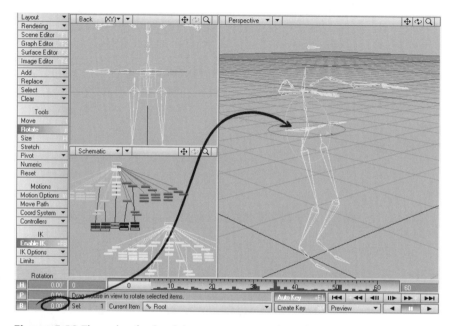

**Figure 5.13** The value for bank in my scene was –90. Changing the pivot's bank to 0 swings my character's spine and pelvis onto its side.

10. Select the pelvis bone of your original mesh.

11. Make sure you are at Frame 0.

12. Enter **0, 0, 0** for its rotation (heading, pitch, and bank), and then manually rotate it until it lines up with the orange pelvis bone of the cloned mesh.

**NEWBIE NOTE:**

After getting each of these bones lined up, press Enter twice to create a keyframe for that bone. Even if you have Auto Key Create active, this is a good habit to get into; it reduces the chances of losing precious minutes or hours of work.

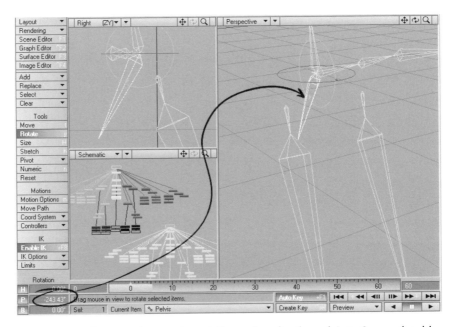

**Figure 5.14** After you change the rotation values for the pelvis to 0, you should only need to rotate it along its pitch axis to line it up with the orange reference bone. Almost always, copying the old value for heading into pitch lines the pelvis and spine bones up perfectly.

13. Repeat step 12 for each of the three spine bones.

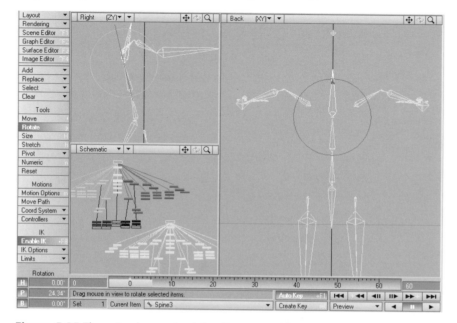

**Figure 5.15** The spine bones, back in alignment with our orange reference bones.

14. Select **RightFoot** in your original mesh.

15. Set its bank rotation to **0**.

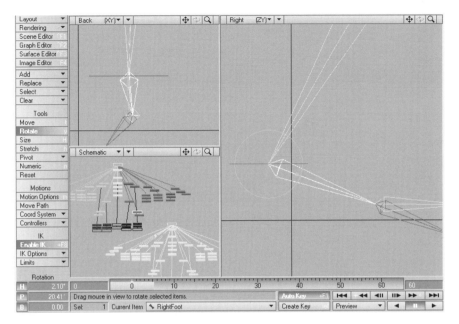

**Figure 5.16** Changing RightFoot's bank should leave it aligned with its orange reference bone (even though RightToes is now misaligned). Tweak RightFoot's heading and bank if you need to.

16. Select **RightToes** (in your original mesh).

17. Swap the values for heading and pitch, and zero-out the value for bank; RightToes should line up with its orange reference bone. Tweak as needed.

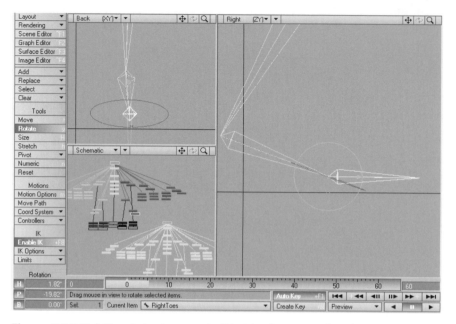

**Figure 5.17** RightToes is back on track. (Nothing is parented to the toes, so they don't have to be exact.)

18. Repeat steps 14-17 for LeftFoot and LeftToes.

19. Check to see that the Head, *Hand_Trans, and *Hand_Rot bones also have a bank rotation of 0 (they are also prone to this odd bank phenomenon). Adjust them as needed.

20. Select the cloned object you've been using as reference and press **-** (or select **Items|Clear|Clear Selected Items**) to clear it from the scene.

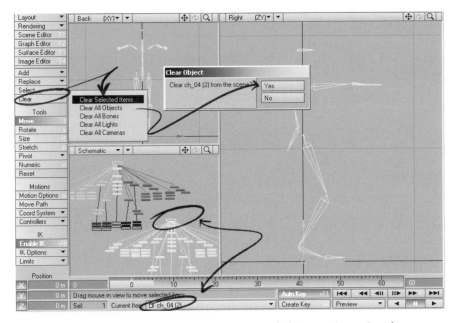

**Figure 5.18** Your character is done with its virtual chiropractic session; be sure you clear the right object!

# 5.4 Bone Hierarchy

We did a lot of hierarchy work in Modeler with skelegons, but there are some hierarchal things that can't be done with skelegons. Modeler forces child skelegons to be attached to the tip of their parent skelegon. Child bones in Layout don't have to be right at their parent's tip. We'll need this kind of relationship for our character's fingers as they attach to the hand.

1. Check to make sure you have Parent in Place active (**Display|General Options|Parent in Place**).

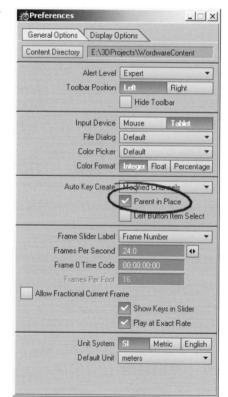

**NEWBIE NOTE:**

With Parent in Place active, LightWave calculates the SRT offset required to keep the selected object in the same "worldspace" (an item's relationship to the LW world versus its relationship to another item; more on this in Chapter 8), even though it inherits SRT data from its parent item. LightWave does a good job of this, but it can be fooled by complex hierarchies where items have had changes made to their pivot's rotation (see Section 5.5). So save revisions and always be watchful for errors in these calculations!

**Figure 5.19** Parent in Place

2. In a full-screen schematic window, click on **RightThumb_Base**.

3. While holding down **Ctrl**, click on **RightHand_Rot**. This is a quick way to make RightThumb_Base a child of RightHand_Rot.

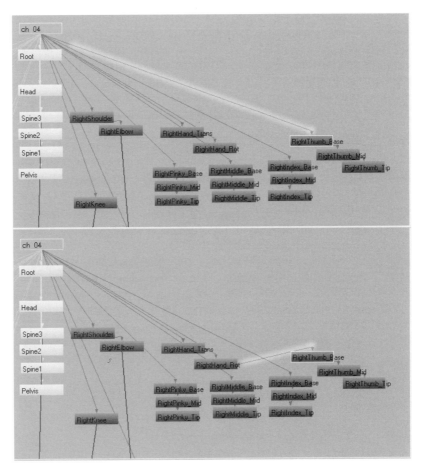

**Figure 5.20** Notice how the line that once connected RightThumb_Base to ch_04 now is connected to RightHand_Rot.

4. Make RightIndex_Base, RightMiddle_Base, and RightPinky_Base children of RightHand_Rot.

5. Make RightHand_Rot a child of RightHand_Trans.

6. Repeat steps 2-5 for the bones of the left hand.

7. Make Head, RightHand_Trans, and LeftHand_Trans children of Root.

8. Make RightShoulder and LeftShoulder children of Spine3.

9. Make RightKnee and LeftKnee children of Pelvis.

10. Make Pelvis a child of Spine1 (Spine1 being a child of Root).

11. Make Head a child of Spine1.

> **NOTE:**
>
> RightFoot and LeftFoot remain children of ch_04.

> **NOTE:**
>
> These are options you'll want to keep in the back of your mind for future reference. I'll go through them in Chapter 8 in the section on how to modify the setup for your personal preference, but this will get your wheels turning as to how to apply changes in setup to the needs of different scenes.
>
> With the way the hands, feet, and head are children of different items (when IK has been fully activated at the end of Chapter 6) when you move the mesh object itself, your entire model will move, statue-like, to its new position. When you move the Root bone, your character's feet will remain where they are, and his entire upper carriage will move, frozen and statue-like. When you move Spine1, your character's torso will move, statue-like, but his head, hands, and feet will stay put.

You'll find some scenes to be much easier having the hands moving with the momentum of the upper carriage (some martial arts katas), and some scenes much more difficult (grappling). Sometimes you'll want the head to be independent of the torso (dancing), and sometimes you'll want it to follow (walking). As you begin work on a scene, think about what kind of hierarchy of head, hands, and feet will make your work easier, and experiment. You'll find your own personal preferences for certain kinds of work. Your solution is likely to involve re-parenting these items. (The head may be a child of Root, Spine1, or Spine3; each will have a different effect on how the head inherits the motion of the body.) Nothing is wrong if it works; creativity is rewarded with a better looking scene with much less effort. Just remember that changes in parenting work best early on in the animation end of things, and that <u>Parent in Place only works when both items' pivots are free of rotation</u>. So save revisions of your scene before making changes in your character's hierarchy.

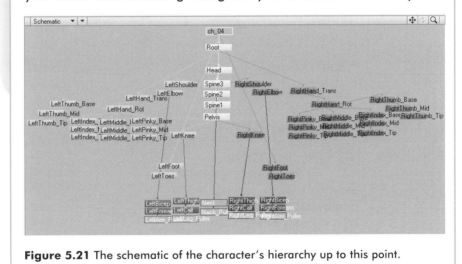

**Figure 5.21** The schematic of the character's hierarchy up to this point.

## 5.5 **Recording Pivot Rotations**

Now we're going to tell LightWave to perceive many of the bones' current directions as if they were 0H, 0P, 0B. This is a big help where gimbal lock may be an issue, especially in the fingers, spine, and IK calculations.

1. Under **Display|General Options|AutoKeyCreate**, make sure you have either Modified Channels or All Motion Channels selected.

2. In the main Layout window, make sure you have the **Auto Key** button active.

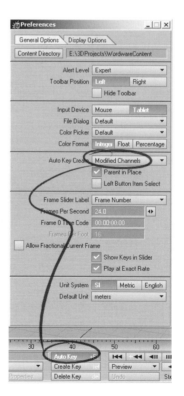

### NEWBIE NOTE:

When you have Auto Key Create active, LightWave automatically records keyframes for items you move. With All Motion Channels selected, a key is created on all axes of scaling, rotation, and translation when you move the item. With Modified Channels selected, a key is only created on the axes of the channels you are modifying. Without Auto Key Create active, all changes in SRT are lost when you leave that frame unless you manually create one for each channel of each item modified. (This functionality was great when Layout didn't have Undo.)

**Figure 5.22** Both need to be active in order for Auto Key to record changes in SRT.

3. Make sure you are on Frame 0.

4. Select the bone named **Root**.

5. Choose **Items|Pivot|Record Pivot Rotation**.

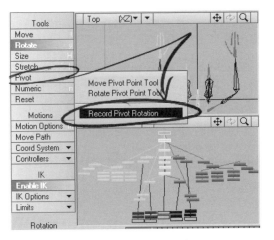

**Figure 5.23** Recording pivot rotation.

6. Select **Pelvis**, and record its pivot rotation.

7. Repeat this to record pivot rotation for all bones.

**NOTE:**

A good way to check to make sure that the pivot's rotation was actually recorded is to look at the rotation numerical input fields. If they're all zeros, rotation has been recorded! This is how I check to see if I've missed anything after doing this step. I just quickly scroll down the bones using the Down Arrow and watch the numeric input fields to see if there are any bones that still have values other than zero!

**NOTE:**

In recording pivot rotation, LightWave (in essence) sets the pivot point's rotation of the current Item to its current rotation. Then it "zeros" its current rotation by setting it to 0H, 0P, 0B. With Auto Key active, a keyframe is recorded at the current frame (preferably the first frame of your scene, usually 0) and LightWave perceives the item as now having a rotation of 0H, 0P, 0B. Without Auto Key active, no keyframe is created (unless you do so manually) and when you refresh the viewport (go forward a frame, then back a frame; save, then load, etc....) the item reverts to its old rotation data, but now this data is added to the new rotation of its pivot.

# 5.6 Recording Bone Rest Information

> **NEWBIE NOTE:**
>
> A bone's rest direction isn't the same as its pivot rotation. Pivot rotation figures in rotational calculations (heading, pitch, and bearing), while rest direction, position, and length keep track of how much the bone has deviated from its initial (rest) direction, position, and length. The points of the object the bone is affecting are pulled along accordingly.

1. With **Root** once again selected, record its rest position, length, and direction by pressing **r** (or selecting **Objects|Bones|Rec Rest Pos**). (See Figure 5.24.)

2. Record the rest position for <u>every</u> bone in your model.

3. Save a revision of your scene!

Give yourself a healthy pat on the back! You've just completed the first half of character setup! In the next chapter, you'll finally begin to see the power of the setup you've been creating as we start to activate IK.

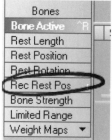

**Figure 5.24** Record rest position.

## Chapter 6

# Putting IK to Work

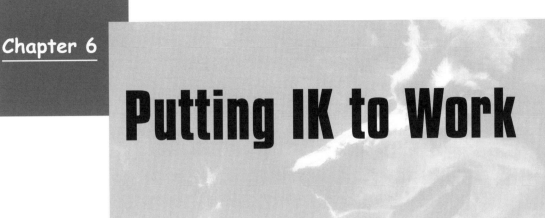

Everything is all set to bring the "big guns" of computer animation to bear. We're ready to activate the power (and limitations) of Inverse Kinematics! In this chapter, you'll begin to see the result of all your hard work in the previous five chapters. And after this chapter, there is only one more step until you can begin to see your character come to life by pulling, pushing, rotating, and scaling the controls you've so carefully crafted!

**NEWBIE NOTE:**

As always, if you feel you need a "leg up" from the last chapter, you can find the scene that has the work of Chapter 5 all done for you in Scenes\chapters\ch_05.lws.

# 6.1 Terminating IK Chains

LightWave must be told where to stop using IK to calculate the rotations of the items in the chain. This is called "terminating" the IK chain (like tying off a rope that holds a string of buoys). We're going to use IK to figure rotations for the neck, arms, and legs only. This means we terminate IK at the bones that are the parents of the neck bone, the bicep bones, and the thigh bones.

1. With a freshly incremented revision of the scene you created in Chapter 5 loaded into Layout, select the **Spine3** bone (which is the parent of Neck).

2. Under **Items|IK|IK Options**, check **Unaffected by IK of Descendants On/Off**. This causes the IK calculations of the child bone, in this case Neck, to stop and go no further.

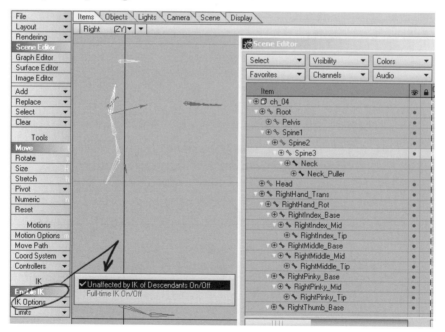

**Figure 6.1** The hierarchal view of the Scene Editor is the quickest way of selecting the bones we'll be terminating. While working with setting up the IK for the bones, I find it helpful to hide the mesh.

3. Repeat step 2 for RightElbow (the parent of RightBicep), LeftElbow (parent of LeftBicep), RightKnee (parent of RightThigh), and LeftKnee (parent of LeftThigh).

> **NOTE:**
>
> You can also set Unaffected by IK of Descendants under the Items|Motions|Motion Options|IK and Modifiers tab for an item (bone, object, camera, or light).

## 6.2 **Creating Goal Objects**

Because LightWave <u>doesn't</u> let you use bones as goals for IK, we have to add a few null objects (which <u>can</u> be used as IK goals) and make them children of the bones we're using as controls so that LightWave's IK can track these bones' positions. (Yes, it's rather backward, but bear in mind, most everything cool in 3D is a "hack" of some kind or other. "Hacking" in this sense is just working within limitations—inane as they may be—to get the result we need. Remember, creativity is your greatest asset in doing anything with 3D. A problem or a stumbling block is simply a gateway to untold possibilities for cleverly wrenching the systems into doing what you think they should do by default.)

1. Select **Items|Add|Objects|Add Null....**

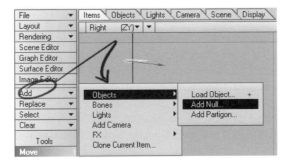

**Figure 6.2** Adding a null object.

2. Name this null object **NeckGoal**.

3. Under **Display|General Options**, make sure that Parent in Place is <u>not</u> checked. (See the following Newbie Note.)

4. Press **m** to bring up the Motion Options window for NeckGoal.

5.  Select the Head bone to be the parent item for this null.

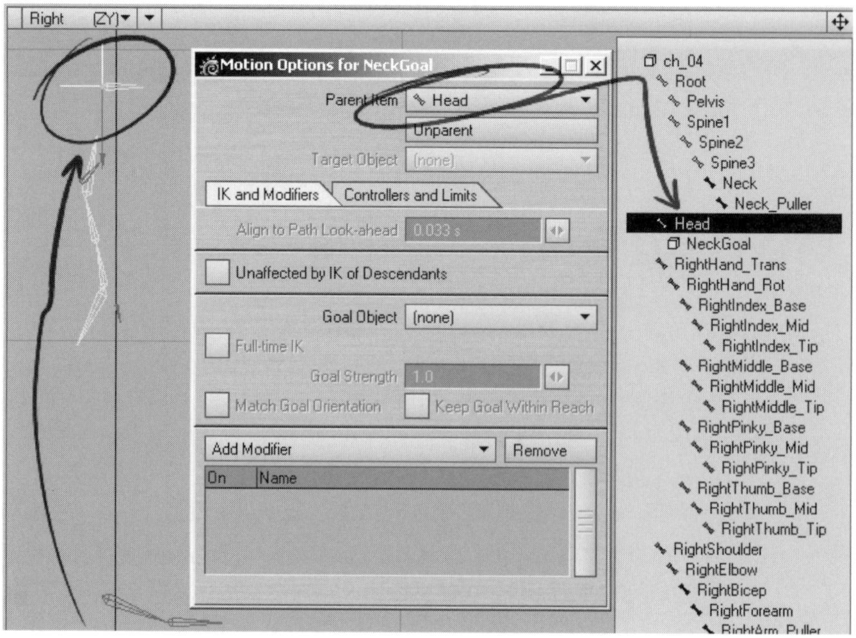

**Figure 6.3** Setting NeckGoal to be the child of Head.

### NEWBIE NOTE:

Because we deactivated Parent in Place, the moment we set Head to be the parent item for NeckGoal, it seems to instantly reposition itself to the base of the Head bone. As a child of Head, NeckGoal's world now revolves (quite literally) around Head's pivot, and wherever Head is, that is where NeckGoal perceives 0X, 0Y, 0Z, and 0H, 0P, 0B to be. From NeckGoal's point of view, it is still at 0, 0, 0. If we had had Parent in Place active when we did step 5, to our perception, NeckGoal wouldn't have moved, but if we had looked at its position in the numeric input fields, we'd have found that it now reads something like 0.1215 $\mu$m, −1.875 m, 50 mm. With Parent in Place active, LightWave calculates the offset (taking into account the parent item's rotation as well as its position) needed to have the selected object stay where it was in world coordinates, which simply means with respect to the world's 0X, 0Y, 0Z, 0H, 0P, and 0B. (More on coordinate systems in a bit!)

6. Create four more null objects, naming them **RightArmGoal**, **LeftArmGoal**, **RightLegGoal**, and **LeftLegGoal**.

**NEWBIE NOTE:**

Parent in Place is to remain <u>off</u> for steps 7-10 in this section.

7. Make RightArmGoal a child of RightHand_Rot.

8. Make LeftArmGoal a child of LeftHand_Rot.

9. Make RightLegGoal a child of RightFoot.

10. Make LeftLegGoal a child of LeftFoot.

11. Hide these objects; they are only used for IK calculations, and we won't need to touch them during animation. Color code them if you are using colors to distinguish items as to which side they belong, and in your schematic, arrange them in a way that makes sense to you. (It may seem like wasted time to have a neat, clean schematic, but its worth pays off tenfold when you're down-and-dirty in a scene and you don't have time to go hunting for something.)

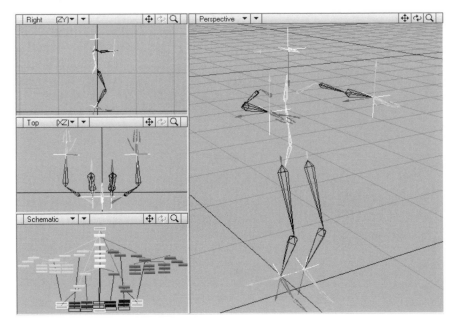

**Figure 6.4** The goal objects.

# 6.3 Activating IK

Now, we've got to activate IK. We'll be telling LightWave which item will be pulling which chain toward which goal object. We won't see the chains move yet; we'll still have to tell Layout which axes IK should take over on each item to be controlled by IK.

1. Select the **RightArm_Puller** bone.

2. Press **m** to bring up the Motion Options panel for this item. (See Figure 6.5.)

3. Select **RightArmGoal** as the goal object.

4. Check the box next to Full-time IK.

5. Set Goal Strength to **80**.

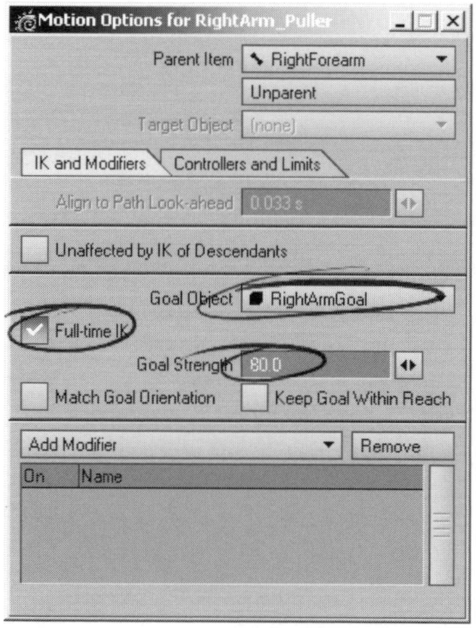

> **NOTE:**
>
> Without Full-time IK checked, LightWave only calculates IK for this chain when you're moving the goal object, and you have to manually set keyframes for each item in this chain that uses IK to figure its rotations. Part-time IK is a holdover from when IK was too much for most computers to continually keep on top of, but it can still come in handy if you need to lighten the load on your CPU as you work on a complex scene.

**Figure 6.5** The motion options for RightArm_Puller.

> **NOTE:**
>
> Goal strength is a level of how much this chain will try to keep the puller touching the goal object as you animate. A low value will let the arm separate from the wrist too easily, and a high value can cause jitters. The number 80 is just an arbitrary value I've come up with that seems to keep things together, while keeping jitters to a minimum.

6. Repeat steps 2-5 for LeftArm_Puller, RightLeg_Puller, and LeftLeg_Puller, setting their goal objects to the respective nulls we created in the previous section.

7. Set the goal object for Neck_Puller to be **NeckGoal**, enable Full-time IK, and set its Goal Strength to **40**. (With only one bone in the chain, a goal strength of 40 seems to do just fine.)

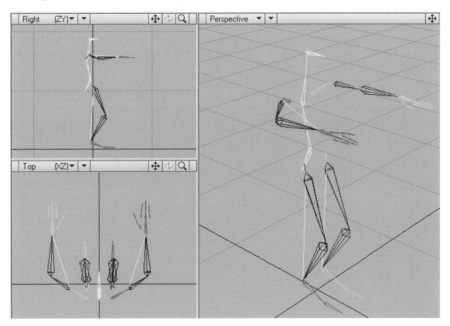

**Figure 6.6** The blue lines on your screen show the active IK chains from the base of the puller item to the base of the child of the Unaffected by IK of Descendants (terminated) item. (These are the "IK chains" which can be shown or hidden under Display|Display Options|Show IK Chains.)

## 6.4 **Activating Individual Controllers**

Next up, we've got to tell LightWave which rotation axes IK will be controlling in our chains. This takes manual control away from whatever axes we select, handing it over to the computer. With respect to the information in Chapter 2 about IK's strengths and weaknesses, this has to be a very discriminating process.

1.  Select the Neck bone.

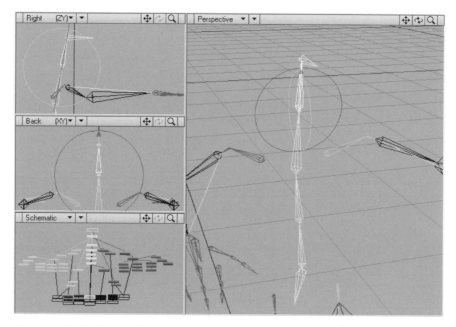

**Figure 6.7** We'll want this joint to pivot along both the heading and pitch axes.

**NEWBIE NOTE:**

With LightWave in rotation mode (LightWave's tool set to Rotate y), you can see colored circles representing the axes of rotation—red for heading, green for pitch, and blue for bank. By selecting Items|Coord System, you can change the axes from World to Parent to Local (you can do this for translation (Move) axes too—X,Y,Z). When you do this, LightWave assumes a new method for calculating rotation and translation. With World selected, LightWave rotates (or moves) the object in alignment with the worldspace coordinates such that Y is <u>always</u> straight up, heading <u>always</u> rotates with respect to the world's Y-axis, etc. With the coordinates set to Parent, LightWave figures movement and rotation with respect to the item's parent. With the coordinates set to Local, LightWave figures rotation and movement as based solely on its own orientation (this is how LW used to figure rotation and movement before Version 6). This may seem confusing. Playing with, moving, and rotating items in different coordinate systems is the only way to really get a feel for what to expect.

**NOTE:**

LightWave's ability to switch between world, parent, and local coordinate systems (see preceding Newbie Note) comes in handy, getting you out of jams or helping to speed up precise placement. But there is a caveat about the systems: LightWave stores rotation and translation data relative to <u>only</u> the parent coordinate system. You can see this by watching the numerical data update (lower-left corner of the default LW layout) as you rotate or move an item along one of its axes while using the different coordinate systems. Only the parent coordinate system always exactly matches what you're doing when you rotate or move a single axis (when rotating along pitch, <u>only</u> the pitch numerical input field updates; under world and local, often two or three fields can be seen to update while rotating a <u>single</u> controller in Layout). What this means for us right now is that in order for us to visually judge which axes we want IK to calculate for, we must be viewing rotations in the parent coordinate system.

2. Press **m** to again bring up the Motion Options panel, but this time, click on the **Controllers and Limits** tab.

3. Select **Inverse Kinematics** for both heading and pitch controllers. (See Figure 6.8.)

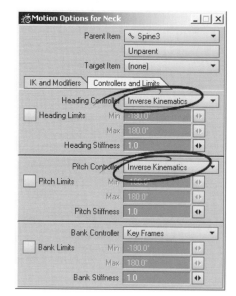

**Figure 6.8** IK has been activated for controlling the heading and pitch axes of the neck bone.

### NOTE:

If you're like most people, you want to move the head bone to see that the neck bone does indeed track to it. (Neck will have to be temporarily unhidden in order to see it while it is not selected—just be sure to hide it again after you're done.) Whenever you do something like this to test a control or a setting, be sure to move the time-slider away from Frame 0 (you can easily delete all keys from a frame other than 0, and get back to your character's "rest pose"). This is important even if you're <u>almost</u> entirely sure you don't have Auto Key Create active. It's always a good idea to cover your behind and give the computer as little opportunity to frustrate you as possible (an ounce of prevention and all that). This is just one small habit to get into to save you from having to utter the phrase, "What do you mean I can't Undo?" along with some choice expletives. (You need your character in this rest pose—where all bones are exactly where they were created as skelegons—in order to properly set skinning attributes/weight maps. And it is always best to have your character load in the same, balanced pose. If you make a modification to the key at Frame 0, you won't be able to get back to this exact pose. And if you delete the key at Frame 0, and that happens to be the only key in the scene for that item, that item has a high probability of being grossly misplaced when you reload the scene.)

**ADVANCED NOTE:**

If you're moving the head bone and are thinking to yourself, "Hey, I can move the head a mile away from the neck! What gives?" Don't worry. Under moderate control, it just gives the feeling of good old-fashioned squash-and-stretch in action. It has been my experience that viewers don't notice if a neck, wrist, or ankle elongates a little during animation. This kind of setup is the only way I know that will allow you to lock a character's hands (which will function the same way as the head) to a surface like a tabletop and still have full range of motion for the rest of the body. This setup allows you to not fret that the wrong twist of the body will pull the hands away from the table. As for the head, yes, it is possible to make an IK setup where the control for the head/neck simply moves the joint between the head and neck, with the head staying attached while pointing in the same direction as the control. However, if you also use IK to have the eyes point toward targets in the scene, having them in a hierarchy that is already controlled by IK (the head/neck) seems to give the solver fits. I've experienced solving errors for the eyes from missing their goal objects by a few degrees to rotating in the exact opposite direction from what you'd expect (often the only way to be sure of this sort of thing is to attach a wireframe two-point poly that is invisible to the camera and not casting shadows to the eyeball extending in its exact "line of sight").

4.  Select **RightThigh**, then bring up the Motion Options panel.

5.  Set both the heading and pitch controllers to use Inverse Kinematics.

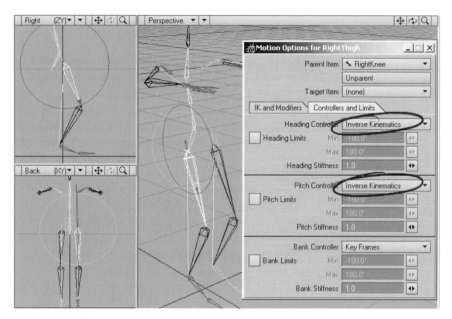

**Figure 6.9** The RightThigh, set to use IK for heading and pitch.

6. Select **RightCalf**.

7. Set only Heading Controller to use Inverse Kinematics.

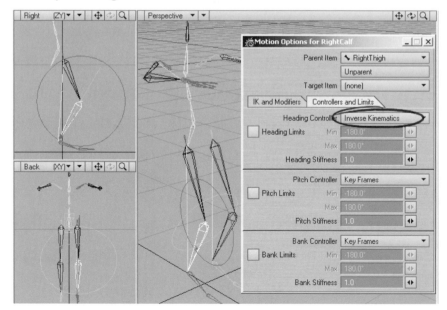

**Figure 6.10** The RightCalf, set to use IK for heading.

---

**ADVANCED NOTE:**

For those of you who are wondering, "Why heading? Shouldn't pitch be the axis that the calf would rotate to swing in a normal, 'calf-like' motion?" You're absolutely right; this would be the normal way of things, except that we used skelegons to create it and its parents (the reason we tweaked the spine, pelvis, and feet in Section 5.3). Could we futz with things to make it work as we think it should? Yes, we could, but should we? Not really. IK will be used to control this bone, and LightWave will have to go through the mental calisthenics of "When I think pitch, I really mean heading." The only reason to tweak an oddity like this would be if we were going to manually control an aspect of this bone where it would get frustrating to have axes not be what we're used to. (We'll have to do this for the feet and toes.)

---

**NOTE:**

Your character's leg should now follow his foot when you move RightFoot. (Just make sure you're on some frame other than 0 when you test it, and delete the keyframe if one is automatically created!)

---

8. Set the heading and pitch controllers for LeftThigh to **Inverse Kinematics**.

9. Set the heading controller for LeftCalf to **Inverse Kinematics**.

Now for the arms: We're going to have to break a rule for the arms. The rule we're going to break is that rule of never having IK solve for more than two of an item's axes. It's a good rule, one that does indeed have a lot of merit. But remember, in this business, the most creative solutions are often the ones most strongly rewarded.

I have found, over the course of many evolutions of setups, that arms, because of their extensive and complex range of motion, need special handling. The skin can bunch or tear, and the IK that drives them is prone to flipping and solving errors. The zones that cause flipping change locations with each different base position you have for your skeleton's arms (how your skeleton's arms are in their initial pose, whether they are straight out in front, or to the sides, or a combination of the two as we have for our character). The relationship of forearm to bicep to the bicep's parent all factor heavily in how easily IK can figure rotations of these items. The setup we've created here has the bicep and forearm and their rotation points in a relationship to each other such that IK can <u>reliably</u> solve for all three axes of the bicep. With the arm bones positioned as they are, the usual problems of having a joint solve for three axes actually work for us, and the resulting movement more realistically mimics life than with any other setup I've used.

> **NOTE:**
>
> I have to mention this just to help illustrate that all-important point that you have to push beyond the bounds of being "safe" (when you have the time to fully R&D that is), that creativity in how you solve problems is a virtue in this work. When I was R&D-ing this setup for a project some time ago, I figured that the arms of the character should be in the position we currently have them because it puts them within the average range of motion; skin would need to stretch and compress less than if the character were spread eagle. All the preliminary math also suggested that this should be an extremely stable IK setup. In reality, when I first put this together, and was using IK only for the bicep's heading and pitch (as I had been taught), the setup was one of the most jittery, flippiest IKs I've ever seen in LightWave. I beat my head against the math for weeks, trying every solution I could think of to force it to work; everything I knew about IK said it should work, and yet it didn't. I was just about to scrap the whole thing. After about two weeks of fighting with the arm's IK, going through every clever variation I could think of, on a whim I turned on IK for the bicep's bank. The deadline for having the characters working was looming, and I had tried everything else; I <u>should</u> have just gone back to an old setup I knew would work relatively well. Much to my surprise, with IK solving for h, p, and b, the arm instantly began functioning just as all the preliminary math said it should! The result is the setup you're building right now, one of the strongest, most realistic, and reliable IKs I've used in any package. Never be afraid to try something weird. Flying in the face of convention is often rewarded, just so long as you've got the time to backtrack to something you know will work.

10. Select **RightBicep**.

11. Set IK to control RightBicep's heading, pitch, and bank.

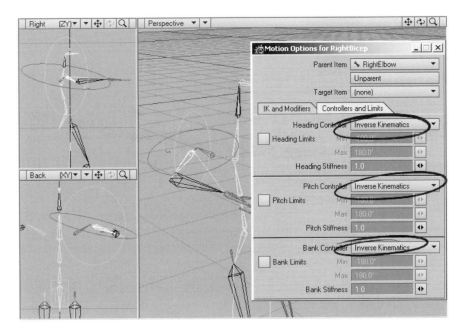

**Figure 6.11** Using IK for all three of RightBicep's axes.

12. Select **RightForearm**.

13. Set IK to control RightForearm's heading.

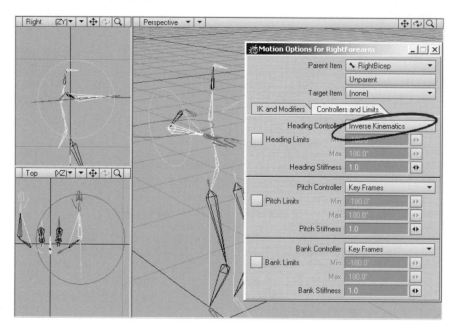

**Figure 6.12** Using IK for controlling only the heading of the RightForearm. (Which, incidentally, unlike the calf, is aligned with heading, pitch, and bank as we'd expect them to be.)

14. Repeat steps 10-13 for your character's left bicep and forearm.

---

### ADVANCED NOTE:

There are some setup artists who use rotation limits ("constraints" in other packages) to keep a forearm or a calf from bending beyond its normal range of motion. I don't find there to be much need for this if there is enough of a helping "pre-bend" between the forearm and bicep, or the calf and thigh. I've actually found that it can increase the possibility of jitters or flipping because it gives IK yet one more thing to think about. Jitter or no, LightWave's rotation limits (currently) cause an item to stop like it hit a brick wall when it reaches the end of its range of movement. This is enough reason for me to strongly advise against using rotation limits in character animation.

---

## 6.5 **Deactivating Individual Manual Controls**

Here, we're going to deactivate the manual controls for items that shouldn't be moved, rotated, or scaled. This keeps you from accidentally sliding a control out of alignment while you're in that animation Zen-zone (quite an easy thing to do, really). If a control does get moved, scaled, or rotated by accident and you don't notice it quickly enough to undo, sometimes you can delete the offending keys on the offending axes. You can sometimes go to Frame 0, and create a key on the offending frame for the offending axes with the SRT data of Frame 0 (by pressing Enter and typing in a different frame number on which to create the keyframe). Often, your scene is just FUBAR. This step, though slightly tedious, helps to keep these problems at bay.

> **NOTE:**
>
> If you are using LW 6.0 or an early release of 6.5b, you can still click on a handle (Layout's little icons for scaling, rotation, and translation) and affect that axis <u>even when that axis has been disabled for manual interaction</u>! Beware! And if you can, upgrade to 7, or at least to the final release of 6.5b. I've seen many promising scenes badly mangled by an animator accidentally clicking on a handle for a control that shouldn't be moved. (If you absolutely can't upgrade for whatever reason, a stopgap solution is to turn off Show Handles—Display|Display Options|Show Handles. It isn't a pretty solution, but it does work.)

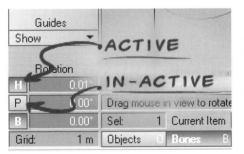

**Figure 6.13** To deactivate a control, click on the button next to its numeric input field. Controls must be deactivated individually for each axis for Move t, Rotate y, and Stretch h.

**NOTE:**

In the case of *Hand_Trans and *Hand_Rot, I find it to be much easier to get the exact follow-through I'm looking for if I use *Hand_Trans for heading and bank, and *Hand_Rot for pitch and bank. You can use all three axes for a single hand control if you wish (and sometimes you may have to in order to get the exact placement you need), but this greatly limits your control of how the hand rotates between keyframes.

**NOTE:**

The bones in this list are laid out in the order in which they were created as skelegons in Chapter 4. You can move down to the next one by pressing the Down Arrow, and up to the previous one by pressing the Up Arrow.

The following is a list of all the items in our scene that pertain to our character. Axes with an "X" in that column are axes that are to be active. Axes marked with an "o" are optional; I generally don't use them, but feel free to if you want. Those left blank indicate controls to remain inactive.

| Item | Move X | Move Y | Move Z | Rotate H | Rotate P | Rotate B | Stretch X | Stretch Y | Stretch Z |
|---|---|---|---|---|---|---|---|---|---|
| Ch_04 (Character Mesh) | X | X | X | X | o | o | X | X | X |
| NeckGoal | | | | | | | | | |
| RightArmGoal | | | | | | | | | |
| LeftArmGoal | | | | | | | | | |
| RightLegGoal | | | | | | | | | |
| LeftLegGoal | | | | | | | | | |
| Root | X | X | X | X | X | X | X | X | X |
| Pelvis | | | | X | X | X | X | X | X |
| Spine1 | X | X | X | X | X | X | X | X | X |
| Spine2 | | | | X | X | X | o | o | o |
| Spine3 | | | | X | X | X | o | o | o |
| Head | X | X | X | X | X | X | X | X | X |
| RightHand_Trans | X | X | X | X | o | X | X | X | X |
| RightHand_Rot | | | | o | X | X | | | |
| RightShoulder | | | | X | X | | | | |
| RightElbow | | | | | | X | | | |

| Item | Move X | Move Y | Move Z | Rotate H | Rotate P | Rotate B | Stretch X | Stretch Y | Stretch Z |
|---|---|---|---|---|---|---|---|---|---|
| LeftHand_Trans | X | X | X | X | o | X | X | X | X |
| LeftHand_Rot | | | | o | X | X | | | |
| LeftShoulder | | | | X | X | | | | |
| LeftElbow | | | | | | X | | | |
| RightFoot | X | X | X | X | X | X | X | X | X |
| RightToes | | | | o | X | X | o | o | o |
| RightKnee | | | | | | X | | | |
| LeftFoot | X | X | X | X | X | X | X | X | X |
| LeftToes | | | | o | X | X | o | o | o |
| LeftKnee | | | | | | X | | | |
| RightIndex_Base | | | | X | X | | o | o | o |
| RightIndex_Mid | | | | | X | | o | o | o |
| RightIndex_Tip | | | | | X | | o | o | o |
| RightMiddle_Base | | | | X | X | | o | o | o |
| RightMiddle_Mid | | | | | X | | o | o | o |
| RightMiddle_Tip | | | | | X | | o | o | o |
| RightPinky_Base | | | | X | X | | o | o | o |
| RightPinky_Mid | | | | | X | | o | o | o |
| RightPinky_Tip | | | | | X | | o | o | o |
| RightThumb_Base | | | | X | X | X | o | o | o |
| RightThumb_Mid | | | | | X | | o | o | o |
| RightThumb_Tip | | | | | X | | o | o | o |
| LeftIndex_Base | | | | X | X | | o | o | o |
| LeftIndex_Mid | | | | | X | | o | o | o |
| LeftIndex_Tip | | | | | X | | o | o | o |
| LeftMiddle_Base | | | | X | X | | o | o | o |
| LeftMiddle_Mid | | | | | X | | o | o | o |
| LeftMiddle_Tip | | | | | X | | o | o | o |
| LeftPinky_Base | | | | X | X | | o | o | o |
| LeftPinky_Mid | | | | | X | | o | o | o |

| Item | Move X | Move Y | Move Z | Rotate H | Rotate P | Rotate B | Stretch X | Stretch Y | Stretch Z |
|------|--------|--------|--------|----------|----------|----------|-----------|-----------|-----------|
| LeftPinky_Tip | | | | | X | | 0 | 0 | 0 |
| LeftThumb_Base | | | | X | X | X | 0 | 0 | 0 |
| LeftThumb_Mid | | | | | X | | 0 | 0 | 0 |
| LeftThumb_Tip | | | | | X | | 0 | 0 | 0 |
| Neck | | | | | | | | | |
| Neck_Puller | | | | | | | | | |
| RightBicep | | | | | | | | | |
| RightForearm | | | | | | | | | |
| RightArm_Puller | | | | | | | | | |
| LeftBicep | | | | | | | | | |
| LeftForearm | | | | | | | | | |
| LeftArm_Puller | | | | | | | | | |
| RightThigh | | | | | | | | | |
| RightCalf | | | | | | | | | |
| RightLeg_Puller | | | | | | | | | |
| LeftThigh | | | | | | | | | |
| LeftCalf | | | | | | | | | |
| LeftLeg_Puller | | | | | | | | | |

## ADVANCED NOTE:

As always, rules are made to be broken. If you feel that you can get the exact silhouette you need only by moving, rotating, or scaling an item that I've said shouldn't be moved, rotated, or scaled, by all means, go for it! But be sure and save a revision before doing so, just in case you find it's a blind alley. Play, have fun, be creative... and always CYA!

## Chapter 7

# Point Weighting

For this chapter, we'll be going back into Modeler to assign the points in our character's mesh to move with the different bones we've created. There is an art to this. And to be honest, there are people out there who are much better than I am. I'll be giving you a foundation to build on. Creativity is rewarded. Use your imagination. Observation and extrapolation are the only true keys to point weighting. (Move your own arm and see just how much of your shoulder moves when your bicep swings forward and back.) Through close observation of the "real world," you will see where the subtleties lie that will get the points of your model moving in the most believable way possible.

> **NOTE:**
>
> The most believable way may not always be most realistic. Animation has always been about giving a visual representation of how it <u>feels</u> to do a thing, not necessarily exactly how it <u>looks</u> to do a thing.

# 7.1 **Point Weighting Basics**

Point weighting is something that has to be done whenever you are using a continuous mesh model (versus using a set of separate objects to comprise your character). Point weighting has to be done in Softimage, Maya, MH3D, 3DS Max, and LightWave. External programs, plug-ins, and scripts can help but only to a degree. Point weighting always, <u>always</u> needs an observant, artful human touch.

In short, point weighting is telling which point to move with which bone. It is telling each point how much to move with one bone versus another. (How much does a point 1 cm from your elbow move with your bicep? How much does it move with your forearm?)

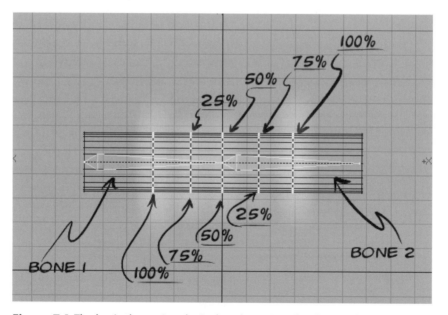

**Figure 7.1** The basic theory I go by is that the points that lay on the meridian where the tip of Bone 1 meets the root of Bone 2 are affected 50% by Bone 1 and 50% by the Bone 2. Move a little way into Bone 1, and Bone 1 has 75% influence over the points while Bone 2 has 25%. A little more into Bone 1, and it has complete (100%) influence over these points.

This basic theory has to be adapted on a case-by-case basis. It is only through applying point weighting, bringing the model into Layout, and moving it through key poses that you can tell if the weighting is correct. In the case of a production environment, the lead or directing animator will usually put together a quick set of movements that take the character through some extreme poses or antics. The animator works only with the IK'd skeleton while the artist in charge of skinning works on the first pass of point weighting. The artist doing the weighting then puts his weighted model onto the animation, scrutinizing how the skin pulls, twists, and bunches. The point weighting artist refines problem areas, confers with the animator, and makes any notes of tight spots in this general-purpose setup that may need to be replaced with a special-purpose setup.

> **NOTE:**
>
> Often, special-case models and/or weightings have to be made for close-up shots where the model is in a pose that can't be handled correctly by the general-purpose point weighting.

# 7.2 Beginning the Point Weighting Process

We're going to start off with something simple, the leg from the thigh down. This is an area that doesn't have more than two bones exerting influence over any given point.

1.  Load the model you used for Chapters 5 and 6 into Modeler. (For me, this is Objects\chapters\ch_04.lwo.)

2.  Save this model to a directory where having lots of versions of it won't cause clutter. Name it in a way that will make sense to you if you stumble across it years later. (Objects\Work\ch07\ch_07_w01.lwo, where "w??" is my current revision number, is what I'll be using.)

3.  Center in on your character's right knee.

4. Set the rendering style for the Perspective window to **Weight Shade** (see Figure 7.2).

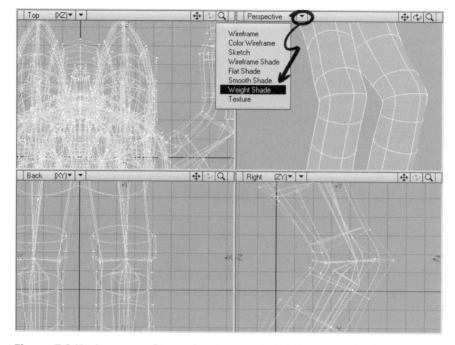

**Figure 7.2** Having zoomed in on the character's right knee, set the Perspective window's rendering style to Weight Shade.

## NEWBIE NOTE:

Weight shade is a rendering style you can set for <u>any</u> window. Points that have values closer to +100% (for the currently active weight map) color their adjoining polygons and patches deeper and deeper red. As points approach –100%, the adjoining polygons and patches will become deeper and deeper blue. I will often activate weight shade for a particular viewport just to get a quick "second opinion" on how the weighting has been applied, comparing that isometric view to the Perspective window. (Sometimes, you'll find it handy to examine your model with multiple views set to perspective and weight shade.)

> **NOTE:**
>
> In the way I point weight, I never set a point to have a cumulative value below 0% or above 100%. Values below 0% can make the point move in the <u>opposite</u> direction of the bone. A value of 200% can make that point move twice as far as the bone has moved. This can be corrected by using the weight normalization setting found in both Layout and Modeler (see Section 7.5), but I find that it is much easier in the long run to simply keep my values precise.

It is easiest to plan point weight groupings with the skelegons in the Background layer to serve as a guide.

5.  With the **Polygons** ^H selection mode active and nothing selected, press **w** to bring up the Polygon Statistics window.

6.  Click on the + next to the Skelegons field to select them.

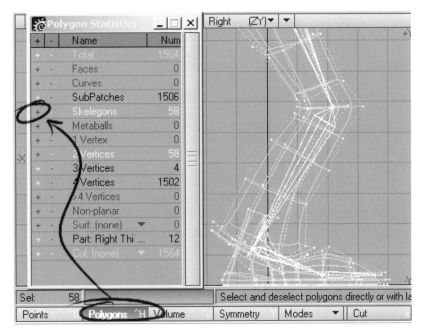

**Figure 7.3** Selecting the skelegons.

7. Press **x** to cut the skelegons from the current layer.

8. Paste the skelegons into Layer 2, then select Layer 1 to be your Foreground layer, and Layer 2 to be your Background layer. (See Figure 7.4.)

9. Hide everything in the Foreground layer but the polygons of the right leg and foot. (This will make it harder to accidentally select the points of the left leg while assigning weight map values to the right.)

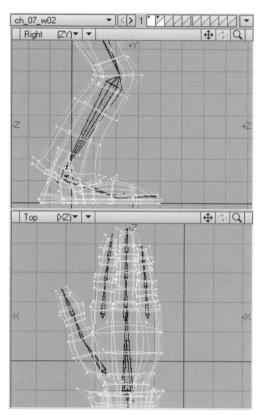

**Figure 7.4** With the skelegons in a Background layer, we can more easily see where the skelegons/bones will need to exert their influences.

> **NOTE:**
>
> If you don't have any maps listed under the weight map list selector (i.e., you're using a character of your own or the maps were cleared) you'll need to (re)create them (see Chapter 4, Section 4.6, Step 24). With both the Mesh and Skelegon layers in the foreground, select **Map|Weight & Color|More|Bone Weights**. Enter **0 m** for Threshold Value, and set Use Threshold to **Clip**. Click **OK**. (You'll also need to pay special attention to the notes in Section 7.3. If we've only just created the character's weight maps, they weren't around when skelegons were converted to bones in Chapter 5 and weren't automatically assigned to your character's bones at that time. We will need to do this manually; see Figure 7.24.)

10. With the W button active in the lower-right corner (for Weight Map mode), click on the selector bar and choose **RightThigh**. (See Figure 7.5.)

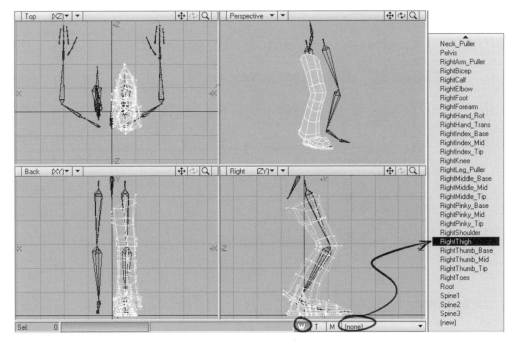

**Figure 7.5** With all but the right leg hidden, select the RightThigh weight map as the active weight map.

11. Select the points that lie on the junction of the thigh and calf.

12. Click on **Map|General|Set Map Value**. See Figure 7.6. (I've assigned the F10 key to this command. Because this command is used a lot in point weighting, I'd suggest that you also assign a keyboard shortcut to it.)

13. Because we have RightThigh already selected as our active weight map, RightThigh appears as the default map in the Vertex Map selector (you could change this selector to any other map, should you wish).

14. Enter **50** for Value 1. (We only need to worry about Value 1 for point weighting; LightWave automatically assumes the value to be a percent.)

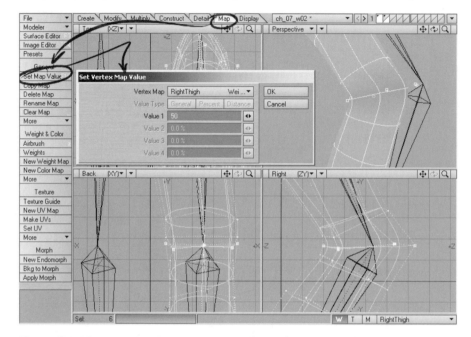

**Figure 7.6** After pressing **Enter** in step 14, the surface surrounding the isoparm defined by the points we have selected turns the shade of red corresponding to the value of +50%.

15. In the lower-right corner of the screen, select the **RightCalf** weight map. (The red coloring will disappear from the Weight Shade window because only RightThigh has values assigned to its points right now; RightCalf does not.)

16. Activate **Set Map Value** again, and enter **50** for Value 1.

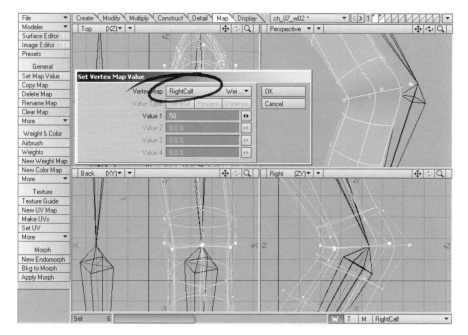

**Figure 7.7** These points will now move with 50% of their influence coming from RightThigh and 50% coming from RightCalf.

17. Select the points that influence the isoparm directly above the knee joint. (See Figure 7.8.)

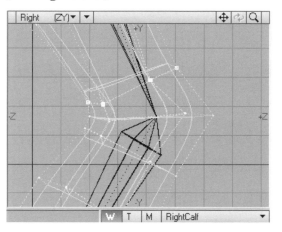

**Figure 7.8** These will be influenced 25% by RightCalf and 75% by RightThigh.

18. With the RightCalf map still as the active weight map, activate **Set Map Value** and enter **25** for Value 1. (See Figure 7.9.)

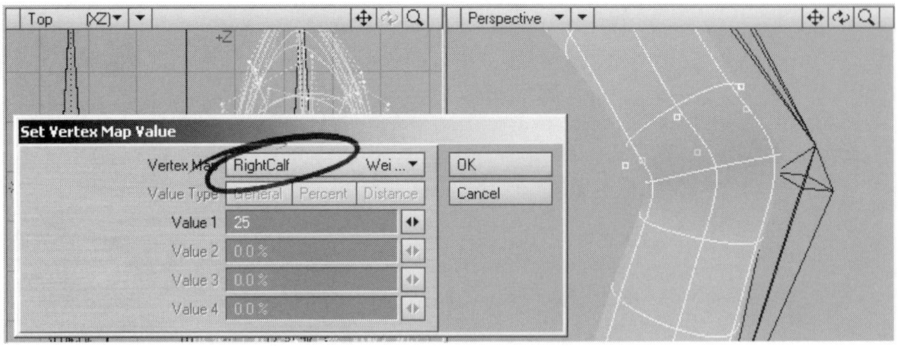

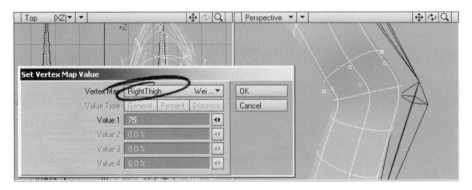

**Figure 7.9** RightCalf now has 25% influence over these points.

19. Select **RightThigh** as the active weight map, and set Value 1 for these points to be **75**. (See Figure 7.10.)

**Figure 7.10** RightThigh now has 75% influence over these points.

20. Select the points that influence the next higher isoparm. (See Figure 7.11.)

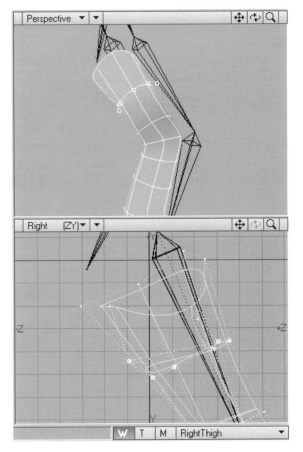

**Figure 7.11** These points will be set to follow RightThigh 100%.

**123**

21. Bring up **Set Map Value** again and enter **100** for these points.

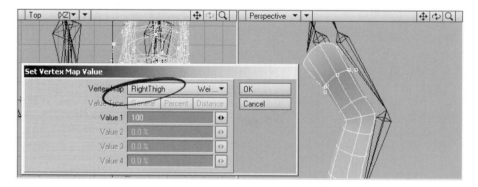

**Figure 7.12** These points will now follow 100% of RightThigh's motion.

22. Set the points of the next highest isoparm to a value of **75** for RightThigh. (See Figure 7.13.)

**Figure 7.13** These points will move 75% with RightThigh and 25% with Pelvis.

23. Select the Pelvis weight map (in the lower-right corner), and set Value 1 for these points to **25**.

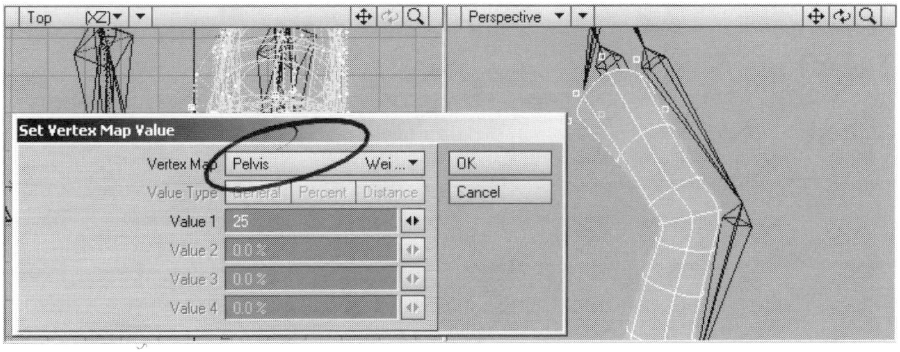

**Figure 7.14** These points will now move 25% with Pelvis.

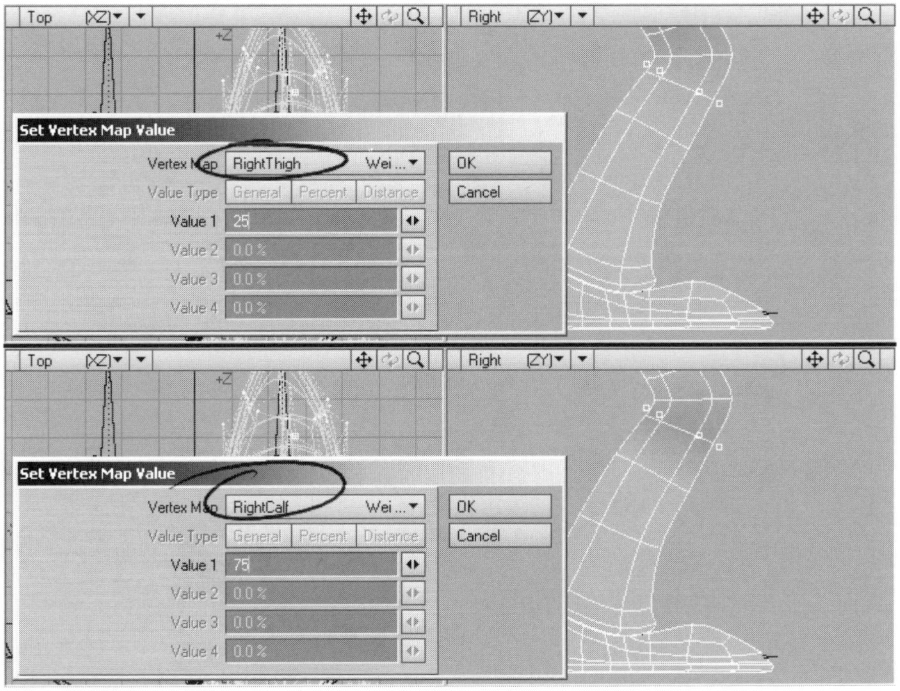

**Figure 7.15** Set the points of the isoparm just below the knee to move 25% with RightThigh and 75% with RightCalf. (Two images are shown together for illustrative purposes.)

125

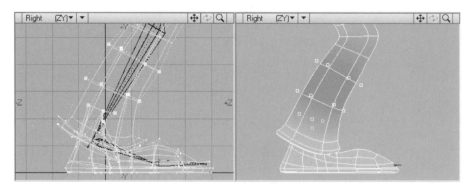

**Figure 7.16** Set the points of the next two lower isoparms and the points that make up the top of the foot to move 100% with RightCalf.

24. Hide the foot so we can be sure to only select the points of the pant leg.

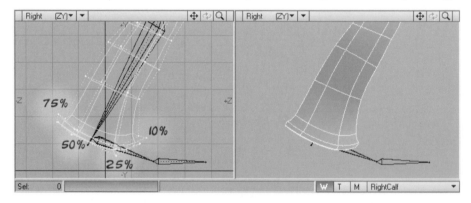

**Figure 7.17** Using this illustration as a guide, assign RightCalf weight maps for these points.

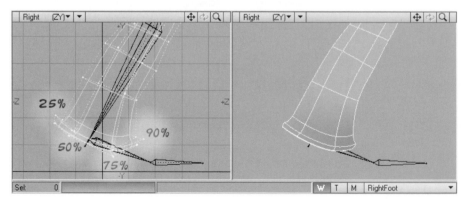

**Figure 7.18** Using this illustration as a guide, assign RightFoot weight maps for these points.

25. Press \ to unhide everything in the model.

26. Rehide everything except the right foot.

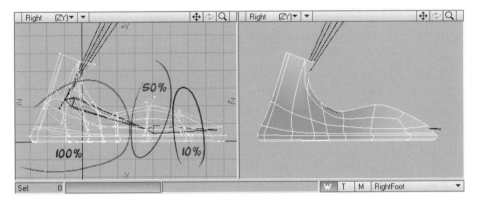

**Figure 7.19** Using this illustration as a guide, assign RightFoot weight maps for these points.

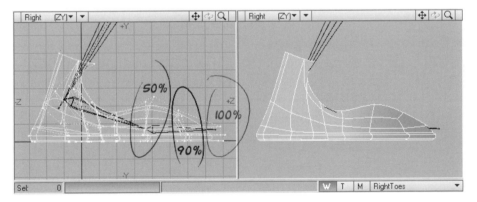

**Figure 7.20** Using this illustration as a guide, assign RightToes weight maps for these points.

This method is the basis for all point weighting. As you gain familiarity with this process, you will develop your own ways of working, your own tricks and shortcuts. Where multiple bones exert multiple influences, such as in the shoulder where a point may be affected by Spine3, RightShoulder, and RightBicep, you simply visualize how much influence each bone should have on the point and assign the values accordingly.

The values on each point must add up to 100%. If the combined values on a point add up to less than 100%, it will get "left behind" as you move the model. (The closer to 100% this cumulative value is, the less noticeable the lag, until the character is moved significantly from its starting position. Be very watchful of these values.) If you have the combined values on a given point add up to more than 100%, that point may "leap ahead" of the motion described by its controlling bone. (LightWave has a bit of a fix for values over 100%: activating Weight Normalization under the Bone Properties panel of Layout. It is far better to be precise with your point weighting than to depend on software to fix it.)

# 7.3 Swapping Models and Testing Weight Mappings

The only way to really know if your point weighting is working is to take it for a test spin in Layout. In this section, we'll check out the weighting we just did for the right leg. In order to do that, we've got to swap out an old model for a new one. Using this technique, and having common bone and weight map names, you'll be able to use almost every animation you do with almost every character you make!

1.  In Layout, load up the scene you created in the last chapter.

2.  In a working directory set aside for Chapter 7, save a version of this scene with a name that will make sense to you if you come back to it years later. Something like "Scenes\Work\ch07\ch_07_MappingTest_01_w01.lws" will do nicely.

> **NOTE:**
>
> If you need to use mine, it can be found in Scenes\chapters\ch_06.lws

3.  In the Scene Editor, make sure that your character model's visibility is set to **Shaded Solid**.

4.  Press **f**, and type **10** to jump to Frame 10. (We're going to be playing with the controls on Frame 10, so we can check that our character comes in properly on its "rest pose," Frame 0.)

**NOTE:**

If, while you're working, bending your model around, you accidentally hit r (an easy thing to do) LW will record the selected bone's current position and rotation as its rest position. If this happens, your model's skin will be fouled for that bone. To fix it, you need to go to the frame where the skeleton is at rest and press r for the offending bone. So, once again, just to drive a point well into the ground: You always need to have a frame in your scene where your skeleton is at rest. This can be at 0, –20, –100, or whatever. Just don't get caught putting the final touches on your masterwork scene (which, because of being "in the groove," wasn't saved for several hours) and accidentally tap the r key; otherwise you'll likely wind up exploring new and more creative combinations of expletives than you ever thought possible.

5. Select the **RightFoot** bone, and move it up and forward.

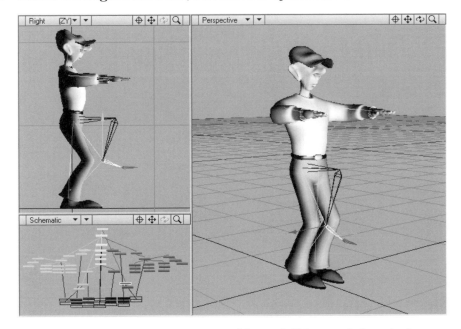

**Figure 7.21** Moving the RightFoot up and forward. This scene is from the last chapter, and in it we were using the model from Chapter 4. No points are weighted, so nothing moves, yet.

6. With the mesh (object) selected, choose **Items|Replace|Replace With Object File**....

7. Select the latest revision of the model you've been working on in this chapter.

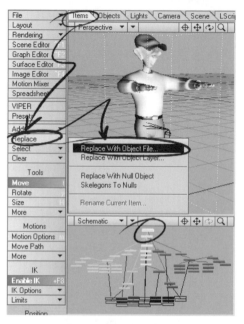

**Figure 7.22** Replacing the old mesh with something newer...

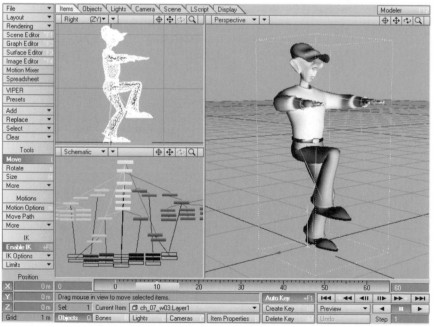

**Figure 7.23** If everything is as it should be, your replacement mesh loads in with the newly assigned weight maps for the right thigh, calf, foot, and toes. The points of the right leg are now controlled by the bones of the right leg. (If not, look to the following notes for troubleshooting information.)

**NOTE:**

If your new mesh isn't doing quite what you think it should be doing, double-check your mappings in Modeler to make sure that no points are mapped that shouldn't be, and that all points that should have mapping have correct values.

**NOTE:**

If your mapping values are correct, and you're still not getting the results you expect, or if the model isn't moving at all, you might need to check to see that bone weight maps are properly assigned for each bone.

When you convert skelegons into bones, and you have already created weight maps (which we did in Chapter 4, Section 4.6, Step 24), bone weight maps are automatically assigned to the bone (skelegon) of the same name. If no weight maps exist on the skelegons at the time you convert them into bones, no weight maps are assigned. If this is the case, you have to assign each weight map to each bone manually.

1. Select the root bone.

2. Press **p** to bring up the Item Properties window for Root.

3. Under Bone Weight Map, make sure that the map **Root** is selected. (See Figure 7.24.)

4. Press the **Down Arrow** to scroll through all the bones and make sure that Bone Weight Map matches Current Bone for each bone.

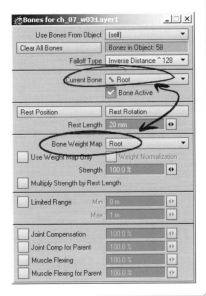

**Figure 7.24** The bone weight map should match the current bone for every bone in your model.

## ADVANCED NOTE:

Another way to apply motion from one model to another is to use the Use Bones From Object setting in the Bone Properties window (see Figure 7.25). (This is a fantastic way of comparing two ideas you might have for weighting a problem area, like the hips.)

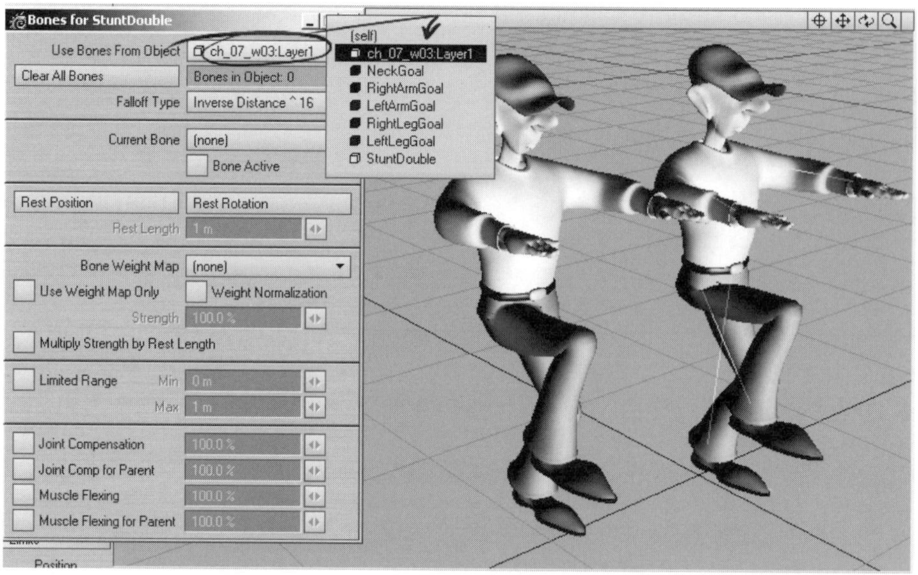

**Figure 7.25** A version of the character named "StuntDouble" was loaded into the scene. Under the Bone Properties window for StuntDouble, I chose ch_07_w03:Layer1, the model I am currently using to test point weighting. All SRT from all bones of ch_07_w03:Layer1 is applied to StuntDouble.

All motion from the bones of ch_07_w03:Layer1 is applied to StuntDouble. (This is an excellent technique for rudimentary crowd scenes.)

8. Using the RightFoot control (bone), stretch the character's leg out and rotate the foot in ways a foot would rotate.

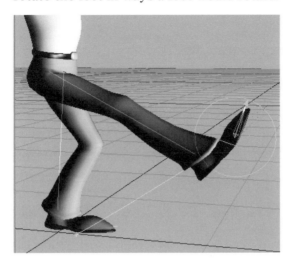

**Figure 7.26** Rotating the RightToes as well, watching the areas of the knee, ankle, and toes to see if the point weighting looks believable for this character. (Remember, we haven't really blended the weighting up into the hips, so we're not looking at that area yet.)

> **NOTE:**
>
> It isn't necessary to cover all possible ranges of movement, just things that may be common positions for this character. If you need specific poses that are distant from the character's normal range of movement, you'll need to build special-case models/point weightings to handle unique instances where the general-purpose setup breaks.

> **NOTE:**
>
> Here is where your own sense of artistry comes into play. You have to judge. A balance of your own (or your director's) stylistic sensibilities and what you think you'll eventually need this character to do determines how much the weighting needs finessing.

And that's all there is to point weighting! All the points in the model are handled in the same way. Use your best judgment when assigning weights in Modeler, toggling between subpatches and polys, then test your decisions in Layout, making changes where necessary.

Point weighting is a logician's dream. It is a process that follows the pathways of reason and empiricism. There are no magic wands or silver bullet solutions to point weighting. Thus far, I've yet to find an "automatic" plug-in that can even give you a good base from which to start. I find it much easier and quicker to just start from scratch, and proceed as we have done with the right leg. (Yoichiro's Mirror Weights plug-in—available free, online at http://www.flay.com—is something I do, however, recommend. It can copy weights from one side of your model to the other and is a real time-saver.)

The following is a list of the weight maps that need to be assigned. All other weight maps (for control bones that shouldn't have any direct influence on the model) need to be left untouched:

Pelvis, Spine1, Spine2, Spine3, Head, RightHand_Rot, RightShoulder, LeftHand_Rot, LeftShoulder, RightFoot, RightToes, LeftFoot, LeftToes, RightIndex_Base, RightIndex_Mid, RightIndex_Tip, RightMiddle_Base, RightMiddle_Mid, RightMiddle_Tip, RightPinky_Base, RightPinky_Mid, RightPinky_Tip, RightThumb_Base, RightThumb_Mid, RightThumb_Tip, LeftIndex_Base, LeftIndex_Mid, LeftIndex_Tip, LeftMiddle_Base, LeftMiddle_Mid, LeftMiddle_Tip, LeftPinky_Base, LeftPinky_Mid, LeftPinky_Tip, LeftThumb_Base, LeftThumb_Mid, LeftThumb_Tip, RightBicep, RightForearm, LeftBicep, LeftForearm, RightThigh, RightCalf, LeftThigh, LeftCalf, Neck

> **NOTE:**
>
> Don't use Map|Clear Map_ to remove a map we've created from all the vertices in the mesh. If you do, that map will be removed from the character. It will no longer be there for Layout to associate with the bone of the same name. Even bones that have no direct influence on the character (like *Elbow) need to still be associated with a map. Having a bone associated with a "blank" map (for this manner of setup) is the most efficient way to keep it from exerting unwanted influence on the model's points.

# 7.4 **The Use Weight Map Only Option**

There are differing views on whether or not to let LightWave's mathematical falloff for bones play a part in skinning. Letting LightWave use its falloff to influence the points affected by bones can indeed help quickly smooth problem areas, and can sometimes give a point that doesn't have its values add up to 100% that extra oomph it needs to stay on track. My issue with using falloff is that it is very difficult to control details where bones are close together as in the fingers. It can also make it very difficult to troubleshoot problem points with values less than 100%. Most importantly, depending on falloff to clean up after you can make for sloppy weighting habits. If you can make it work by hand, you really understand what you're doing.

My general MO is that when given a choice to do something right by hand or to depend on a computer system that might break when you need it most, I always opt for the more controllable of the two. (If the system needs adjusting under a deadline, you can spend more time trying to find and fix a problem in which the computer intervenes heavily than it would have taken to do it correctly by hand to begin with.) You will have to decide for yourself which works best for you. (If you are building animations for a video game, chances are the game engine won't have the spare clock cycles to calculate falloff, so you <u>must</u> use the Use Weight Map Only option.)

If this is your first time point weighting, I'd strongly suggest using the Use Weight Map Only setting. Using it, there's nowhere to hide errors. When you have a weighting that works, you know you did it right.

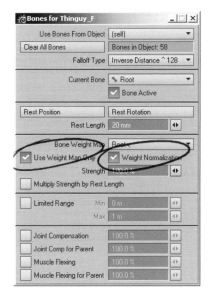

**Figure 7.27** Use Weight Map Only and Weight Normalization.

> **NOTE:**
>
> When you activate Use Weight Map Only, Weight Normaliza-
> tion is automatically checked as well. As much as I am against
> using a subroutine to cover for untidy weighting, I'd suggest
> leaving this active (unless, of course, you are working on a
> video game, in which case you'll have to ask your core pro-
> grammer how he has the game engine deal with cumulative
> values greater than 100%).

Under Item Properties for all bones in your character, activate **Use Weight Map Only** (if this is how you will be working).

## 7.5 **Finding Stray Points**

So now you've got all your points weighted, or at least you're pretty sure you do. You swap the model into Layout, and using the Schematic window to select Root, RightFoot, and LeftFoot, you drag your model a couple of meters –Z. You notice, as in Figure 7.28, that some parts of the skin aren't looking quite right.

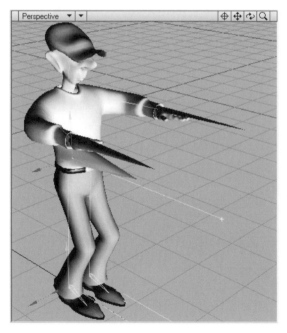

**Figure 7.28** The points that are "left behind" have cumulative weighting values that don't add up to 100%.

This is a technique for letting the model itself tell you where the problem points are:

1.  Switch to Modeler. (If you're not running LightWave with the HUB active so that Modeler and Layout can pass information between each other, you'll have to manually save and reload the model where appropriate.)

2.  From the Current Object pop-up button (to the left of the layer buttons), make sure you have the mesh on which you are currently working in Layout selected. (For me, this would be ch_07_w07.lwo.) See Figure 7.29.

3.  With the mesh layer active, press **Tab** to convert sub-patches into polygons.

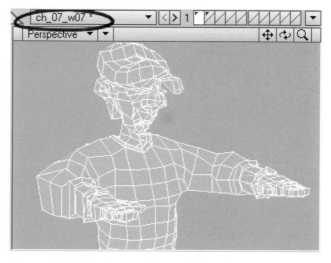

**Figure 7.29** The character's mesh, in polygons.

4.  Switch back to Layout. With the HUB active, you should now be looking at your scene with your character as a polygonal mesh, instead of sub-patches. If this doesn't happen, you may have to save the object in Modeler, then reload in Layout to update the changes.

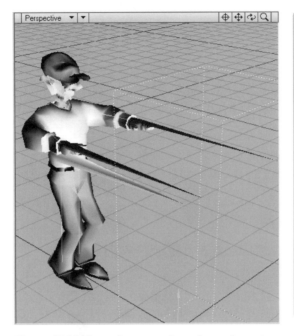

**NOTE:**

If Layout and Modeler seem to not be passing information back and forth properly through the HUB, I'd suggest saving a revision of your scene, closing both Layout and Modeler and forcing the HUB to quit as well. When the HUB stops being reliable, Layout and/or Modeler are often not far behind. Closing everything, the HUB including, and reopening Layout and Modeler is often the best preventative against a nasty crash.

**Figure 7.30** The polygon version of our character now in Layout.

5.  Choose **File|Save|Save Transformed Object....** (A dialog box will come up warning you to "Select a different filename for the transformed object if you want to keep your original object geometry.")

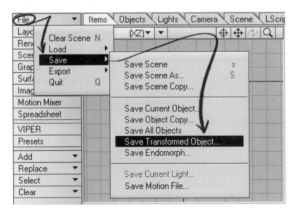

**Figure 7.31** Saving transformed geometry.

6. Name the transformed object **BadPointFinder.lwo**.

7. Switch back to Modeler and load **BadPointFinder.lwo**.

8. Copy the mesh and paste it into Layer 3 of your current working model. (See Figure 7.32.)

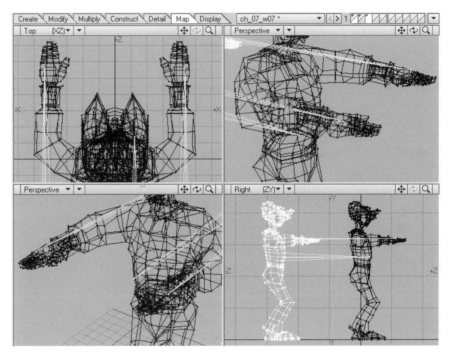

**Figure 7.32** With Layer 1 visible in the background, the mesh of BadPointFinder.lwo points directly to the points that need weighting adjustments!

# 7.6 **Straightening the Feet for Animation**

I saved this part for last because while point weighting, I like to see bones stretching from where their real-life socket would be to where their real-life tip would be. The feet have a notable "L" shape to them, where the ankle is and where the toes connect. Because of this, when we built the foot control bones, we built them at a bit of a downward angle. This works great for getting a visual bearing on point weighting, but in order to animate well, the foot control bones have to be realigned to 0P.

---

**NOTE:**

Were we to leave the feet at this angle, it would be hard to keep them flat on the floor when we rotated them in worldspace H. Even using world coordinates, the feet dip a bit as they rotate in H because LightWave uses parent coordinates to store animation data, regardless of what coordinate system we use to manipulate the controls.

---

**ADVANCED NOTE:**

There are several methods we could use to align the foot controls. This method is the one I use because it requires no "eyeballing."

---

1.  In Layout, make sure you are on Frame 0, that all parts of Auto Key Create are active, and that Parent in Place is <u>deactivated</u>.

2.  Hide your mesh so we can just look at bones for the moment.

3.  Select **RightFoot.**

4.  Choose **Items|Add|Clone Current Item....**

5.  Enter **1** for Number of Clones.

6.  Select **RightFoot (2)**, and choose **Items|Replace|Rename Current Item ....**

7.  Set the new name for this bone to be **RightFoot_Anchor.**

8.  Set RightFoot_Anchor as the parent of RightToes.

9.  Set RightFoot as the Parent of RightFoot_Anchor. (So the hierarchy would be: RightFoot => RightFoot_Anchor => RightToes.)

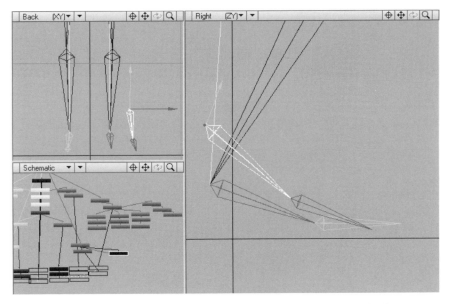

**Figure 7.33** Because Parent in Place is off, things get shifted around a bit. Don't worry; they'll be back in line before you know it.

10. Change RightFoot_Anchor's position to **0X, 0Y, 0Z.**

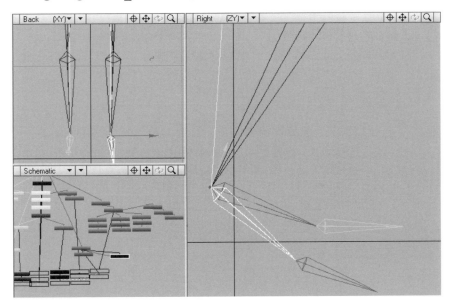

**Figure 7.34** RightFoot_Anchor is now back at the pivot of RightFoot.

11. Select **RightFoot**.

12. Activate **Items|Tools|Pivot|Rotate Pivot Point Tool**.

13. Enter 0 for all axes of the pivot's rotation.

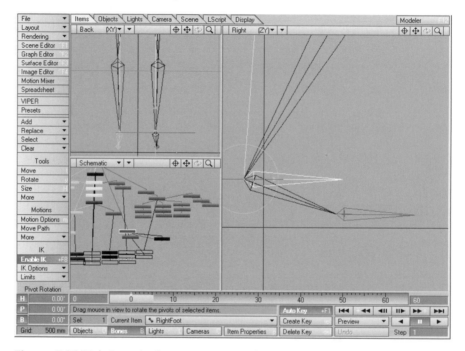

**Figure 7.35** RightFoot_Anchor now assumes the positioning once held by RightFoot. RightToes follows right along into place (being a child of RightFoot_Anchor).

14. Under **Objects|Bones|Rest Length**, set the rest length of RightFoot to **0.020**. (This is just a visual preference thing; I don't like to see a spike sticking out from my character's ankle.)

15. Press **r** to record this new rotation as the bone rest position for RightFoot.

16. Select **RightToes** and press **r** to record bone rest position.

17. Select **RightFoot_Anchor,** and press **r** to record bone rest position.

18. Press **p** to bring up the Item Properties window for RightFoot_Anchor. Uncheck the box labeled Bone Active to deactivate it.

19. Select **(none)** for the Bone Weight Map for RightFoot_Anchor.

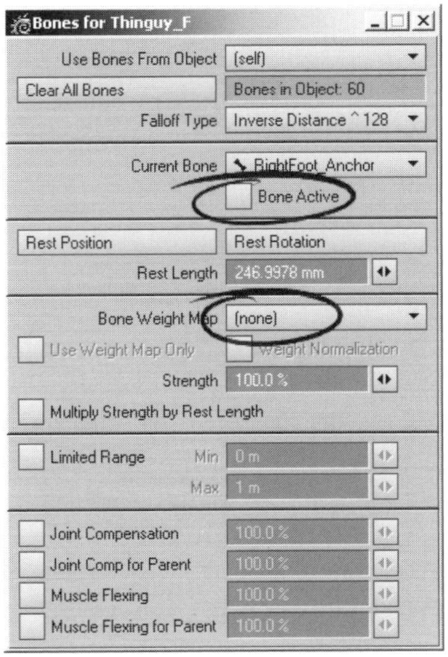

**Figure 7.36** RightFoot_Anchor is just something to keep RightToes in place. It doesn't need to exert influence on the character's points.

20. Hide RightFoot_Anchor and position it neatly into your schematic.

21. Repeat steps 3-20 for LeftFoot.

22. Unhide your character's mesh, and you're ready to get this guy moving!

## 7.7 **Putting Him Through the Motions**

All the points are weighted, nothing lags behind. But is the weighting going to work for the animations the character will be performing? Does he form the silhouettes you want as he's put through a series of poses? Ankles, armpits, buttocks, elbows, knees, shoulders, toes, and wrists have to be critically evaluated, tweaked, and reevaluated.

In a production environment, you would normally have the lead animator for that character or the animation director do a little animation for this character so the motion technical directors (the guys in charge of skinning and a great deal of other things as well) can scrub through the animation frame by frame to see if and where their point weighting could be improved. To this effect, there are two scenes that you can load and swap your model into:

▶ Scenes\chapters\ch_07_PoseTest.lws is a series of poses to see how your character's skin stretches when in common and extreme poses.

▶ Scenes\chapters\ch_07_MotionTest.lws is a short animation for you to see how your character's skin stretches as it moves through a quick bit of action.

> **NOTE:**
>
> In the following chapters, I'll go over the animation controls, and you'll be putting your character through a series of poses. If, as you work, you notice something that doesn't quite seem to be working in the point weighting department, you can always go back into Modeler and finesse the weightings, updating your "final" model at any point of the production process.

# 7.8 **Tidying Up**

Just a few more "housekeeping" kinds of things remain before we move on to animation training itself. Don't worry: They're quick and easy, and they'll be over before you know it.

1. In Modeler, cut and paste the skelegons back into Layer 1 of your character. Clear away any unused data in subsequent layers so you've got everything all neat and tidy on Layer 1.

2. Save a version of your Model in a "Finals" directory, naming it so that you know it is the final version of your character. (Objects\Final\Thinguy_F.lwo works for me.)

3. If you're working on an OS that lets you set "protection bits" (read-only properties) for a file, activate this bit so you don't accidentally delete or write over it. (A backup copy in a separate archival folder is always a good thing, too.)

4. In Layout, swap out the model on which you've been working with your final model.

5. Delete all extraneous keyframes from your scene (so your character is keyed to his rest pose at Frame 0), and hide RightBicep, RightForearm, LeftBicep, LeftForearm, RightThigh, RightCalf, LeftThigh, and LeftCalf (so they can't be accidentally clicked on and selected during animation).

6. Save this scene in a Final directory, designating that this is your setup scene for this character. (Scenes\CharacterSetups\Thinguy_Setup.lws is what I use.)

7. Set the protection bit (and/or make a backup copy) for your setup scene so you will always have something clean and familiar to start all your animations.

And that's it! These are the secrets to character setup (or at least some of them). Everyone has their own way of doing things; everyone finds ways that work best for them. You can use this information as is, or you can blend and mold it to fit your specific needs. Hopefully, even if you're new to LightWave and/or character setup, this section has given you the tools and the understanding to be able to take the mystery out of this all-important foundation of computer animation.

Computer animation is in a constant state of evolution. Setups are devised and abandoned, evolved upon and stripped down. If you happen to stumble upon (or forge through sheer effort) something great, share it with others. You'll be helping the world of animation as a whole, and bettering the impression of animators and technical directors in general!

## Chapter 8

# Using the Controls

OK, so you've done a sizable amount of work on this character setup stuff, from pre-bending to point weighting. It almost makes modeling seem easy in comparison. There's a lot of technical stuff there, but what does it all do?

If you're like most creative people I know, your motto is Run and find out! You've probably played with the controls already and put our guy through some poses. But I'm sure some questions arose, like, "Why do things this way?" or "How do I get it to do this?" or "What's the best way to do that?" In this chapter, I'll show you how to work the controls we've created. And this is simply my favored way of working, nothing more. Now, granted, it works smashingly for me, but remember, you are not limited to this way of working. After going through this chapter, play with what you've learned and see what works well for you. Based on what you've learned about how setups work, you can modify anything and everything to create the controls that work exactly the way you wish to work!

> **NEWBIE NOTE:**
>
> If you would like to work from my setup, it can be found in Scenes\CharacterSetups\Thinguy_Setup.lws on the companion CD.

> **NOTE:**
>
> If things do not work as described, there may be problems with the character's hierarchy or IK settings (i.e., chains not terminated or IK set to solve for the wrong axis). If you are finding errors, and you wish to understand what went wrong, you may have to backtrack as far as Chapter 4 to find where the errors are.
> Double-check your scenes and hierarchies with the final scenes for each chapter provided on the companion CD. Usually, it is something simple that was overlooked and is easily fixed.

# 8.1 The Model Itself

When I first started building setups, I would build in a special control for moving the character to where he was going to start his scene. I gave this up because it is just one more thing to build, one more thing to keep track of. I now just use the model itself for the gross positioning control.

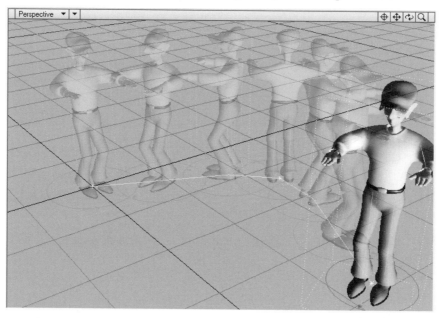

**Figure 8.1** Using the model itself (Objects\Final\Thinguy_F.lwo in my case) to orient and position the character to where he will start his scene.

▷ The model may be moved and rotated on all axes.

> **NOTE:**
>
> For translations, it is usually best to have the coordinate system set to world. For rotations, I generally work in the parent coordinate system, but switch to world or local when gimbal lock makes things tedious.

## 8.2 Root

The Root bone will move everything but your character's feet. (See Figure 8.2.) You can use this bone to get general upper carriage movements while your character's feet stay rooted firmly to the "floor."

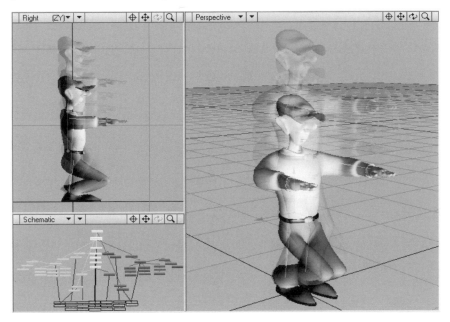

**Figure 8.2** Moving Root in –Y, you get the character's upper carriage to move downward. The character's feet stay locked in place.

▷ Root is designed to move and rotate in all axes.

# 8.3 Pelvis

The Pelvis bone is what you will use to swing the character's hips about.

> **NOTE:**
>
> Even if you're not planning on having him do Middle Eastern dancing, this is an important control. Most people stand with more weight on one leg than the other, "popping" one hip up; the shoulder on the same side swings down. The technical term for this is *contra-posto*. The ancient Greeks were the first to use contra-posto in their sculpture. Having the hips and shoulders rotated in opposite directions is an easy way to add life to any pose.

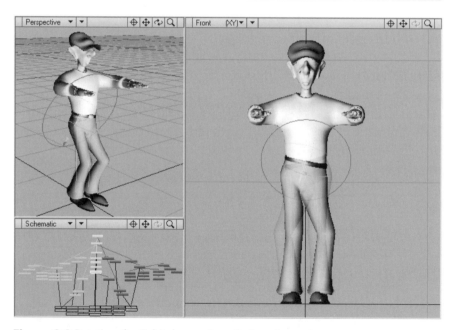

**Figure 8.3** Rotating the Pelvis bone along its heading axis.

▶ Pelvis is designed only to be rotated. It may be rotated in all axes.

## 8.4 **Spinal Bones**

The bones of the spine do pretty much what you'd expect; they rotate to curve the spine of the character into the shapes you need.

Spine1 does double-duty, however, in that it also is used to position the character, leaving the hands and feet rooted in place. (This is useful in a scene where you've got his hands planted on a tabletop and he is getting up from a chair; his hands and feet won't move until you move them with their separate controls.)

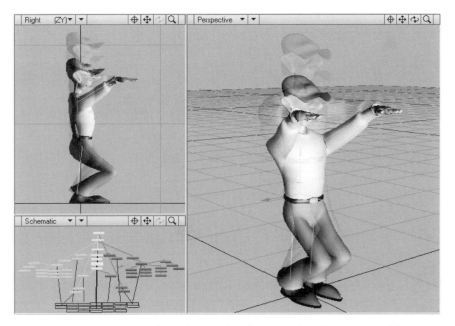

**Figure 8.4** Moving Spine1 in –Y lowers the character, but his hands and feet stay where they are.

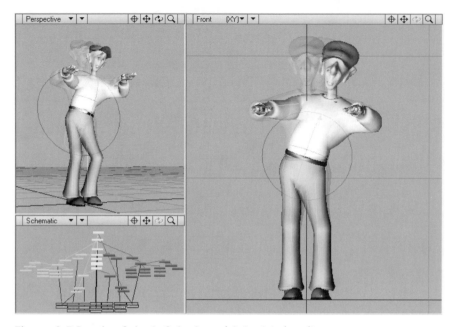

**Figure 8.5** Rotating Spine1, Spine2, and Spine3 in heading.

▸ Spine1 may be rotated and moved on all axes.

▸ Spine2 and Spine3 may be rotated on all axes.

> **NOTE:**
>
> Head is a child of Spine1; it will move when you rotate Spine1 but will remain in place when you rotate Spine2 and Spine3. I've made the setup this way so that the head can follow the larger movements of the character's center of gravity, but remain unaffected by the finer detail movements of the upper two spinal bones. This holds the head more steady when you've got a lot of expression in the shoulders for a walk or antic. I've found it easier to move the head to keep it on top of the neck than to try to counter-rotate it to keep it from wobbling as the shoulders swing about. (Often, I'll have Head as the child of Root or of the model itself so I have absolute control over it in a powerful scene.) Feel free to experiment with having Head as a child of different controls to find what is most intuitive for you.

**NOTE:**

Use Spine1 and Spine2 for the larger curves of the spine. We have a lot more flexibility in the lower part of our backs than we do in the center of our rib cage area. Spine3 is best used for small bits of rotation to add a little bit of visual "final touch" to a pose.

**NEWBIE NOTE:**

I like to have only either heading and bank or pitch and bank active when rotating controls (or using the "handles"). I find it easier to switch back and forth between activating and deactivating heading and pitch than to try to move the mouse exactly in a straight line for precise positioning.

## 8.5 Head

The head is pretty straightforward. You can translate and rotate it to your heart's content. You can pull it away from the body for a frame or two to give the quick-and-easy impression of old-fashioned squash-and-stretch.

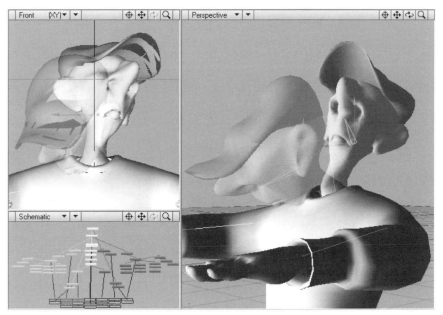

**Figure 8.6** Moving and rotating the head control.

▶ The Head may be moved and rotated on all axes.

# 8.6 **Hand Translation Controls**

RightHand_Trans and LeftHand_Trans take care of moving the hands, and they control the hands' heading and bank rotations. It is better to have a completely separate control for pitch (*Hand_Rot) than to fight with the gimbal lock that is possible when you have H, P, and B all on one control. Even with LightWave now implementing world, parent, and local space coordinate systems, I still recommend a "nested" setup like this. Sometimes, when using world or local coordinate systems, odd values get fed onto an item (where something was 0H, and by rotating it just barely in worldspace, it suddenly has –360.5H). With nested controls, you can more precisely control what axis gets rotated, when it rotates, and how much. With so much expression carried by the hands, I feel this small inconvenience of dealing with two controls to rotate the hands is well worth it.

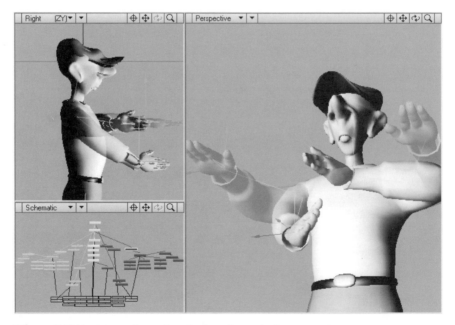

**Figure 8.7** Moving and rotating the hand translation controls.

▶ RightHand_Trans and LeftHand_Trans may be moved in all axes, but they should only be rotated in heading and bank. (In a pinch, you can rotate in pitch, but only sparingly, and get pitch back to 0P as soon as you can.)

# 8.7 **Hand Rotation Controls**

RightHand_Rot and LeftHand_Rot rotate the hands in pitch and bank. They fine-tune the hand rotations.

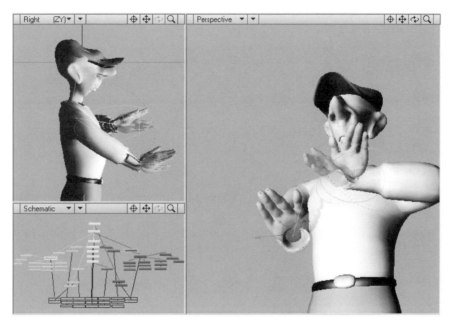

**Figure 8.8** Rotating the hand rotation controls in pitch and bank.

▶ RightHand_Rot and LeftHand_Rot should only be rotated in pitch and bank.

# 8.8 Shoulder Controls

RightShoulder and LeftShoulder allow you to shrug your character's shoulders and cave or expand his chest. Rotating these controls in heading will raise and lower the shoulders. Rotating these controls in pitch will swing the shoulders forward and back.

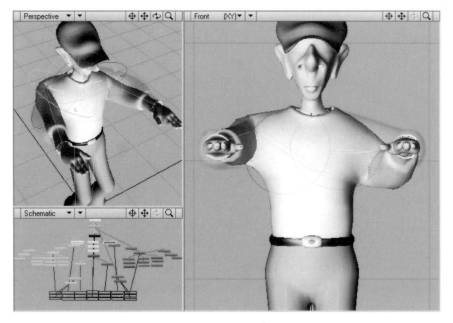

**Figure 8.9** Rotating RightShoulder in +P and rotating LeftShoulder in +H. The character's right shoulder swings back while the left shoulder drops down.

▶ RightShoulder and LeftShoulder should only be rotated in heading and pitch.

# 8.9 Elbow Controls

RightElbow and LeftElbow raise and lower the character's elbows. It is equivalent to the rotator cuff within our own shoulders. This control is limited in how much it can do. Try not to rotate these controls too far; it can be easy to accidentally get a value of +/–360 or more and not realize it. If the elbow rotates from 0 to +/–360 over the course of an animation, it will flip.

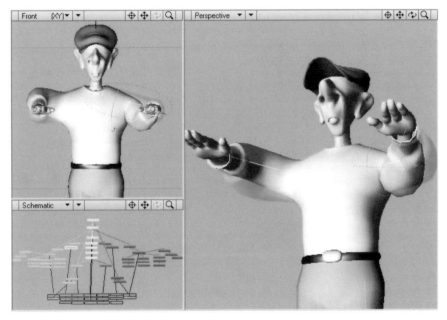

**Figure 8.10** Rotating RightElbow and LeftElbow in +B swings the right elbow up, and the left elbow down. They are mirrors of each other, so you have to watch this when animation gets fast and furious.

▶ RightElbow and LeftElbow should only be rotated in bank.

> **NOTE:**
>
> I find that if I'm having problems getting the elbow into the exact position I'm trying for, I'm probably trying for a pose that would break a real-life arm. There's usually a way to work through a problem pose by taking a look at how my own arms would most naturally strike that particular pose.

# 8.10 **Foot Controls**

RightFoot and LeftFoot take care of all rotations and translations on the feet. Because foot motion is usually much less complex and demanding than hand motion, it usually isn't necessary to nest controls as we have for the hands.

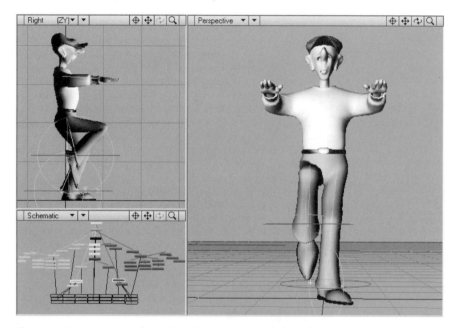

**Figure 8.11** Moving and rotating RightFoot and LeftFoot.

▶ RightFoot and LeftFoot may be moved and rotated on all axes.

# 8.11 **Toe Controls**

RightToes and LeftToes rotate the toe section of the foot. Don't just use these controls to keep the traction section of the foot in contact with the ground; play with them to give some added expression to otherwise stiff poses!

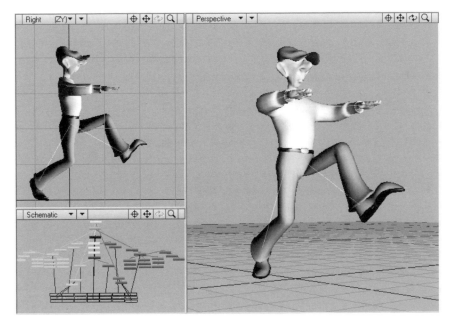

**Figure 8.12** Just using the feet and the toes.

▶ RightToes and LeftToes may be rotated in all axes (though usually pitch and bank will get most jobs done).

## 8.12 **Knee Controls**

The knee controls work almost identically to the elbow controls. The same considerations should be taken into account not to rotate them too far.

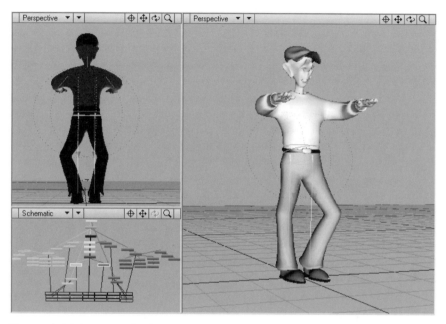

**Figure 8.13** Swinging the knees wide.

▶ RightKnee and LeftKnee should only be rotated in bank.

## 8.13 **The Fingers and Thumb**

The base of all the fingers can be rotated in both heading and pitch. The other two bones of each finger, mid and tip, should only be rotated in pitch.

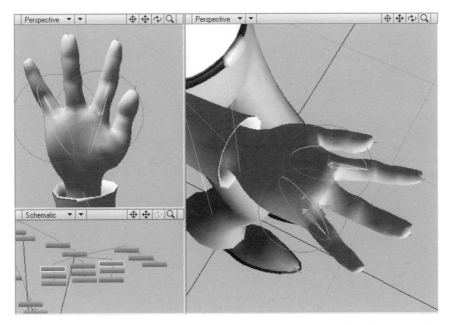

**Figure 8.14** Rotating Index_Base and Pinky_Base in H to spread the fingers wide.

### NOTE:

Because now LightWave allows you to select multiple items at once, you can grab all the finger bones and quickly bend them around an object. Be careful, however, because if you have one of the base bones selected too, the base bones can and will rotate in H, even though the mid and tip bones will not. You have to keep an eye on this so you don't make more work for yourself. (Watching the rotation from multiple views as you bend the fingers can help keep everything as it should be.)

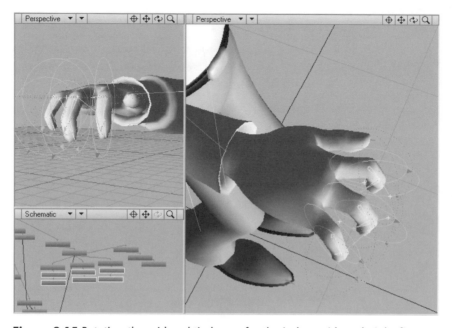

**Figure 8.15** Rotating the mid and tip bones for the index, mid, and pinky fingers.

The thumb's base can rotate on all three axes. This is to mimic the somewhat complex action of our real-life thumb's base joint close to the wrist. You will almost always need to use a combination of pitch and bank to properly simulate the way our opposable thumbs work.

▶ The base bones of the fingers may rotate in heading and pitch.

▶ The base bone of the thumbs may rotate in all axes.

▶ The mid and tip bones of all digits only rotate in pitch.

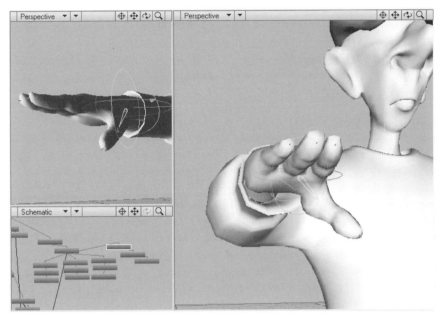

**Figure 8.16** Swinging the thumb down and around with pitch and bank to get that good ol' opposable thumb action.

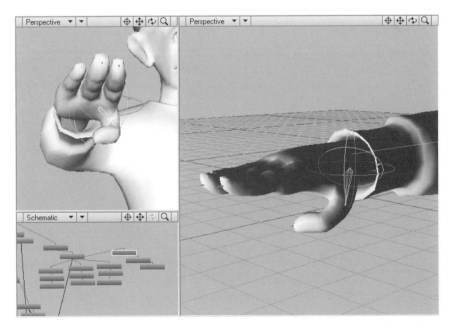

**Figure 8.17** The other two bones of the thumb work just the same as the mid and tip of the fingers.

# 8.14 **Notes on Modifying the Setup**

Those are all the controls you'll need to make your character walk, dance, act, emote, and pretty much everything else you can imagine. After playing with them a little, you will probably take to them like a natural—most people do. However, some bits of the setup may seem foreign no matter how much you use it, always expecting a control to do something other than what it does. That's OK, too!

This setup is simply my way of working. It has evolved over many years, since my first feeble setups on an Amiga, long before LightWave implemented IK. It has been streamlined to balance control, speed, and intuition. Still, this is only what I consider to be intuitive. You are all individuals out there, and if something seems redundant or overly complex for how you want to work, modify it! With what you've learned over the course of the last seven chapters, you now have the ability to craft the setup you've always wanted.

Some people don't like the nested controls for the hands; I can't live without them. (I actually prefer to nest the feet as well.) Some like the spinal controls to have their pivot rotations aligned differently. You've got the tools now to do almost anything you want. Experiment! Play! Learn!

This is your show now. Above all, this animation stuff is supposed to be fun!

**NOTE:**

Some possible setup modifications include:

- ▶ Making Pelvis a child of Root so it does not rotate with Spine1.
- ▶ Making Head a child of Root or of the mesh itself to have it hold very steady during martial arts or sensual walks.
- ▶ Making Head a child of Spine3 so it never pulls away from the torso when posing the spine.
- ▶ Making *Hand_Trans a child of one of the spinal bones so the hands inherit the torso's movement.
- ▶ Removing *Hand_Trans, so *Hand_Rot is the sole control for all movement and rotational axes of the hands.
- ▶ Making one of the hands a child of the other's rotation control (useful when swinging a bat or a sword).

## Chapter 9

# Life Drawing—The Next Logical Step

Life drawing? In 3D? You betchya! Life drawing is the best way to learn how to break down shapes and to understand what is actually going on to create those wonderfully complex and deceptively simple poses. As you work with life drawing in 3D, you'll begin to see exactly what makes a pose look and feel the way it does.

Why does a good animation drawing have the emotional impact it does? It has that kind of impact solely because of the poses the characters are in. Animators are often considered draftsmen; there is no more precise art form than animation. (In a standard-sized animation drawing, the deviation of a line by even 1/32" can completely change the emotional read of the drawing.) Yet, at the same time, everything must appear effortless and inevitable. You achieve this level of proficiency by mastering the sets of skills required. You master these skills to the point that they become so much a part of you, you can't do anything but execute them perfectly, precisely, and without thinking. All it takes to get to this level of proficiency in anything (animation being no exception) is simply to practice at least a little each and every day, to know where to start and how to proceed—how to get to the "next logical step."

Finding the next logical step is all getting anywhere with anything is. All of us can move steadily from one step to the next. We all start this path the same way. The troublesome thing with these next logical steps is that it is only when you begin to achieve mastery that you begin to understand what they are. Looking back from the plateaus of mastery, you can see where all the steps were, and where you got lost along the way. From the plateaus of mastery, you can also see the next logical steps that will carry you to where you would like to be. (No matter how good others may think you are, you must always, always be looking for that next logical step. There is always something more.) This is why it is so vitally important for teachers of anything to not only care about what they're teaching and be able to communicate it, but to have achieved a level of mastery to be able to see these steps. Mastering animation takes humility, dedication, passion, and time. But with these steps, mastery should not be painful; you should always be able to see your path before you. Moving from one simple signpost to another, studying and understanding, learning how to see motion, how to understand the conveyance of feeling. Each step builds on the successful completion of the last. Each next logical step has an "Ah-ha!" factor that is often so simple that it could all too easily hide forever in plain sight.

And so, the next logical step from where you are right now is to get to know those controls you labored long to create. You need to know them so well that they become second nature to you. (And if there is something in the setup you simply cannot work with, go back and change it until it feels right to your way of working.)

If, after going through the life drawing models in this chapter, you still feel you need more life drawing before moving on, flip to Chapter 14 where you'll be directed to many more models to "draw" from. (Don't be afraid to go back and revisit these old models. It's always good, throughout your career, to go back and reaffirm the things you know.) Move forward only when you feel comfortable. Doing so will make the whole process of learning animation that much more enjoyable and rewarding.

# 9.1 The Standing Model

Posing a character is the art of translating what you have in your mind into the 3D coordinates that will make your character fit that vision.

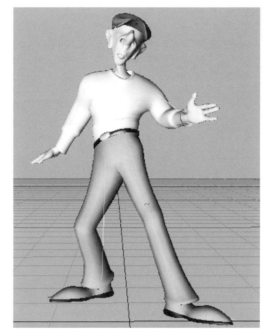

**Figure 9.1** We'll be starting with a standing model. The pose is interesting enough to keep us from getting bored, but still easy enough to be recreated with relative ease.

Now, you might be asking, "How do I know where in 3D space to put these things that I'm seeing on this flat, 2D page?" In very short order, you'll get the hang of being able to translate the subtleties of slight differences in angle and size on a page into 3D coordinates. (LW's grid lines are very helpful; I wish all life drawing classes had their plinths marked with grid lines.) We'll be starting with a technique that will have you well on your way before you know it.

On one project I was given hi-res scans of models I would eventually have to animate. The project didn't have the budget for Paraform (a program designed to make animatable NURBS models from hi-res scan data) and we knew the client was going to be a stickler for having the models perfect. After reducing the poly count somewhat with qemLOSS2, just to make the scans manageable on a 500MHz PII, we changed the surface of the scanned model to be partially transparent. We then built our subpatch model around that framework. We could see exactly when our subpatch was passing through the scanned model's surface, and it turned out to be a rather quick way of not only getting an animatable subpatch model, but also in getting a whole lot better at modeling very quickly. (Running my own studio, I've had to learn to wear a lot of hats to get jobs out on time. I'll always be a better animator and director than I'll ever hope to be a modeler, but every new thing you can add to your set of skills is an asset.)

We'll be using that same technique to get you started in life drawing here. You'll know when you have enough angle here, enough distance there to support the character's weight. You'll know when your character carries the essence of the pose, and you'll know when your character is spot-on. You'll be able to turn the view and explore from every angle. You'll see, right there in front of you, whether your model covers the drawing model or not!

1. Load in your setup scene and then save the scene as something that will let you know this is life drawing model 01. (Scenes\Work\ch09\Life-Drawing_01_w01.lws works for me.)

2. Load in Objects\chapters\Ch_09\LifeDrawingModel_01.lwo.

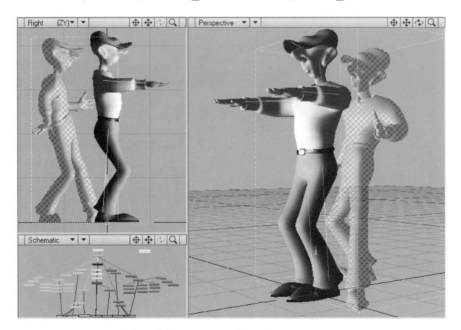

**Figure 9.2** Your model and the pose you'll put him into.

3. Using Chapter 8 as a reference if you need to, start moving controls!

If you find yourself in a bind, don't be afraid to scrap your work and start over (with a saved revision, of course, just in case you really were on the right track). As they say, "Animation is the art of revision." Also, don't hesitate to come back to this pose at some time in the future, using what you've learned to see if there are better, faster, more elegant ways of getting him to assume this pose.

There are a few things I'd like to point out about the pose itself before moving on. If you look at it from any angle—back, front, side, or top—the character looks balanced. Even though he's got his weight shifted back and to the right, his legs support him in a way that he could hold indefinitely without falling over. Weight distribution is a very important thing. Every stationary pose must read as balanced from all angles, not just the camera angle. The character's center of gravity must appear properly supported; he can't look like he's about to fall over.

> **NOTE:**
>
> Another thing to watch on the whole weight issue is that when you have a character moving he has to have the proper weight distribution for the speed and direction of his movement. Walking is just falling forward and catching ourselves every time we step. Running means that we're leaning forward farther to get more offset for the forward thrust. Every pose, whether moving or stationary, must be balanced or the character must be about to fall over.

The best way to assess the balance of a pose is to turn your head away from the monitor, close your eyes, and turn your head back to the monitor. Open your eyes for no more than 1/4 second. The afterimage you have in your mind will have a feeling to it; it'll either feel comfortable ("Yeah, I'd buy that") or awkward ("Man... there's just something not quite right about that"). Do this from every angle, even if your final output will be to film or another 2D medium. Human minds work better than we might sometimes guess, and though your audience might not know exactly why something doesn't look quite right, they'll feel the difference between a pose that carries its weight properly and a pose that is off balance even slightly.

> **NOTE:**
>
> A properly animated scene should look good from all angles. (This is especially true if you're doing work for a 3D video game and you can't control the camera.) True, there will be angles that look better than others, but no angle should look unbelievable. Watching your scene from the worst angle you can find is a trick you can use to make it read all the better from the intended angle. It is like flipping a drawing over and looking at it on a light table from the other side. You disassociate yourself from what you've been thinking for the past hours or days and are able to look at it from a more objective point of view. From that unflattering angle, make the tweaks you see that need tweaking, then look at the scene from the camera angle; you'll be surprised at how much more believably it reads.

We've also got contra-posto, the reversal of angles between the hips and shoulders, going on in this scene. The character's hips are swung down and back on the <u>right</u> side. The character's shoulders are swung down and back on the <u>left</u> side (though in relationship to the shoulders' initial pose their new angle doesn't appear that different). This makes the pose read with more life than if the hips and shoulders were parallel.

Hands are important with every pose. Much of the emotional read of a pose is carried in the character's hands. This is as important with wild action as with subtle acting. When working with a run or other vigorous activity, don't forget the importance of the hands. If you were ever on a track team, do you remember your coach telling you that the way to run faster is to pump your arms harder and faster? This balance and counterbalance works throughout our entire bodies. Our non-conscious minds have ways of picking up on these *non-verbals*—cues given by the way someone stands, the timing with which they do something, and many other subtle cues that have nothing to do with spoken words. Non-verbals have ways of translating themselves directly into an emotional read within the viewer. Understanding everything you can about what it is your character is doing, putting yourself into that situation, and letting all of that wealth of information flood through you as you work is the key to believable animation.

Another thing to pay attention to in this pose is the handling of the finger groupings. Rhythm plays a very important role in animation. Having the fingers equidistant, either close together or spread apart, is monotonous and boring. A common technique to break this up is to pop the pinky or index finger out from the other two by rotating its base in heading. It is a simple thing, but adds a lot of life to a pose. Making sure the fingers aren't all bent the same amount is another important thing to remember. Often, you'll see a pinky bent slightly when all the rest of the fingers are straight. Watch for opportunities to add these techniques to your own poses, but make sure that the emotional read it adds goes along with the read of the pose you're trying to create.

4. Look over your scene closely. Are all areas of the life drawing model covered by your model? If so, congratulate yourself! You've just taken a huge next logical step on the path that leads toward being a fantastic animator!

# 9.2 **The Seated Model**

This exercise is just the same as 9.1. We'll be loading a life drawing model into a fresh scene and moving our character until he "assumes the position" (as it were).

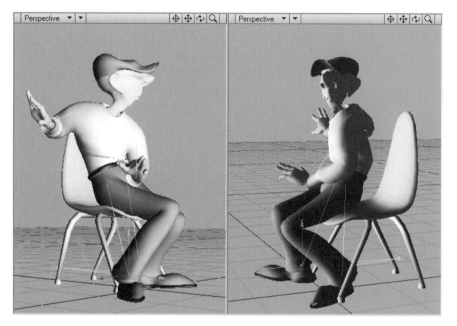

**Figure 9.3** This is the pose we'll be working with for this exercise. It looks like there is a lot more going on, but it is actually just as easy to manage as the previous pose. Do watch the fingers and thumbs; there's a little more action going on there.

1. Load a copy of your setup scene, then save the scene in your Chapter 9 working directory as something that'll remind you that this is life drawing model 02.

2. Load in Objects\chapters\Ch_09\LifeDrawingModel_02.lwo.

3. Load in Objects\Props\Chair.lwo.

4. Start pulling controls until your model fits the pose held by the life drawing model.

> **NOTE:**
>
> *Twinning* is an industry term for anything that mirrors something in the scene, either in motion or in pose. Hands and arms can twin. Feet and legs can twin. Fingers can twin, and entire characters can twin each other in a scene. <u>Watch out for this!</u> Twinning is something that almost never happens in real life. It is easy to fall into, and it makes your pose read flat and unbelievable. Luckily, twinning is something that is easily caught and fixed if you have a watchful eye out for it, both during the creating of the scene and in watching it when you think it might be finished.

Some notes on the pose itself: The character's feet are both at different angles and positions with respect to the center of the pose. Even so, both feet are braced against the chair legs, giving a feeling of tension and readiness to bolt. Not only is the character perched on the edge of the chair, he is off center to the chair's right, adding to the feeling that something more is going on than what the audience knows. His knees are together in a way that reads of fear and protection. The focus of his torso and hands is away from where his head is turned, giving a reading that there may be separate things making him uneasy. The hands form two distinctly separate shapes that don't twin regardless of what angle they are viewed from, yet they both read of surprise and trepidation within this pose.

Everything comes together in this pose to give a reading that this guy isn't happy about being where he is. As you work, try to understand and internalize what subtleties build these feelings within you. Animation is a lot like jazz in that you build riffs that you know work well to produce certain feelings within certain contexts. You put them all together in a piece, transposing, modifying, and working on the fly. Always be on the lookout for new riffs that you can add to your repertoire. Real life, film, television, comic books all abound with different takes on experience and response. When a scene comes along where you can use one of these new riffs, you'll feel like a kid in a candy store: "Oh man! I've been wanting to give this a try!"

> **NOTE:**
>
> Animation is supposed to be fun. The surest way to take the fun out of it is to not have the time you need to get the job done right. Whatever the situation, always strive to give yourself the time to feel good about the end result. Don't rush things. When you walk away from your desk, it is important to want to walk back.

# 9.3 The Reclining Model

Now we're going to do a couple of models lying on the ground, one face-up, the other face-down. It is best to get familiar with doing things as many different ways as possible. This is called "filling the well." When a situation arises and you need to do something differently from your normal way of doing things, it won't catch you by surprise.

I'm going to recommend using the model itself to lay the character onto his back for the first pose, and using Spine1 to get him there for the second pose. You not only get a feeling for different controls, you get used to seeing the model all out of joint—hands, feet, and head dragging behind—but knowing that there's a method to the madness.

1. Load a fresh copy of your setup scene, then save a revision as we've been doing.

2. Load in Objects\chapters\Ch_09\LifeDrawingModel_03.lwo.

3. Using the mesh itself to lay the character onto his back, start pulling controls; see how you do!

As you work with the hand controls in this pose, pay attention to what happens when you rotate the *_Rot control first, or the *_Trans first. Certain poses are easier to get when you move one first, versus the other. Also, don't be afraid to break some rules. If you see what you want, and all you need is to rotate *_Trans in pitch, go ahead and rotate it in pitch. In making this pose, I found it much easier to rotate the RightShoulder control in world H than to fight with parent H and P.

**Figure 9.4** This is a pretty straightforward pose; you should have very little problem with it. It is also a bit of a standard life drawing pose; it's the pose the model usually assumes when he knows he's going to be there a while.

## NOTE:

Something that will help you as you work is being aware that LightWave has a *solving order*, the order in which it calculates heading, pitch, and bank. LightWave figures heading first, then pitch, and lastly bank. This makes sense when you think of bank as being the child of pitch, and pitch being the child of heading. Rotating bank doesn't affect any of the other two axes. Rotating pitch affects the angle of bank (hence the wonders of gimbal lock). Rotating heading affects both pitch and bank. When rotating something into what may be a bit of a complex space, try working backward—bank first, then pitch, and finally heading.

> **ADVANCED NOTE:**
>
> If any of you techno-wizards out there find yourselves working on an expression that will "cancel out" the rotation of a previous item, say to have a platform always be level no matter how its support arm rotates, the solving order info will help. What you've got to do is to have a hierarchy similar to: SupportArm => Cancel_B => Cancel_P => platform. With either the LWFollower plug-in or by using an expression, have Cancel_B rotate at the bank rotation of SupportArm multiplied by –1. Have Cancel_P do the same for SupportArm pitch, and have the platform itself do the same for SupportArm heading. (I know this may seem like something out of left field, but believe it or not, this has saved my behind in a character setup.)

Something else that will help you as you go: Before you start, actually lay down in this position and see how it feels to lay like that. Doing this will help you more than just about anything else you can do. Animation is a *kinesthetic* art, an art based on movement and feel. If, while you're working, you can remember how it felt to be in that pose, it will make your work go much more easily, and you'll get a much stronger, more readable, believable pose. Animation is getting the viewer to feel what it feels like to do or to be something. When you believe in that feeling as you do the work, it will show through your art. And don't worry about appearing weird by standing up at your desk, going through a motion, or striking a pose—all animators do it! The halls of any place I've worked have at least one or two animators acting out their scenes at any given time. And because animation is all about feeling, watching yourself on videotape only goes so far. If you are using videotaped reference, as you watch try to put yourself there in that action; feel what's going on, both kinesthetically and emotionally.

4. Take a close look at your pose from all angles. Did you get everything covered?

When you feel comfortable with the work you've done, we'll move on to the next reclining pose.

5.  Save your scene and load in your setup scene again.

6.  Load in Objects\chapters\Ch_09\LifeDrawingModel_04.lwo.

7.  Save a working revision of this fourth life drawing scene.

8.  Avoiding the use of the mesh itself and the Root control, start posing!

**Figure 9.5** This pose has a lot going on. There is heavy curvature of the spine, twisting the pelvis and the shoulders onto very different lines. The right side of the pelvis is raised to accommodate the right knee's angle at the side of the body; the right shoulder is pulling forward, reaching for the hand's position. The fingers aren't just flat on the ground, they spread and reach, reading of support and intent. All in all, it is a very cat-like pose, and the curves read strongly from every angle. (Poses where the curves read well from every angle are what to strive for in video game work where you don't know where the viewer's camera will be.)

9.  Take a step back and look at how you did! (Hide and unhide the life drawing model. Move it off to the side so you can compare the two at once. Do they both give you the same gut-level feeling?)

Does your pose need more work? Do you need to scrap it all and start over? (Remember, you can save yourself a lot of time in the long run by doing this.) Were you able to get your pose to match the model's? Try to remember the order in which you rotate the controls. If you're having problems, zero-out those controls, and try rotating them in a different order.

> **NOTE:**
>
> Often times, when something isn't quite coming together, I find that there are usually just one or two things that keep the pose from reading the way I want it to. Taking a quick break to get a cup of tea, take a quick run around the building, or do something else that gets my mind off the ways I was thinking usually does wonders. When you come back to the scene, almost always there's an, "Oh, duh! Of course!" and you make a few quick changes and wham—everything has fallen into place!

When everything is reading well, your character covers the life drawing model perfectly, so congratulate yourself! This is one of the harder poses I could think of for you to try. Animation consists of two things: timing and posing. You're well on your way to having posing down pat!

## 9.4 **The Character and Weight**

How do you get a character to read as if he is carrying something heavy when all we've got are the tools of pose and timing? We have to show the audience by how the character responds to and interacts with the weight. (You never want the character saying, "Boy, Phil, this 500-pound weight is heavy." That's bad directing.)

**NOTE:**

Actually, everything in filmmaking (storytelling) is about showing how characters respond to things in their environments. The characters' responses will tell an audience how heavy, happy, or scary a thing is. The audience will empathize with what they see, pulling from their own experience. The best example of this in a recent film is in the 2001 version of *Lord of the Rings*: When the ring wraiths enter the Inn of the Prancing Pony, we see a big man who looks to be a cook. His response of utter, childlike fear, hiding as the wraiths enter, lets us know beyond the shadow of a doubt that this is a very bad situation.

**Figure 9.6** Based entirely on the memory of how it feels to carry a heavy household appliance, we read everything from how heavy this weight is to the character's outlook on carrying it.

1. Load in a fresh copy of your setup, saving it back out as the revision with which you will be working for this sitting.

2. Load in Objects\chapters\Ch_09\LifeDrawingModel_05.lwo.

3. Animators, start your engines!

Notice with this one how the model really feels like he's working with this weight? It's all about posture, silhouette, and how we ourselves have experienced similar things and empathize with how he looks. An interesting thing is that you can get a totally different read on this pose by swinging the knees inward to touch. Try it. The model goes from this hefty dude to someone looking like he's about to lose it. Different angles of the head give the impression of catching this guy at different points of lifting this weight. With his head tilted down, as it is, he gives the impression of someone concentrating on the task at hand. If you tilt his head up, he looks like someone just picking up this weight and trying to get it settled for the long haul.

Another interesting thing to note is (and I'll go over this again in the section on silhouette) that with good, strong poses, you've usually got one side of the character smooth, like this guy's back. The other side is all full of interesting jutting shapes to catch and hold the eye. Again, this is rhythm. This visual sense of rhythm—smooth vs. bumpy, straight vs. curved—is the key to making a pose read of highest quality.

Also note that the character's hands are beyond the reach of his forearm bones. This stretches the wrists out of the shirtsleeves and adds to the visual feeling of the hands being "pulled" by the weight. In an animation, the moment the hands were to come back in touch with the ArmPullers, the arms would pop a bit, making a quick motion which is noncontiguous with the surrounding motion. This happens any time you pull a goal away from its puller, and then let it come back in contact. It's a good idea to try your hardest to make sure the goals always stay within reach of the pullers assigned to them. If, in a pose like this, it really needs to be that way, you can cover that pop by having a bit of quick action surrounding the motion, or by making several, precisely controlled keyframes of the control that moves the goal so that when the joint does start moving again, it isn't so abrupt.

> **NOTE:**
>
> Strong poses are poses "drawn" with verbs, not nouns. Pose an arm stretching, a back reaching, a leg compressing, or a neck craning. Always pose with verbs, even when a character is doing nothing.

How did you do? It's a relatively simple pose when it comes right down to it, but there are a lot of subtle points to make sure you've covered. Take a step back, brew a cup of really good tea, and analyze.

# 9.5 The Timed Pose

Whenever you take life drawing, you usually start with a series of quick, :30 (thirty-second) poses. You then move on to 1:00 poses, then 3:00, 5:00, 10:00 poses, and then to long poses of 30:00 to 2:00:00. The idea behind this is to loosen up not only your drawing arm but your mind (and heart) as well. During the quick poses, you remember to not get all mired in the minutia; you focus on the big picture, the things that get the pose to read at a glance.

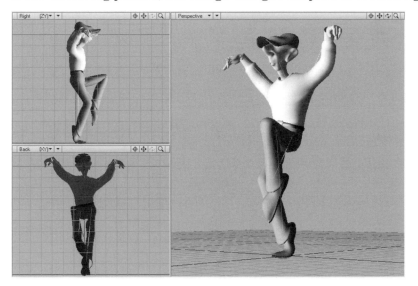

**Figure 9.7** This pose is simple but still interesting for this timed pose set. There's enough going on here to keep your attention for 30:00, and broad enough to get good, strong gestures in :30.

1. Load in a fresh setup; save it as a working scene revision as usual.

2. Working only from Figure 9.7, give yourself 3:00 (three minutes) and see how you do.

> **NOTE:**
>
> Working solely from the figure is the next logical step in what we're doing. You've already become familiar with the controls, what they do, and how to use them to pose your character from a model directly in the scene with him. Now, you've got to be able to take an image (real or imagined) and turn that visual into the 3D coordinates that delineate a character's pose.

3. Take a step back from you work. How did you do? Did you work any differently from when you have the life drawing model right there in the scene with you? Did you approach the scene any differently than when you know you have an unlimited amount of time?

4. Save a revision of this scene, load up a fresh setup, and get ready to tackle this pose again.

5. Try this pose again, just from the figure, and this time give yourself 10:00 (ten minutes). See how you do.

Try to start the scene the same way you did when you had 3:00. Rough in the broad gestural lines first, then work on fine-tuning the details.

6. Again, take a step back and compare the work with the figure. How do you feel about it? Did you start this pose the same way you did the 3:00 one? (If you had saved a revision as the 3:00 mark passed, would it look similar to what you had done in the last sitting?)

> **NOTE:**
>
> There will almost never be enough time for you to be completely, 100% happy with a scene while working in production. Some productions will give you more time than others, but you will always have something more you want to do with the scene. Like a painting, an animation is never finished; it simply stops in interesting places. Being able to rough in the important details first, being happy with silhouette, weight, and emotional read, and then being able to noodle the details is what will make you content with your work and yourself as an animator when you see your scene in the final product.

7. Load in Objects\chapters\Ch_09\LifeDrawingModel_06.

8. Move (only in X and Z) and rotate (only in heading) the life drawing model until he comes as close to being in the same position as your character as possible.

Compare and contrast. Your character, after 10:00, should match the life drawing model fairly well. There will, of course, be details not quite there yet, and exact positioning will probably be off. But the overall feel of the pose should be the same.

9. Save this scene as a revision.

10. Load in a fresh setup, saving it out again as a working scene.

11. Using what you've learned, give yourself 30:00 (thirty minutes) working just from the figure. While still starting the same way you would if you only had 3:00, try to get things to totally match the model.

You've become very familiar with this pose. You know which controls to move now and how much to rotate them. You know what it takes to put this guy into this pose you now feel deep in your own bones. You don't just see the pose in your head, you expect to move him into it and you plan on moving specific controls to achieve this pose. This is the Zen zone of animation. You've achieved it already. All it will take is a little more practice with posing to get that same knowing feeling about any pose you visualize.

12. Take a step back again. Get up and shake it off. When you come back to your desk, load in Objects\chapters\Ch_09\LifeDrawingModel_06 and see how you did.

Your pose should be very close to the life drawing model's. Based on where you know you deviated from the model in the 10:00 sitting, you were able to expect and correct in this sitting. You've had the time to get the fingers and all the other little details posed just right. Things are pretty darn close. If you had the chance at this pose again, you know what you'd do to speed up the process and make it even more effortless.

Here's your chance.

13. Save this scene as a revision, reload a fresh setup, and save it once more as a working scene.

14. Giving yourself only 3:00 (three minutes) this time, pose this guy from the figure alone, using all you've learned from the previous three sittings.

> **NOTE:**
>
> Animation being the "art of revision" as it were, you will more than likely run into a scenario where you will have to go over and back over a scene that was perfectly good the first time you did it. More and more often, directors of animation succumb to the notion of, "I don't know what I want, but I'll know it when I see it, and that ain't it." It's really too bad. It can be disheartening to an animator, and it really only reflects the director's own lack of vision and confidence. Sure, the scene may not be exactly what the director had in mind, but does it move the scene forward? Are the characters true to themselves? Is there good acting going on? Do you believe in and feel for the characters? These are the things that once mattered under the great directors of animated works. These are the things that let animators fall in love with their characters and their scenes. These are the things that let that love read fresh and bright through the screen and move the audience to tears and joy. These are things that hopefully will matter again. "Making an animated film is like workshopping a play"? Not hardly! Not unless you want to dishearten your crew and blow a whole lot of dough. Revise to improve, not simply to make different!

15. Take a step back. How did you do?

16. Select **File|Load|Load Items From Scene**, and choose the scene you saved after your first 3:00 sitting.

17. Using the mesh itself, move the characters side by side.

18. Compare and contrast.

Your more recent scene should radiate a lot more confidence that you as an animator had in posing out the character. You should be able to see your knowledge of the things that will catch the viewer's eye in an instant—the broad strokes, leaving the finer detail work for later (or for an assistant).

> **NOTE:**
>
> When you first get issued a scene, a good idea is to spend no more than three to five minutes on each pose as you're roughing in the action. You'll be thinking in broad strokes, seeing if the silhouette is giving you the reading you wish it to. And if you don't like what you see, you won't have that much time invested in the scene. You won't feel compelled to stick with something that could be better if tackled from scratch from a different angle.

## 9.6 The "Cool Walk"

Everyone has got to have a "cool walk," right? Well, this is our character's. Even though this pose is a bit more complex than the last, it's still very straightforward. You should be able to take what you've learned in the previous sittings and nail this pose pretty quickly. Pay special attention to the shifts in weight and the multi-axis contra-posto going on. The character is walking, so he would indeed fall over if he tried to hold this pose indefinitely, but the amount he is off-balance is congruent with the perceived speed of his assumed forward momentum.

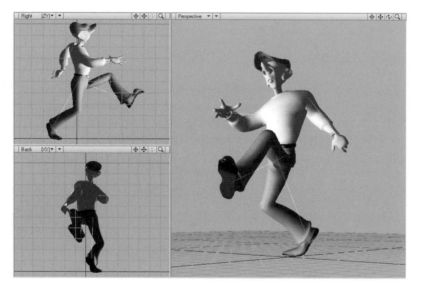

**Figure 9.8** This pose has a good, clear line of motion (the line or arc that clearly defines the pose or action) running right down the character's head/neck/spine/right leg—a very prominent "S" when seen from the back view. Look for this line (or arc) of motion in all your future poses and scenes.

1. Load up a fresh setup, and save it as a working scene as usual.

2. Using only Figure 9.8, put your character into this pose, giving yourself all the time you need to do so.

You may want to stop after the first three or ten minutes, save a revision of what you've done, and start over from scratch. As I've said, it isn't uncommon for an animator to throw away his first drawings until he gets into the groove of the scene. More often than not, it'll get you a better quality finished pose than you would have had, had you kept right on going from the start.

3. How did you do?

4. Take a step back, take a bit of a break, and then compare and contrast your work with the figure.

Do you get the same emotional read from your pose as the figure? Do you have the same feeling of a jaunty, rakish lilt to his step?

5. Load in Objects\chapters\Ch_09\LifeDrawingModel_07. Compare and contrast.

How closely did you match the curvatures of his spine, the placements of his appendages? In the sections on animation, we'll get into improvisation, but right here, we're trying to build your ability to see and to interpret that information into as precise 3D coordinates as possible. Make notes and do the pose again, if you feel the need!

# 9.7 **Clickin' Them Heels**

This is another relatively simple pose with a strong arc of motion. Work with this the same way you worked with the previous life drawing model. When you're ready to compare and contrast, the model can be found in Objects\chapters\Ch_09\LifeDrawingModel_08.

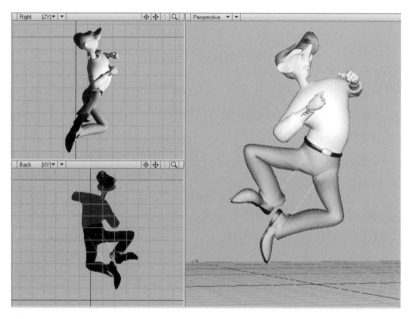

**Figure 9.9** Notice how the model's left side is all about stretching. You can almost feel the pull along your own back muscles. The model's right side is all about compression. You can almost feel the pressure along your own rib cage. This gives us a strong, definite arc of motion. We also have one side that is relatively smooth, the model's left, and the other side that is quite interesting. Rhythm and arc of motion make this pose one that reads in an instant.

Pay close attention to the lines of the shoulders and feet. A lot of the strength of this pose is carried in the ways these angles balance straight lines against curved lines.

## 9.8 Batter Up!

This is the hardest pose we'll get into right now. It has a lot of complex weight balancing going on: Some compound curves and a very tight angle for the right shoulder require a lot more attention to get him into place. The positioning and angle of the pelvis can make the knees a bit vexatious as well.

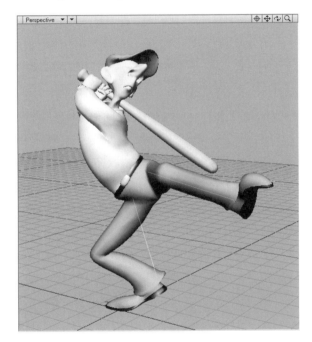

**Figure 9.10** I want you to work with just this one perspective angle first. See how far you can get before using Figure 9.11, which has the other two angles you have become accustomed to using.

Turn this model around in your mind first, before jumping right in. Try to visualize where the different body parts are in relationship to the others. Do this for a good three minutes before starting to move controls. Look at the figure, close your eyes, and see if you can turn the model over in your mind. Based on what you know of the pose and your experience with the controls, where do they have to be to get the character into that position?

After you've gone as far as you can go just looking at Figure 9.10, compare what you've done with Figure 9.11. Keep working a bit if you need to. Try to get that same moment-before-he-swings kind of feeling to your pose. Break down the angles in your mind, and dissect what combinations of angles and curves, stretches and compressions, arcs and balance make this pose read the way it does.

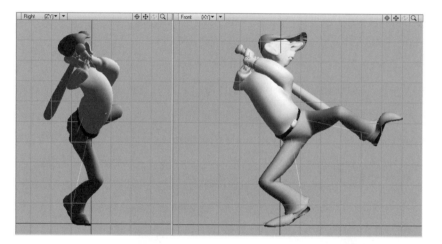

**Figure 9.11** The right and front views of the pose.

When you feel you've got this guy as close as you can by just looking at the illustrations, load in Objects\chapters\Ch_09\LifeDrawingModel_09. Compare and contrast how closely you were able to hit the pose. Make mental notes, hide LifeDrawingModel_09, and make changes. Unhide the life drawing model and see how close your changes brought him to the model's pose.

# 9.9 **Life Drawing**

Animation truly is only two things: posing and timing. Working with posing the character in this way (life drawing in 3D) is integral to becoming a quick and intuitive animator. It is the only way to get the guesswork of figuring how to get the pose you're looking for behind you. The more life drawing you do, the sooner you will find this stuff internalized, ready for use without even thinking about it. When all of this has been internalized (and when timing has been internalized, too) is when animation can become this wonderful foray into imaginary worlds where you and the character are one for as long as you're working on the scene. This is when animation is pure magic.

Always keep on top of your life drawing. When you have downtime, flip to Chapter 14, where you'll be directed to other poses to work from. Go through magazines and books, and "draw" from both photographs and animation drawings. Take a course on life drawing and bring your laptop! Pose your characters from the people you see around you every day. Movies, television, real life—there is a wealth of knowledge waiting in experiences that don't stand still.

No matter how good you get, always keep up on your basics. Life drawing is a plinth from which the masterworks of animation rise up.

## Chapter 10

# Reviewing Animation Basics

Every animator, no matter how accomplished, always goes back to studying the basics at different times throughout his career. These are the foundations that support all the techniques of advanced animation mechanics. Actually, you could probably get through an entire career just on these basic principles alone, and you could do quite well. Having them at your fingertips, ready to use at a moment's notice without the burden of thinking about them, is what to work for in your studies.

## 10.1 Timing

As I have mentioned before, animation is really only two things: posing and timing. Timing is the placement through time in a scene of when events occur. Understanding timing is simply understanding how things appear to happen as actions play out over time.

As an animator, you will need a stopwatch. Go out and get yourself a good one (if you haven't already got one). Keep it with you always and just start timing everything around you. Find out exactly how long it takes to do everything you see. Time different people doing the same thing. Time someone getting up from a chair. Time people looking at their watches. Time someone giving you a mean look for being so intrusive. (Time how fast you can run away.) You get the idea.

The only way to understand timing is to take notice of it as it exists all around you. When you get up from a chair, you don't just stand straight up, you lean forward, putting your center of gravity over your feet, and then you straighten. Each of these motions require some amount of time to complete. There is a pause between the lean forward and the rise. That takes time, too. Explore and understand real-life timings. Once you get a feel for them, start to modify and play with them.

*Anime*, Japanese animation, makes great symbolic use of modified timings to convey different feelings. Characters hang in the air much longer than they "should" before crashing back down to the ground with an impact that belies their apparent mass. This obvious departure from reality crafts feelings of great power and otherworldliness. Anime uses timing to sculpt how you, the viewer, feel about what you're seeing. Something just barely perceptibly outside of reality makes a viewer feel uncomfortable. Slowed timing appears dreamlike. Often, when timing is artfully used to sculpt feelings, the audience only gets the impact of the feelings, and is unaware of the reasons why.

Timing is also a rhythmic device. Just like music, animation has beats, rhythms, and tempos. You want to keep things interesting for the viewer and not have everything fall on the same timings. This makes a scene read dull and flat. If your scene has keyframes every eight frames, it will read like mush. You have to break up the keys, stagger them, and syncopate them. Get the audience to expect something by setting up a pattern, and then break that pattern (ONE, two, three, four, one, two, three, four, one, TWO, three, four...). Keep them on their toes, when their toes need to be kept on. Slow, languid scenes need this special attention to timing even more than frenetic scenes to keep the audience from losing interest, yet maintaining their dreamy flow.

Timing is also important to get across the relationships between objects and mass. Massive objects don't get moving as quickly as slight ones do, but when they do, they're quite a challenge to stop. A light object or character can leap up from the ground more quickly than a heavy one. Lighter items can seem to float a bit more before gravity begins to exert its effect. Heavier items can seem to be pulled greedily back down to Earth.

Everything you do with timing helps the audience to differentiate between the shapes they see on screen.

> **NOTE:**
>
> Animation is experience. If you don't live it in your heart, it won't come out of your scene.

> **NOTE:**
>
> Since stopwatches are such physical objects, and you may leave for work and forget it, I've included a small animation timer on the CD under Extras\AnimationTimer\. There are two files that are, in essence, the same thing. One is just the bare .swf (Flash4 file), the other is an .exe (executable program) exported as a stand-alone from Flash to run on Windows machines. If you're on a Mac, open up your Internet browser (with the Flash4 Plug-in installed from http://flash.com ) and drag the .swf file into the open Internet browser window. You can also choose File|Open and browse to the .swf file. You can e-mail this tiny .swf (only 68K) to yourself so you'll never be without a way to time animations! It does frames, feet/frames, SMPTE, and seconds. It converts between these formats, and you can use it to do some rudimentary frame-offset calculations. (Click on the "Help?" icon to find out more!)

# 10.2 **Squash and Stretch**

Squash and stretch is one of the keystones of good animation. Even the most realistic of animations needs to have some element of squash and stretch in it. Animation is all about the emotional impact of experience; you alter the outline of a thing (not the volume) to give the audience a visual interpretation of the forces impacting it.

1.  Load Objects\Props\Ball.lwo into Layout.

2.  Make a 21-frame sequence (from 0-20) where the ball bounces similar to Figure 10.1.

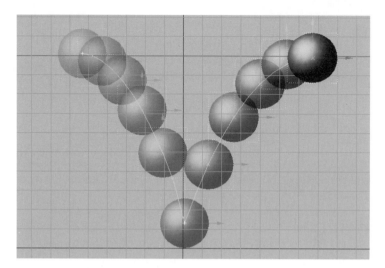

**Figure 10.1** This bouncing ball has good timing to it: It accelerates toward the ground, springs back up, then decelerates as it nears the top of its rebound. The timing may be good, but it has no squash and stretch to it. (You can find the scene to study in Scenes\chapters\ch10\Figure_10-01.lws.)

In order for the ball to really give the impression that the force of gravity is <u>pulling</u> it down to the ground where it impacts and springs back up again, we have to push reality a bit.

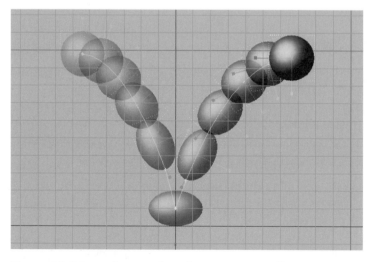

**Figure 10.2** Just using stretch and rotate to put rudimentary squash and stretch on the ball gives a visual read to the forces acting upon it. (See Scenes\chapters\ch10\Figure_10-02.lws.)

> **NOTE:**
>
> A more believable take on this would be to use bones to flatten the ball around the area of impact where it hits the ground. I also like to stretch objects into wedge-like shapes with the point of the wedge leading the eye into the coming motion.

3. Now, using whatever techniques you'd like, add some squash and stretch to your bouncing ball scene.

> **NOTE:**
>
> LightWave, having introduced Bezier interpolation for splines, has made it a whole lot easier to get nice, smooth motion curves. Don't be afraid to drop the old TCB splines in favor of these more controllable curves. However, because you have more ability to noodle with the Bezier handles, you can more easily throw things out of whack. I've also noticed that Bezier splines almost always need some kind of adjustment and are rarely interpolated correctly (for my tastes) by default.

Compare what you've got with Scenes\chapters\ch10\Figure_10-02.lws if you need to. <u>Always remember to preserve the volume of the object</u>. When you squash in Y, the object has to expand in X and Z in order to preserve the mass we perceive it to have. We're not getting rid of mass, we're displacing it. (Think of a water balloon. When you squeeze or stretch it, there's still the same amount of water in it—until it pops, that is.)

NOTE:

Something to be said about working with spline curves is that they should have the absolute minimum number of keyframes needed to keep the item moving as it needs to, and they should be as elegant as possible. "Elegant" is a relative term and does not necessarily mean "smooth." The curves should be a linear interpretation of the action. I like to think that the curves should be pretty if the motion is to be flowing and beautiful, or harsh if the motion is to be percussive and violent.

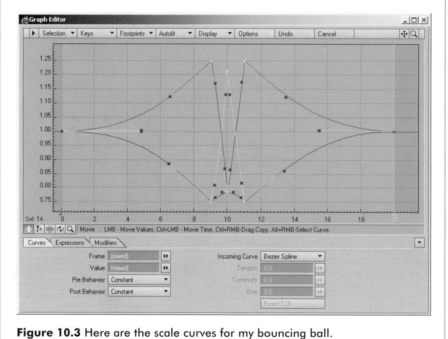

**Figure 10.3** Here are the scale curves for my bouncing ball.

**NEWBIE NOTE:**

Squash and stretch doesn't just happen with entire objects, it happens with parts of objects separately, too. It happens with legs, hands, arms, torsos, fingers, heads.... It happens with any part of the character that can visibly have a force acting upon it. Drop a weight into our character's arms and his legs should squash to show the impact the sudden introduction of the weight has on his body as a system. As our character's hand whips up to catch a fly ball, his hand and fingers elongate over the course of the frames. The hand travels the greatest distance to accentuate the feeling of speed. (You can think of this like handcrafting motion blur.)

The way our character is set up, stretching the neck, arms, and legs is easy. We pull the controls for the head, hands, and feet away from where the IK chain can reach and things stretch. You can squash individual parts of his body by scaling that individual control; all children of that control will be equally affected (squash the hand and the fingers will also squash). You can even squash and stretch the bones controlled by IK, like the thighs, calves, biceps, and forearms, but be careful when doing so. IK calculations are complex, and adding stretching into the mix can make normally dependable IK chains unpredictable.

As always, when you're done squashing and stretching and your character is at rest, make sure you return him to his original, at rest proportions. Multiple instances of squashing and stretching can be going on simultaneously in a complex and explosive scene, but you always need to return the parts that aren't being acted upon by extreme forces to the proportions the audience has come to expect.

## 10.3 **Gesture and Line of Motion**

*Gesture* is the most important part of an animation drawing (or pose). Gesture is what makes a silhouette read with purpose and intent and helps the viewer understand the motives behind the character. Gesture is the ultimate distillation of an idea into form (2D or 3D). *Line of motion* is the path that flows through and defines the gesture.

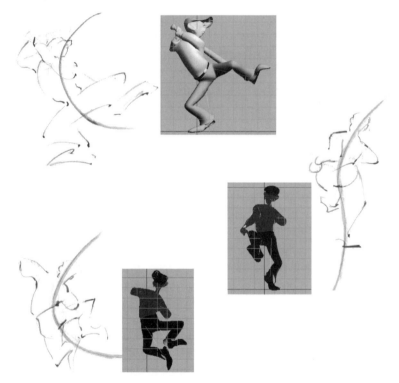

**Figure 10.4** Some poses we've visited before, and the *thumbnail drawings* (quick, loose drawings to get the gesture, idea, and feel of a pose—not the anatomy of a pose) that inspired them. Notice how clearly the line of motion (represented by the thick line running through the center of each thumbnail drawing) reads through both the thumbnail and the finished pose.

The line of motion is the "big picture" read we get from a pose. It tells us what is going on and where we should look. It gives us an idea of what has happened a moment before and what to expect to happen next. This line of motion should be clear and readable in all your poses. The more simple and readable it is, the stronger it will be. You can think of it like a graphic design element with arms and legs. It has to telegraph as powerfully as any sales pitch you've ever had. The line of motion has to read clearly, even on the *break downs* (the main poses you have to put between the key poses that keep a character's motion true to the vision you have in your mind) and inbetweens (all the frames that come between keys and break downs).

Lines of motion should be clearly readable and have at least some curve to them, unless you are using that straight, rigid graphic concept for effect (like using the character as an arrow). Lines of motion should also be no more complex than an "S" shape. Our minds generally don't bother to figure out the complexities of a super squiggly line; it just reads as chaos. Unless you're using that chaos for effect, it will have much less power than a strong, simple shape.

Reversing the line of motion keeps it interesting and builds strength in the pose. You can also have parts of your pose reverse their arcs, too, like an arm that reverses the direction of its curve as the hand rises from rest. Reversing a curve is a powerful graphic element; the audience's eye will be drawn to it. Because of this, you should carefully orchestrate these reversals, like a symphonic conductor. Too many reversals in a short span of time will exhaust the viewer. Too many reversals happening all at once over different parts of the character will splay the audience's focus and lose their interest. Through an animation, line of motion is like the bass beat that drives the scene.

> ### ADVANCED NOTE:
> The concept of curves and reversals can be extended throughout multiple characters in a scene, paying attention to how each interacts with another to create an overall line of motion that moves over the visual plane of the screen.

## 10.4 **Anticipation**

*Anticipation* is leading the eye with motion. You are using a preceding action to lead the audience's eye to what is going to happen next, or to an important area that they will need to be focusing on. The concept of anticipation really comes from stage magicians who need you to look at their right hand while their left puts a pigeon into a wine glass.

Filmmaking has always been about leading the audience's eye. (When we take the 3D information and squeeze it onto a 2D plane, the audience needs help so they don't miss what's important.) Lots of motifs have been developed to help catch the audience's eye, from carefully planned editing, to a splash of color in an otherwise dull set, to a breeze that ruffles the curtains right before the hero enters.

> **NOTE:**
>
> Motion leads our eye. In the wild, a fox can seem to disappear in a field not three feet away if he stands still. When he moves, our eyes lock onto that movement. Anticipation is moving an important part of the character's body to draw our eye to that spot so we don't miss the action that follows. Before some fast action happens with the character's hand, flex his fingers just a little while the rest of his body remains still or in a moving hold (see Section 10.8). You can use "leading the eye with motion" (anticipation) as any other rhythmic device at your disposal. You can tease the audience with it, building patterns and getting them to look in a certain direction expecting more of the same, then wait until their expectations have died down before hitting them with that big knockout punch! (This is classic horror movie timing.)

1. Load your setup scene.

2. Save it as a revision for Section 10.4 in your working directory for Chapter 10.

**NOTE:**

The exercises in this book are about to get a lot more subjective. For the exercises that follow, there is no "right" way and there is no "wrong" way. There is only what looks good for the scene. It isn't my goal to turn you into a clone of me. I'm going to do my best to give you the tools, and let you decide what you do with them. What it will take to let the exercises truly do their best for you is for you to honestly and humbly appraise what it is you see in your finished scenes. You have to ask yourself, "Is this something that would fit flawlessly into the best animated feature I've ever seen?" You have to be honest with yourself about the answer. If the answer is "no," then you have to go through both the animation basics and the advanced animation mechanics as checklists to see if your scene has everything in it that it needs. Evaluate your animation from as many different viewable angles as you have time. When all angles read convincingly for your character's intent (and being), your scene should give you a bit of a shudder and an innate knowledge that if you saw this on the big screen, sandwiched by the best animation you've ever seen, it would fit right in.

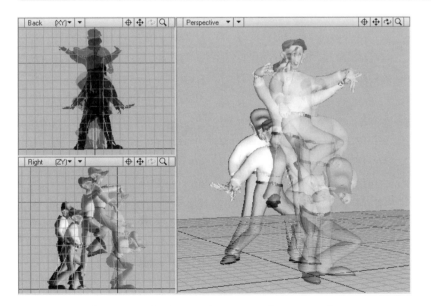

**Figure 10.5** This composite image shows my take on our character anticipating, jumping, and landing. (He "jumps down" before he jumps up.)

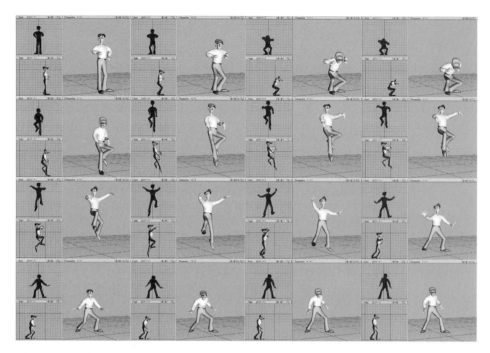

**Figure 10.6** This is an image sequence of the same animation. (Shown on *twos*, a new drawing for every other frame, running at 24 fps.)

## Pose Copying

I'd like to make a concerted effort to not leave anyone behind, even if you've never animated before. There are a few scenes included on the companion CD where you'll be able to do a kind of "moving life drawing in 3D," which will get you further ahead in beginning your understanding of animation than any amount of reading ever will. Remember, though, this is simply *copying* animation. In order to get the full impact of that particular section, once you've done a spot-on copy of the animation, take a short break and go back and (without referencing anything but your own imagination) do the animation from scratch. Make it *your* animation. Take what you've learned by copying and push it farther, explore and experiment. You will be building confidence by going through the motions (building what they call "muscle memory") and then using the experience to make your own decisions. Do this with as many of the exercises as you need; you can cover a lot of ground this way.

To do this exercise as an exploration of moving life drawing:

1. From your working revision (created in step 2 of this section), select **File|Load|Load Items From Scene…**.

2. Choose **Scenes\chapters\ch10\Figure_10-05.lws**. (In response to the request to load lights as well as objects, choose **No**.)

3. Select the **Thinguy_F (2)** object.

4. Choose **Items|Replace|Replace With Object File…**.

5. Select **Objects\Final\Thinguy_LifeDrawing_F.lwo** and click **Open**.

6. Under **Display|Display Options|Schematic View**, make sure **Drag Descendants** is checked.

7. In a schematic view, with Thinguy_LifeDrawing_F still selected, drag it and its hierarchy away from Thinguy_F's hierarchy so it doesn't get in the way as you work.

8. Change the end frame to 29 (assuming you're working in 24 fps, as both my setup and animation are) and you're ready to start matching my animation, pose for pose, frame for frame!

9. Scrub through the animation. See where the extremes are and copy those poses first.

10. Once you have the extremes in, scrub back through the animation and reposition him to the model where he drifts farthest from the model's animation. (This is in essence what a break down is.)

11. Repeat this process until your character matches the model's animation perfectly.

As you copy the poses, look for the other animation principles going on in the scene as well. There's squash and stretch, drag, follow-through, circular motion, overlapping action, and there's even altering realistic timing to get him to snap up from the ground as he leaps. As you go over these points in this and the chapter on advanced animation mechanics, think back on what you did here. Think not only of how things in my scene worked but how you can make them better!

3.  Animate the character anticipating, jumping, and landing.

**NOTE:**

If you choose to have your character's fingers clench into fists as I have done, you'll run into that lovely issue of gimbal lock. I had to switch to local coordinates in order to get the *Base bone of the two outer fingers to not leave a gap between themselves and the character's middle finger. The problem is that when you go back to parent coordinates, you find yourself presented with a problem: There are some huge numbers (+/– 90 or more) in heading and bank. If you have already created other keys for these bones where heading and bank are more reasonable (+/– 80 or less), those fingers will look wrong when they inbetween from one keyframe to the other. My solution was to click in the numeric input box for heading, and leaving the value intact, type in "180 – " to the left of the current value (say 117.00). When you press Enter, LightWave figures what 180 – 117 is and leaves "63.00" as the value for heading. I repeated this for bank, and got something that was a pretty darn close approximation of what I had gotten using local coordinates. The only difference between the rotations is that this set inbetweens just fine with a keyframe of 0H, 0P, 0B.

**NOTE:**

Before I animate anything, regardless of whether it is for money or just practice, I try to come up with a reason for the character to be doing the action. It helps to get personality into the scene so it doesn't read as a flat and boring (even if it is a well-animated) bit of purposeless action. Before getting into this scene, ask yourself, "Why would this guy be jumping?" Is he startled? Did he win a lottery? Is he avoiding a sweep kick, and why is someone throwing a sweep kick at him (how does he feel about having someone throw said sweep kick at him)? When you're comfortable with the answers to these questions, those answers will read through the scene as the character's intent and purpose. Even if this little snippet is all the world ever sees of this guy jumping, there will be a feeling that this guy has a life, a soul, an opinion about and a reason for jumping. (Think Degas—a slice out of time. You want the audience to feel that the character came from some moment before, and that he's gone somewhere a moment after the scene ends.) Doing this will leave your audience wanting more.

"...which is a kind of integrity, if you look on every exit, as an entrance... someplace else."—The Player (*Rosencrantz and Guildenstern Are Dead*)

## 10.5 **Drag**

*Drag* is a pretty simple concept. Hold up a (clean) shirt. Move your hand moderately fast to the right. The bottom of the shirt lags behind your hand. This is drag.

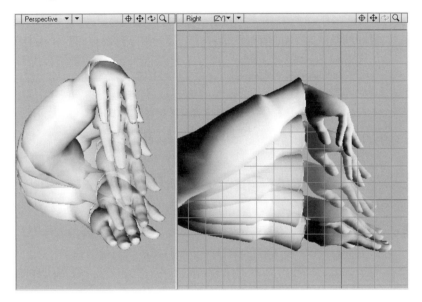

**Figure 10.7** As the wrist moves up, the fingers and palm drag behind.

Drag happens on nearly everything in animation. You can make a scene look multitudes better by making sure drag is appropriately applied to hands, fingers, toes, elbows, and heads. It's like squash and stretch in that it may not really happen in real life quite as much as we show it in animation, but it gives a visual representation of how an action feels.

If you were to see someone next to you in the café acting with the amount of drag that feels natural on a cartoon character, you'd probably seriously think about changing tables (or restaurants). Drag isn't about what looks real, it's about what looks good.

Sensuous villains tend to let drag and follow-through unroll their every action. ("Oozing charm from every pore, he oiled his way around the floor..." —Professor Higgins, *My Fair Lady*.)

Cartoon items can show their mass with respect to other cartoon items by how much drag (and follow-through) they have as they animate.

Almost every animated action, even the most realistic acting, needs to have some element of drag in order to make it read well to an audience.

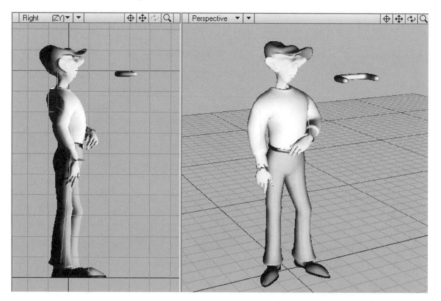

**Figure 10.8** We'll be using this scene to practice drag.

1. Load in Scenes\chapters\ch10\Section_10-05_Setup.lws.

> **NOTE:**
>
> All of the scenes I'll be handing you to work with are at 24 fps. If you need to practice at another frame rate, feel free to make adjustments accordingly.

> **NEWBIE NOTE:**
>
> Newbies, my take on the scene is: Scenes\chapters\ch10\Section_ 10-05_F.lws. Load items from the scene and copy if you need to!

2. Paying special attention to drag on the fingers and palm, animate ThinGuy reaching up with his left hand and grabbing that floating handle.

As you work, here are some suggestions to bear in mind: Raise the character's hand above the handle first, then let it settle down upon it (don't just go straight for the handle, that's boring). Take a quick read ahead in the next section on follow-through to help you refresh your mind as to what happens when the hand reaches the top of its arc and begins to settle onto the handle. Let the fingers unfold with their own follow-through, but make sure they don't do it all at the same time; try to keep at least 1 to 2 f difference between each digit.

Give your scene as much screen time as you need to have your character's intent play out. Is he scared of the handle? Does the handle represent some kind of long-sought-after goal? Is he going to save the world with this handle (if it were part of a switch assembly) or destroy it?

> **NOTE:**
> You'll notice that this scene starts on Frame 0. The character's rest pose is on frame −100. With the rest pose at −100, I can still go back to it in case I need to straighten anything out, but it is far enough away from Frame 0 that it won't have too much of an adverse effect on the motion curves (causing the character to inbetween in an unwanted way from 0 to the first keyframe). If you do notice the motion paths going off their intended course between 0 and the first keyframe, you can always set the frame counter at 0, and make a keyframe for all items at −1. (This works best if you're using TCB splines. It doesn't work quite as well for hermite or Bezier splines.) Remember, though, to rekey −1 if you make adjustments to the pose on Frame 0!

3. When you're satisfied with your work, load in Scenes\chapters\ch10\Section_10-05_F.lws and compare your solutions with mine.

Are there any ideas that come to mind as you're watching and comparing the scenes? Can the solutions I came up with for drag, anticipation, or timing help you in making your scene better?

4. Take another pass through your scene. See if there are ways in which it can be *plussed* (pushed beyond where it is) to make it more entertaining or read better.

## 10.6 **Follow-Through**

*Follow-through* is the counterpoint to drag. When you hold up that (clean) shirt, and move your hand to the right, then stop, the shirt flows beyond the stopping point of your hand. This is follow-through. (The shirt then settles gently back to where your hand stopped. This is *settling*.)

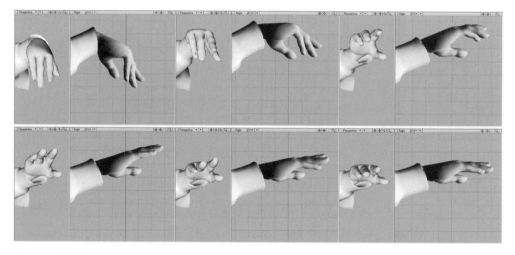

**Figure 10.9** The wrist moves upward, beyond its settling point, then comes back down to rest. The palm and fingers continue to flow upward (they follow-through), even as the wrist begins to settle back down. (The palm and fingers then drag behind the wrist to settle slightly after it does.)

> **NOTE:**
>
> Some of the subtlety of the animation is lost in the above figure. (There are many things about animation that can be best understood when seen as animation.) Load in Scenes\chapters\ch10\Figure_10-09.lws. As you watch it as a preview or scrub through the frames, watch the graceful, fluid nature of the hand. See how the motion almost unfurls but still has some snap to it as the fingers follow-through. Notice also that the pinky settles first, then the middle finger, and finally the index finger and thumb. (This variation in timing keeps the fingers from twinning and is almost unnoticeable unless you go looking for it, but adds a wealth of life to the motion.)

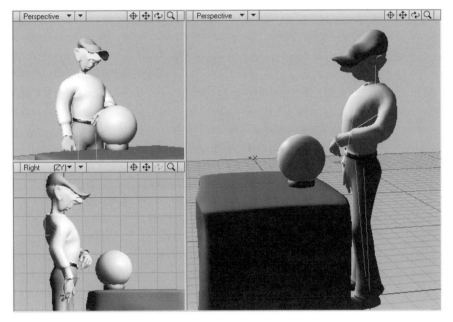

**Figure 10.10** Here's the scene we'll be working with for this exercise. The character's initial pose is almost identical to the previous exercise, but his intent is entirely different.

1. Load in Scenes\chapters\ch10\Section_10-06_Setup.lws.

> **NEWBIE NOTE:**
>
> Newbies, between the last couple of exercises, you've learned a lot. I want you to work this scene from scratch with the rest of us. If you're really unhappy with how you do on it, you can always go back and work with posing to my scene. But I think you'll surprise yourself with how well you actually do on your own here.

2. Giving yourself three seconds of screen time to complete the action, I want you to have our character place both his hands on the crystal ball.

We're going to be working with some acting here. The scene is still very much open to interpretation, but I want you to make his movements very fluid and mystical. He is moved by an irritable power he doesn't quite understand but doesn't fear; the blood of his gypsy ancestors runs deep in his veins. He raises both his hands over the scrying sphere and lays them gently, reverently, almost sensuously along its sides to gaze deep into the mists of time.

> **NOTE:**
>
> An animator is an actor with a pencil, stylus, or mouse. In this sense, being an animator is the best job in the world.

As you work, focus on all that you know, all that we've gone over so far. Make sure there's appropriate anticipation, drag, and follow-through. With the exception of the scene length of three seconds, you have carte blanche as to how much action to put in there. Make sure that whatever action you do put in reads clearly; that there is enough action to keep the scene interesting (by the end of the scene, the audience will want to see what happens next), but that there isn't too much going on and we overwhelm the audience. (You don't want total sensory overload; people lose interest very fast when they're overwhelmed.)

After you've finished the scene and you're watching it play out before you, ask yourself if your character reads with the same personality you envisioned him to have before starting the scene. Has he remained true to your vision? If not, has he improved? Did you find new ways of making his characteristics show through even more?

This is a scene that should have a lot of fluidity to it. It should really play up the drag and follow-through, not just on the fingers and hands but on the elbows back and head, too. You're allowed to go over the top with the whole "mystical" thing on this scene. Ham it up!

> **NOTE:**
>
> It's a lot easier to pull something back from the edge of overacting, toning it down, than it is to try to get something that is dry and straight to read with more warmth and richness. When in doubt of what the director wants with a scene, I usually err on the side of subtle intensity. I can always pull it back if the director thinks it's too much.

3. Before you go on, jot down on paper some notes about your scene, where you feel things could be improved (there should always be at least some areas you feel can be improved). Take note of the good things going on, too, the things that read well and touch on what we've gone over so far.

4. Save a revision of your scene.

5. Take a look at what answers I came up with for this scene in Scenes\chapters\ch10\Section_10-06_F.lws.

As you watch what I did, keep in mind that there are no "rights" and no "wrongs." There is simply my take on things and yours. Since there is no overall story arc to which we are adhering, we don't have to worry about our guy being in character; all we have to concern ourselves with is: Does the action look believable? Does the action look good? Are there any areas in which things can be improved?

> **NOTE:**
>
> Scenes\chapters\ch10\Section_10-06_F.lws is just to give you ideas, give you another viewpoint on how things can be done. The greatest thing you can do for yourself as an animator is to explore as many ways to do a thing as possible. Find as many different solutions to problems as you can. Talk with other animators, get their ideas on things, find new angles and insights, and share what you have learned. The broader the range of experience you can bring to your work, the more deep, rich, and fulfilling it will become, not just to do, but to watch as well.

In watching my take on the scene, are there any ideas you get about things you can do to your scene? Are there bits of the ways I've used drag and follow-through that give you ideas on how you can plus your scene?

**NEWBIE NOTE:**

Newbies, if you feel you could benefit from posing through my animation, take time to do that now. Then retry this scene from scratch.

6.  Take another look at your scene. Work from the notes you've made about your scene to bring this animation to a level you feel would fit seamlessly in a collection of the best animation you've seen. Take as much time as you need before moving on.

**NOTE:**

As far as quality goes in animation, you only get as good as you let yourself. By that I mean you have to give yourself the time it takes for you to do feature-quality work before you can pare that amount of time down to that which might be given on a TV series. If two weeks is what it takes to bring a certain complexity of scene up to feature-level quality, do your best to make sure you have that time given to you. Eventually, after working and streamlining your processes, you may be able to get a scene of similar complexity done in one week. But being given only one week to do scenes of that complexity time and time again, you can work forever and never reach that level of feature-quality animation. Our brains give to us what we ask of them. We have to ask for that level of quality, and give the amount of time it takes for feature-quality habits to be formed.

## 10.7 **Easing In/Easing Out**

We've already been doing this in our practice scenes. *Easing in* or *easing out* is simply slowly bringing our character into or out of a motion. We saw easing in in the gentle settling of the fingers in Figure 10.9 and its corresponding animation. The wrist, palm, and fingers eased in to their resting point. In Scenes\chapters\ch10\Section_10-06_F.lws, the character's hands eased out of their initial pose at the beginning of the animation.

Easing in and easing out are ways of taking the sharp "edges" off of an animation. Care must be taken so that the "edges" aren't smoothed so much that the animation becomes "mush." Use varying amounts of easing in and easing out to build rhythm in a scene. You can allow one part of the character to take more time to slowly enter or exit a motion than another to prevent your character from twinning.

**NOTE:**

The best kind of spline curve for easing in and easing out is a Bezier curve. Working with Bezier curves means that you often spend as much time working in the curve editor (motion graph) as you do actually animating. The hard work pays off with a scene that has the barest minimum of keyframes needed to keep the animation on track; you have absolute, precise control of how the curves enter and exit a keyframe.

**NOTE:**

You can get a pretty good ease in and ease out effect with TCB splines, too, by moving the time slider one or two frames before the keyframe into which you want to ease. You create a key for that item one or two frames before the frame the slider is currently on. The drawback to this method is that you can end up cluttering your keys. Unless you remember which keyframes are the poses and which are the ones you've created to ease in or out, you can accidentally delete the wrong one while making changes to the animation. (Save revisions of your scene to CYA!)

Easing in and out isn't just used for keeping an item from "slamming" to a dead stop; use it to add texture, rhythm, and flavor to a scene. As you act out a scene before settling into animation, note how you enter and exit moves. Bring that kind of characterization into the easing your 3D actor performs in the scene!

## 10.8 Moving Holds

A *moving hold* is where the character is stationary and one or two parts of him are moving (like an ear or an eye), or when the character moves almost imperceptibly to another pose after settling into his key pose. These are ways in which a character can be kept alive while he isn't performing a *storytelling action* (an action which furthers the story or scene).

To do a moving hold in traditional animation, you had to either animate the parts that did move on a separate layer (the ear or eye that continues to move), or trace back (redraw from the first drawing of the hold) the parts that didn't move. In traditional animation, this can be time consuming. In 3D animation, it is simply a matter of adding a little offset to a control on a future keyframe so the character appears to continue to live while he's "stationary."

One of the biggest criticisms of computer animation, however, is that the characters never stop moving. It is so easy with the splines we have to work with, and the computers to (relatively) quickly handle the inbetweens, that knowing when to lock down a character has now become an issue.

> **NOTE:**
>
> "Splineyness" refers to the problem of a 3D character always being in constant motion, or to the problem of the motion not having enough "crispness" to it. ("I dunno. The motion looks a little spliney.") Don't just accept the computer's interpretation for the spline curves; make sure they are exactly the way you want them to be. Make sure that there is a good balance of "texture" to your animations: soft, sharp, quick, slow, tiny, and broad. Make sure that the storytelling actions read clearly and don't get lost in the moving holds.

Pay close attention to the style of animation you're doing. It may look stylistically best to have your character visibly freeze for a bit, or to have most of him freeze while an ear and his whiskers droop as smoke rises from his head. Remember that animation is all about the conveyance of feeling. Stylistic symbolism is a powerful tool for doing so. Make an effort to understand what kinds of symbolism have been used before. Understand the "language" of symbols that audiences have come to accept. This is a language that has been explored and refined since before the 1920s!

> **NOTE:**
>
> You may even try setting all your splines to interpret as stepped, so your character stays frozen until you put in a keyframe, break down, or inbetween. This gives your motion the same feel as traditional animation; it's handled in exactly the same way!

If you are working on a more realistic piece, take a look at how real life handles its moving holds. Sure, when we stand, we're not perfectly still, but how much do we actually move? How visible is the motion on screen? If a particular motion is visible, where and how does it affect the form? Remember that movement attracts the eye. You want to make sure that the audience's focus is where you want it at all times. Don't let an overactive moving hold distract your viewer from important action (or lack thereof)!

Study all the great actors you can. Watch how things are done on stage, and compare this with how the best film actors of today use their motion or lack thereof to sculpt an emotional performance. Compare this with the greats of the Silent Age of filmmaking. Masters like Chaplin (who at times did more than 50 takes of a scene to get it exactly the way he envisioned it) made sure that every character on the screen was moving exactly as they intended.

> **NOTE:**
>
> Watch films with the sound off. This helps you focus on the action and really see what is going on and how the scenes were crafted. As you watch, ask yourself what these actors were doing to evoke the feelings they do. What were they doing with timing and pacing? How is their delivery of thoughts and ideas? How do they use anticipation, drag, and follow-through?

Use all the resources at your disposal to gain an understanding of how to best use the tools before you. Always make sure that every aspect of your final scene adds to the feeling you want your audience to read, that nothing detracts from it, and that everything that needs to be read, reads clearly.

"Music is the silence between the notes."—Unknown

## Chapter 11

# Advanced Animation Mechanics

## 11.1 Silhouette

Silhouette is the first thing our minds read when we look at anything. This is why it is so vital to pay very close attention to our character's silhouette as we work and as we evaluate. Not only must it read strong and true to every feeling and opinion of our character, it must also clearly carry the intent of his action. (You have to be careful, too, that parts of the silhouette can't be misconstrued for things they aren't.) From the silhouette alone, you should be able to tell what's going on and how the character feels about it.

In terms of reading the character's intent with the silhouette, if the character is evil, every line of his silhouette should radiate with villainy. If the character is a lovable goof, every line should read with pleasant silliness. If the character is sweet and inculpable, every line of the silhouette should emanate innocence.

The silhouette should have appeal. Audiences have to identify with a part of what they read in the silhouette and like what they see. Even if your character is distilled badness, he still has to appeal to the audience; otherwise, they're not going to relate to him or care about what he's doing. This does not mean toning things down, not in the least. This means making sure whatever you do looks cool. The audience has to read the silhouette and think, "I want to be that," or "I want to have one just like that!" Granted, appeal can be pretty amorphous, and what has appeal for one person may not for another. As ethereal as appeal can be, you know when you've nailed it when you see your scene and think, "I gotta get one of those!" (Or at the very least, you feel as if there's a part of you that can connect with what you're seeing on screen.)

> **NOTE:**
>
> Milt Kahl said it best about appeal: "If you're working on a scene and you either want to be that character, or be with that character, you're doing it right." The magical thing about this is that if you're true to yourself, and you do feel this way while doing a scene, the audience will too.

> **NEWBIE NOTE:**
>
> Appeal is a tough quality to nail down. What makes something look appealing, and something else look like a "transporter" accident? You could have an entire book on this quality alone. Yet, one thing is certain; when you try your hardest to make something appeal to everyone is when you most often fail. To start off in gaining an understanding of appeal, watch high-quality animation and take note of when something strikes you close to your heart. Try to exactly copy what you see with your own work. The more you do this, the more you will build "muscle memories" for how to achieve certain specific results. This is important because when you're working, you need to turn off the "thinking" part of your brain, and just go by feel. (My mentor, Tom Roth, said that to get a good quality line, you had to stop trying.) As you're working, you have to watch for the moment your control passes a part of your character through a pose that feels right (maybe you've seen something like it before and it worked in that context). You'll quickly build "riffs" you know will work for certain situations and you'll be able to put your brain on "autopilot" and just enjoy the work. Remember, the key is to understand what makes things great by consciously understanding great things!

The strength of the pose still has to ring, crystal-clear, through the silhouette. There has to be enough visual information, *landmarks* (internalized cues all mammals seem to use to identify based on shape, perceived relative distance, and angle), that the viewer will be able to identify what is going on and relate to his own experience. Landmarks are the shorthand we use to identify a situation at a glance. In a silhouette, they are all we have.

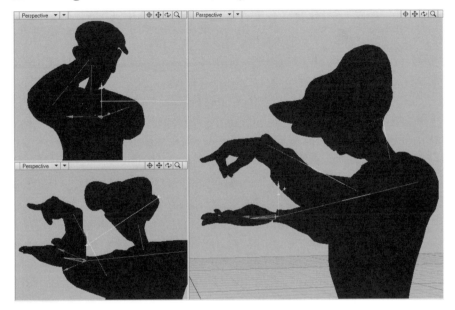

**Figure 11.1** Three views of the same pose in silhouette; each has varying degrees of success and drama.

The image at the upper left is a straight-on shot. You can't really tell what is going on. Things are just a mass of rounded shapes. If you didn't know this was a human character, you might not know what you're looking at.

The image at the lower left reads better, though there is still a bit of confusion about what is going on with the character's hands. We get the idea that this is an *up-shot* (a shot from a low angle pointing upward, also known as a *worm's eye view*). (I'm guessing that it isn't a down-shot (over the (left) shoulder) because of the size differences in what I can make out to be the hand masses. Also, his shoulders appear straight; in order to get the extension of what would be the right arm, he would need to rotate his right shoulder in.) We get a feel of the angle of the character's head from the outline of the character's left ear, what we can discern to be the character's right ear, and what we know of the kind of hat it looks like he's wearing. From there, we're able to pretty quickly guess that the character's left hand is outstretched with the palm upward. We get this because of what we assume to be the thumb, the bump above the plateau of the hand, which would most comfortably be created by the thumb being to the left of the hand mass. (We can guess that this is the left hand because for it to be the right hand (palm down to have the thumb on that side) we would need to see indications of fingers along the bottom line of that hand. The left index finger appears to be outstretched, and the other fingers appear to be curled slightly because of how the angles meet on the underside of that hand. What's going on with the right hand is a bit of a mystery. We can't really tell its placement in relationship to the other hand; its silhouette doesn't give us enough information to accurately guage its size. The right fingers don't give us much either; their definition is hidden in the mass of the hand.

The image on the right has the most information of the three. We see exactly what is going on. The only question we have by looking at the silhouette is which hand is right and which hand is left (something that's fairly minor in the grand scheme of things.) We can all relate (we've all probably done something similar in our lives). So even though we don't know quite what he's got between his fingers, we can see that it must hold some interest because all his attention is focused on it. Because of the landmarks, we can identify in an instant what is going on, and we get immediate ideas as to how this character feels about what he is doing.

Rhythm plays a huge part in how good a silhouette looks. It has to be interesting. It has to hold your attention. There have to be engaging little nooks and crannies, and strong expanses of gently curving lines. (We are referential beings; smooth is only smooth because we have something to compare it with.) And there has to be variance in how big these interesting details are. You need details big enough to grasp the very instant you look at the silhouette, and little particulars that you begin to notice only after several moments.

These rhythmic details will determine how successful your silhouette (and your pose and animation) will be. The idea is that you want to have the viewer want to explore the piece. There have to be large, smooth areas to balance the tiny details. There have to be curves balancing the straight lines. Balance, rhythm, straights, curves, big, small—there's a lot that goes into just this one aspect of silhouette. Remember that the best thing you can do is to find what works (you can hold up a frame from an animated feature and clearly see the difference between that and the average bang-it-out Saturday morning cartoon) and look for what you know should be there making it work.

> **NOTE:**
>
> In painting and drawing, the different levels of detail are called the different *reads* of the piece. The big details catch your eye from across the room. The medium-sized details are noticed as you move across the room toward the piece, and there should also be wonderful little details like brush strokes that you only see when you have your nose almost touching the canvas. <u>None of these sets of details should interfere with the others</u>. Your ability to integrate elements like these into your own work comes not only from looking <u>at</u> other pieces with successful levels of detail, but looking <u>for</u> them.

As far as rhythm goes, there's not much to mention about the image at the upper left in Figure 11.1. It's all about semi-definable curves, with only a few straight lines thrown in here and there. There's nothing to catch and hold our attention; as silhouettes go, it's quite forgettable.

The silhouette in the lower left has some great areas of bumpy details, balanced and offset with large smooth areas. The *negative space* (the area surrounding the character which is interpreted to be contiguous even if broken up by background) is carved into interesting shapes by the jutting hands and head. There's a great balancing of the straight line of the (character's) right forearm where it meets the gentle, broken curve of his right upper arm/shoulder at an almost right angle. That strong, pronounced angle is balanced by the wide, powerful curve on the underside of the elbow. (Notice also that the large shape of the bottom of the elbow is actually a curve that becomes a straight line.) There are many smaller, interesting details as well—fingers, ears, curves of the hat. The balance of large details and small, curved and straight lines, angles and arcs makes for interesting and enjoyable rhythm.

The image at the right of Figure 11.1 again has large, languid curves and flats balanced against the quick little curves of the fingers and mouth. There are lots of great little points where curves and straights meet or blend. And the line of the back reads as a powerful straight against the equally powerful curve of the tummy (made up of two lines that themselves could be considered straight). The rhythm of this angle is more complex than the previous two. It is interesting; it has many areas to explore and large, smooth shapes to balance and carry the finer details. But even so, it doesn't quite have the drama that the silhouette in the lower left does. We read what's going on, do a quick exploration of the details and stop. Our eye doesn't want to re-explore the details, traveling through the composition again and again as it does with the silhouette in the lower left. This is because of the way wedge shapes are used in both compositions.

Wedge shapes are powerful design tools. They lead the eye from their widest part to their tip. In the image in the lower left, the large mass of the torso and arms is a wedge and shoots our eyes over to the detail work of the hands and fingers (especially that pinky). From there, we're caught by the brim of the hat and wedged back into the torso, and our eyes start taking that journey all over again. It is a triangular composition, made up of smaller, directional wedges.

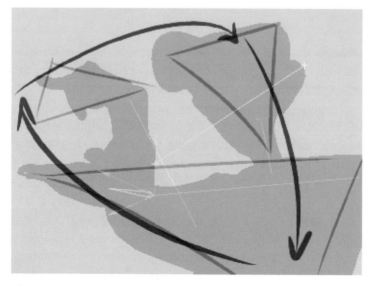

**Figure 11.2** The triangular composition, made up of smaller, directional wedges accelerates our eye around the composition.

The image on the right has wedge shapes as well, but they're less pronounced. The large wedge of the torso mass has its narrowest part down toward the bottom of the screen, leading our eye out of the picture. The head is triangular shaped, but equilateral; we don't perceive a direction in which to be led. The space between the arms is the strongest wedge shape (created from the negative space outside the character); this leads us from the eye-like silhouette of the hand back into the torso, but there is nothing in the torso to hold us there.

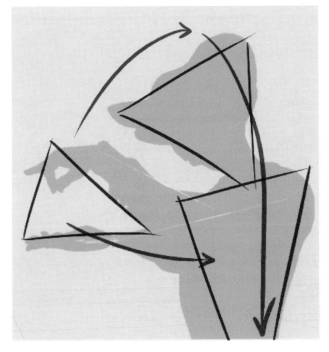

**Figure 11.3** This composition just doesn't work as well as the previous one. We read what is going on with the character, but after a cursory exploration of the parts, our eye "just sits there."

**NOTE:**

The concept of triangular compositions and using directional elements to lead the eye was brought front and center by the Renaissance masters. Look to the works of Rembrandt, Gentileschi, da Vinci, Caravaggio, and Peter Paul Rubens. See what you notice first; turn away, close your eyes, and when you turn back to the painting, what do you see first? Where does your eye move next? Why? Is it a hand pointing? An arm leading toward another area of interest? The way light cuts a silhouette through the darkness or light? Heads that are turned, leading us toward other characters, and pools of light and shadow are subtle, brilliant ways of drawing the audience in and keeping them moving around the two-dimensional plane of the screen. Look for what you know to be there! Understand because you begin to see what was so elegantly hiding in plain sight!

There's a lot more to silhouette than just making the action read clearly. Every scene should be staged and animated so that the silhouettes are instantly readable, dramatic, rhythmic, and executed with attention given to how their design elements impact the viewer.

---

**NEWBIE NOTE:**

All this information on silhouette may seem like esoteric, artsy-fartsy stuff, but understanding, internalizing, and applying it is what will make your work stand worlds above the rest.

---

**NOTE:**

The view I'd stage the scene from is the one on the lower left. Aside from the strong design and compositional elements, the silhouette doesn't give away everything about the scene at once. It gives enough information that it captures the audience's interest the moment it comes on screen, and the playing out of the scene (through character motion and/or camera motion) will reveal the rest. I like there to be a little mystery in what I do; it draws the audience in, makes them wonder—and in that wondering (if they already care about what's going on), they are in essence participating in the scene. This is the name of the game in any kind of storytelling; get the audience to <u>want</u> to know what happens next!

# 11.2 **Exaggeration ("Bad" Poses)**

How far can you push a silhouette and still have it work in a scene? It depends on how "realistic" the animation, but it is always more than you first think.

Good animation often has many so-called "bad drawings." These are drawings where the character is exaggerated so much that were you to see just that one frame, it would look seriously wrong. Even the tightly rendered classics have characters moving through poses that are pushed so far that they look weird out of context.

With most of us, it is harder for us to really push something into exaggeration than it is to take something that is a little too broad and pull it back. (And when we first start out in animation, most of us are so self-conscious of doing something "wrong" that a lot of our scenes look stiff and boring.) It's OK to push things; we're showing the <u>impression</u> of experience, not the photographic representation of an action.

There are two basic kinds of exaggeration: extreme poses and "super-mega-ultra-extreme" poses. (We'll just call these "ultra-extreme" poses.) With both, you need to get your character back to his original proportions and expected silhouette as soon as possible. (The audience will buy into a lot, if there's a bit of relative normalcy for them to cling to as madcap action plays out.)

**Figure 11.4** Extreme poses.

Extreme poses can be moved through for two to three frames. (Anything on screen for four frames or longer tends to cement in the audience's mind.) They heighten the visual impact of the force acting on the character. (This force doesn't have to be physical—remember the Avery cartoons!)

**Figure 11.5** Ultra-extreme poses.

Ultra-extreme poses should only be left on screen for one frame (one frame at 24 fps—you may be able to push an ultra-extreme to two frames at 30 fps, but use caution). Ultra-extremes are meant to be felt, not seen! They are meant to run right by, without the audience even being aware that they were ever there, with only the elusive sense of bright, snappy animation in their wake. They can almost be thought of as subliminals. Their power is in the emotional impact, not in their cognitive retention.

Extremes and ultra-extremes show the intense impact that really gets your character moving. You can have crazy shapes and proportions, insane squash, incredulous stretch; you can have your character stupendously off balance. You can break all the rules for the sole purpose of driving a point home (and have fun doing it). Extremes and ultra-extremes can also be used as *smeared* frames (exaggerated motion blur) as a character turns his head ultra-quick. Use them to add sharp, percussive rhythm and snap to your actions; they are the breve of the animated world.

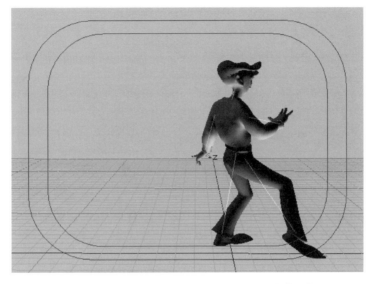

**Figure 11.6** This is the scene we'll be working with for this section; we'll be animating him doing a wild take as something spooks him from off-screen left.

1. Load up Scenes\chapters\ch11\Section_11-02.lws, and save a working revision.

2. Animate our character doing a take, but keep him from going into any extreme poses; keep all his poses strictly believable.

The direction for this scene is: Our character is in a haunted house. He can barely see in the gloom and has lost his companions along the way. He's just paused to better hear something behind him when, without warning, a loud crash explodes from off-screen left. The character needs to end the scene facing screen left.

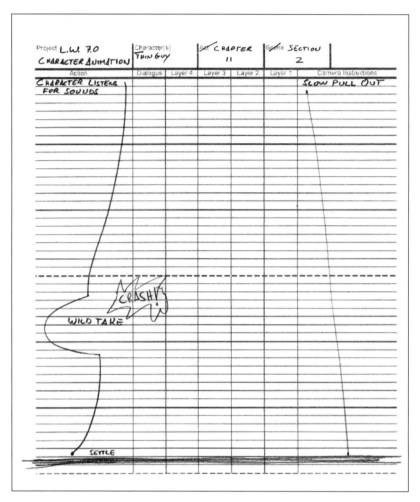

**Figure 11.7** The X-sheet (exposure sheet) for scene 11.2.

> **NOTE:**
>
> X-sheets are mostly used in traditional animation where drawings may be repeated or reordered, and different characters (or parts of characters) may be on different levels of paper. I still use them for 3D animation because the action line is a great way to get a visual feel for how the rhythms of the action will play out over time.

## Reading X-sheets

Reading an X-sheet becomes second nature pretty quickly. Every company you'll work for will more than likely have a different variation on the X-sheet's layout, but the information you need is always there. Project, character(s), act, and scene are self-explanatory. (I've changed "act" to "chapter" and "scene" to "section" to make these headings apply to the exercises we're doing right now. Some animation companies use "sequence" in place of "act.") Every new camera setup (different angle, cutaway, etc.) is a new scene (scene 1, scene 2, scene 1B, or scene 1B-1, if you need to add a scene between scene 1 and 2). Plan your animation well in the storyboarding phase so you don't have to insert a lot of scenes after the planning phase is done and scene numbers have been assigned.

Next, we've got sections for action, where the action is described and (usually) represented by a meandering line. (Usually the action isn't cast in stone; you can push it and pull it to make sure everything reads well on the screen.) Then the dialogue is phonetically spelled out in the dialogue section. (Since dialogue isn't being covered in this book, I'm putting in sound effects, SFX, cues here.)

Then we've got different layers for individual characters (parts of characters) or objects. You can use this area in 3D animation to represent the motions of individual characters or scene elements within the scene. You can also use these layers to choreograph elements to be worked on in a separate scene file to be composited later in post-production if a scene is just too complex to be held in memory all at once.

Farthest to the right is where the camera instructions go. If you were going to have to *dolly* the camera (i.e., move the camera as if it were on a wheeled cart (a dolly) on a track) around the character, *truck in* or *out* (push the camera in or pull it out, again, as if it were on a wheeled cart), zoom in or out, or *rack focus* (pull the focus of the camera using either depth of field controls or with an external post-processing program so that it goes from being in focus to being out, or vice versa), all this information would be here.

This X-sheet is geared for 24 fps. There's a thick, dashed line after every 24th frame, letting you know where each second ends. There are thicker lines every eight frames. These thicker lines help visually break each 24-frame second into three, equal, tractable sections. These eight-frame divisions also help by breaking the scene down into 1/2 foot segments; many studios still measure an animator's output in feet and frames. (Each foot of 35mm film is 16 frames long. This scene is 2' 14 f, it lasts :01.22, or 1.91 seconds, and is a total of 46 frames long.)

Looking at the X-sheet for this scene, we've got the character listening for sounds until the "crash" happens exactly at Frame 27. He does a wild take until about Frame 34. Then he settles until the scene ends at Frame 46. (The folks whose job it is to make X-sheets usually scribble a thick line where a scene ends so you, as an animator, know where to stop. If you find yourself timing X-sheets (also known as "slugging"), remember that you have to take into account any "heads" and "tails" (additional time that is needed to make transitions between scenes when dissolving or using another kind of transition that doesn't instantly cut from one scene to the other) that those in charge of editing the film may need.)

As you work on the scene, examine it from every angle to make sure the character is reading as he should. Make extra sure that the camera view reads solidly (work from the camera's predefined motion).

3.  When you get done animating your scene, compare what you did with my version: Scenes\chapters\ch11\Section_11-02a_F.lws.

See if there are any ideas you can work into your scene, such as ideas on timing, posing, drag, follow-through, and silhouette. Take another pass through your scene if you feel you can push its entertainment value farther. Remember to keep things from exaggerating. Keep the silhouettes strong and "realistic."

4.  Now, save a working revision as 11-02b; we're going to take what we just did and add a little exaggeration to it!

5.  Go back through your scene and push the poses farther. Exaggerate them to the limits of what your eye will believe. (Remember to let the character return to his rest proportions after the impacts that exaggerate him have passed.)

Really push the poses you did in the first pass of this animation; keep them from being ultra-extreme, but really see what you can get away with. Exaggerate everything you've learned so far—drag, follow-through, silhouette, squash, and stretch; make interesting visual shapes that flow well into one another.

6.  Again, when you're comfortable with what you've got, compare it with my barely restrained bizarreness: Scenes\chapters\ch11\Section_11-02b_ Elws. See if there are any more ideas you get about how you can push things.

If my scene does help bring about ideas of ways you can exaggerate things, go back and work them into your scene before moving onward. We're exploring how far you can push things and still have them read as "believable," which is very different than "realistic." Now's the time to play and have fun! Push and pull, and knock yourself out!

7.  When you're content with your scene 11-02b, save a working revision as **11-02c** and get ready to really nail a far-out, super-mega-ultra-extreme pose!

Ultra-extremes work best as an accent to a quick bit of action. In our scene, the only place a "bad drawing" extreme would work is in our guy's wild take, around Frames 30-32.

Ultra-extreme poses are islands unto themselves. They push what you've already got to the Nth degree. They shouldn't affect any of the surrounding frames, so they (usually) can't be inbetweened into; you have to isolate them so they are there-and-gone before the audience has an inkling of their existence. The best way I've found to put in an ultra-extreme is as follows:

8.  Scrub through the action to find the place where you want this ultra-extreme; this is where the character either moves the farthest between two frames or comes to the apex of his action.

9.  Select the mesh object itself, and create keyframes for Current Item and Descendants on all position, rotation, and scale axes on the frames on either side of the frame that will be the ultra-extreme. (If I wanted to have the ultra-extreme pose on Frame 30, I'd go to Frame 29 and create keyframes for Current Item and Descendants, then go to Frame 31 and create another keyframe for Current Item and Descendants.)

By having the mesh selected, you're creating for it and all of its children, bones and all, keyframes to lock in these poses. You're telling LightWave that even though (in my case) Frame 30 will have a bizarre keyframe, make sure everything still passes through these pre-established poses. You may even need to create these "anchoring" keyframes on (in my case) Frames 28 and 32 as well, just to be sure this bad drawing pose doesn't affect the splines in our animation as it currently is. Be sure to save a revision of your scene before putting in your ultra-extreme pose!

10. Go to the frame that will be your ultra-extreme pose and start pulling controls to throw our guy into the most extreme pose you can think of. Move, rotate, and scale things far beyond where you think they would rationally hold up in an animation.

11. Play your animation through, and check it out. Does that ultra-extreme pose add extra snap to the animation!

12. Load in my version of the scene: Scenes\chapters\ch11\Section_11-02c_ F.lws and give it a play through.

13. Go back and modify your animation if watching mine has given you any ideas as to how to make the ultra-extreme in your animation read better.

Ultra-extremes can take a bit of finessing to get them to work within an animation. They need to read as a bit of subliminal smack. They shouldn't jump out of the animation or hold your eye. They should flow right by you, only leaving a sense of added energy in their wake. Once you get the hang of extremes and ultra-extremes, you have yet another tool in your service that can bring added life and entertainment value to even the most mundane scenes!

# 11.3 Snappy Animation (Modified Timings)

There are times when an extreme or ultra-extreme just doesn't quite give your scene the right plussing you're looking for. Consider altering the timing of things to make them snap! You can remove frames, and you can replace an inbetween with a copy of the held-frame from the immediately preceding key. The name of the game is to get your scene to have the feel of what you're trying to get across, and in this game, there are no rules! If it works, go with it!

Remember the animation in Section 10.4 (Scenes\chapters\ch10\Figure_10-05.lws)? I had the character spring up from the ground a bit more quickly than would be considered "realistic." I've pulled a frame from the part of the animation where he would be pushing off from the ground. This gives him the feeling of snapping up from the ground, like something was there that made him want to pull his feet from the ground as quickly as possible. ("Yipe!") Now let's try animating a punch.

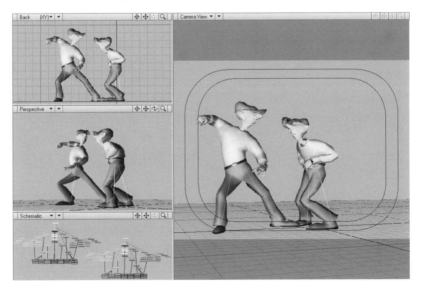

**Figure 11.8** We're going to be animating a punch for this scene.

1. Load in Scenes\chapters\ch11\Section_11-03_w01.lws, saving it as a working revision for this section in your Chapter 11 working directory.

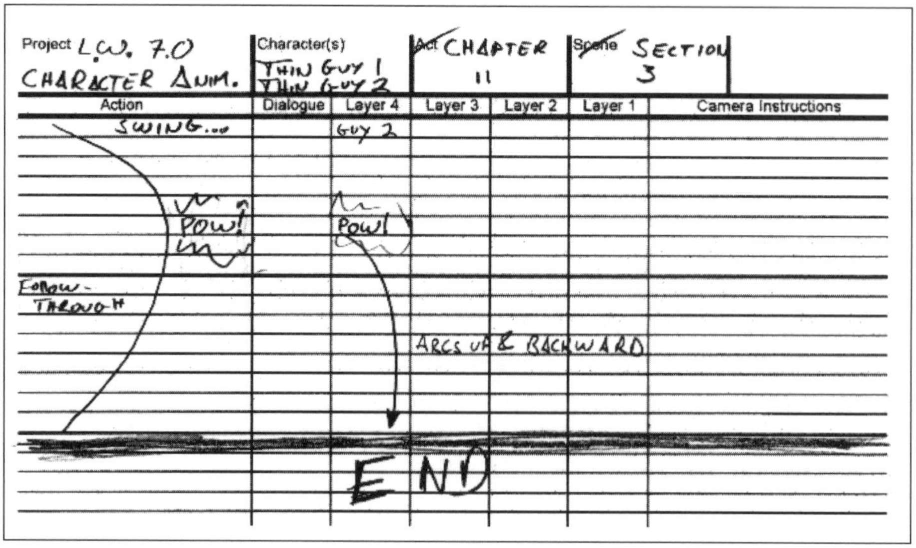

| Project L.W. 7.0 CHARACTER ANIM. | Character(s) THIN GUY 1 THIN GUY 2 | Act CHAPTER 11 | Scene SECTION 3 | | | | |
|---|---|---|---|---|---|---|---|
| Action | Dialogue | Layer 4 | Layer 3 | Layer 2 | Layer 1 | Camera Instructions | |
| SWING... | | GUY 2 | | | | | |
| | Pow? | Pow! | | | | | |
| FOLLOW-THROUGH | | | | | | | |
| | | ARCS UP & BACKWARD | | | | | |
| | END | | | | | | |

**Figure 11.9** This is the X-sheet we'll be animating to.

As you animate, I want you to try something. Don't have a keyframe showing the actual impact of the punch. Instead, put a keyframe a little bit before the impact, and then on the following frame, key a pose a little bit after the impact. You can have Thinguy 2 either already arcing backward or still being propelled by Thinguy 1's fist.

2. Working with the above X-sheet, animate the scene.

Even though we don't actually see a "drawing" of the impact, we as viewers don't have any problem interpolating what happened. We see the lead-in and the follow-through, we see the effect Thinguy 1's swing had on Thinguy 2, and by omitting the one frame detail of actually showing the impact of the punch landing, we maximize the perceived impact and thrust!

3. Compare what you have with the animation I did. Even though our styles may be different, the impact of the animation should be very close! (Scenes\chapters\ch11\Section_11-03_F.lws.)

# 11.4 **Circular Animation**

The concept of *circular animation* says that everything in animation happens along some form of circular, flowing arc. This follows along the same line of thinking as arc of motion, and getting the most powerful reading out of a gesture. You can think of circular animation as an arc of motion through time. It is a way of getting the strongest four-dimensional gestural "drawing" from your work.

**Figure 11.10** Turning the head from screen left to screen right; linear and booor-ing.

**Figure 11.11** Just by adding one break down pose, tilting the head down so that it follows an arc as it turns, you add feeling, heighten interest, and increase the entertainment value of the animation.

Everything (that isn't making use of an intentional linear graphic element) can be plussed by introducing a circular movement to it. Care must be taken to ensure that motions still retain their textures and rhythms; don't let things get so fluid that they turn to mush. You want fluidity that is comfortable for the eye to follow, and retains all the elements of good animation.

> **NOTE:**
>
> Most motions produced by living beings (on this planet at least) are constructed around an arc of some kind. These arcs have a kind of smoothness to them because of an inherent desire to conserve the energy required to generate that motion; it is a needless exertion of energy to apply force to redirect or modify the trajectory of an object when you don't have to. When someone throws a punch, the motion of the punch is controlled by the unfolding joints of the elbow, the shoulder, and the positioning of the body. When that punch reaches the end of its motion, it is pulled back into the body by the same rotational joints; the mass of the fist causes the motion to be smooth and (from a motion analysis point of view) elegant. Everything is a balance of rotation and counterrotation. Our minds accept and understand circular movements more readily than angular or unexpected movements because our minds have evolved to quickly read a situation based on silhouette and movement. We analyze motions in an instant, projecting where they will go next; it is a survival adaptation all animals have. As animators, we need to play to this adaptation, unless we are using our knowledge to intentionally startle our audience or throw them off balance.

Heads, hands, and feet aren't the only things that have circular motion to them. Elbows, knees, torsos, hips, shoulders, every part of the body that moves should be handled with respect paid to circular motion as you create, finesse, and examine your animation.

As you examine your animation, glue your eyes to one part of your character's body, say a knee. Watch that part play through again and again. Does it flow? Does it look believable? In its fluidity, does it still have textures that make it an interesting and balanced part of the whole? When knees compress for a jump, they can start out wide, then swing inward slightly as they propel the character upward, describing a slight ellipse. This is much more interesting than a knee just going straight up and down. Like all things in animation, though, subtlety is the name of the game—subtlety with intent.

> **NOTE:**
>
> If you're having a hard time tracking a movement, or if something doesn't read quite right along a series of frames, grab a dry erase marker and put tiny dots on the monitor's glass tracking a specific body part's progress from frame to frame. (Don't do this on a laptop screen, and do make sure that the marker won't hurt the monitor first!) These dots will show you exactly where that body part deviates from the smooth arc of motion, where it accelerates and decelerates, and where it jumps, pops, and wavers. It is a good idea to do this not just from the camera's view but from side, front, and top views as well.

Remember circular motion with every character, but especially when you're working on those characters with poise and polish. It can make both villainy and gallantry read with heightened impact!

# 11.5 **Successive Breaking of the Joints**

Back in the early days of animation, when an animator wanted an arm to bend or flex, he simply treated it as if it were a rubber hose. This sort of animation was entertaining for the time, but audiences had to have a high level of "suspension of disbelief." As artists became more comfortable with the underlying anatomy of their characters, they began to achieve fluidity with their motions not by treating bones like rubber, but by successively bending the joints connecting the skeletal structures in a fluid, whip-like manner. This is known as the *successive breaking of the joints*.

What this means to us (where it's harder for an arm to bend like rubber than to have it retain its bone structure) is to concentrate on letting motions unfurl, paying attention to all the joints that make that motion possible.

1. Load up Scenes\chapters\ch11\Section_11-05_w01.lws, and then save it as a working revision in your Chapter 11 working directory.

2. Animate the arm in a 40-frame loop (at 24 fps) so that it flows in the same successive breaking of the joints as in Figure 11.12.

241

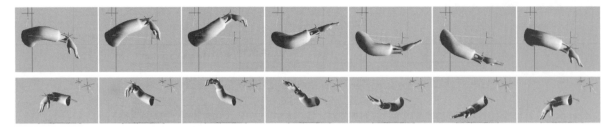

**Figure 11.12** A wave-like motion undulates through the arm. The curve is led by the elbow, which "drags" the rest of the arm down, then "pulls" the rest of the arm back up. All the joints operate well within their normal ranges of motion; this is the successive breaking of the joints.

3.  Compare your work with my final scene when you're done (Scenes\chapters\ch11\Section_11-05_F.lws). Make adjustments to your scene until the motion is smooth and fluid.

Successive breaking of the joints fits into the same category as circular motion. It helps things read better, it shows attention to detail, and it heightens the entertainment value of your scene. These finesse points give "high-dollar" animation the feel it does. By understanding how to artfully incorporate them into your work, the animations you create will read with that level of class too! (Observe, dissect, understand! Continue with the practice scenes in Chapter 14 and watch as the subtle complexity of your work grows in leaps and bounds!)

# 11.6 **Overlapping Action**

*Overlapping action* is an extension of the principals of follow-through. Not all the bits of a character start moving at the same time, and not all of them come to rest at the same time. Each part of a character has its role to play in

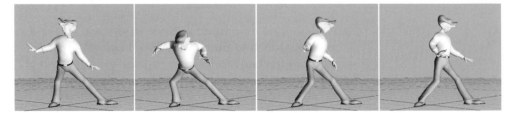

**Figure 11.13** Here is our character doing a bit of a take as he turns around. Technically, these poses would work, but because all his parts strike their extremes at the same time, this appears robotic.

balance, momentum, and acting. Having each part of a character following its own natural timings adds up to a convincing, overall fluidity of movement.

**Figure 11.14** This is the same action but with different parts of the body pulling others into motion in their own time.

In Figure 11.14, the hips start the movement, dragging the upper torso which, in turn, drags the head and hands. The torso then rolls upward as he straightens then settles back to look. Each part of his body reacts in accordance with its own mass, dragging and following through with respect to its own points of rotation. This set of frames reads with more life and fluidity than that in Figure 11.13.

All animations, even the most realistic, will require attention to at least subtle overlapping action. Acting through a scene beforehand and really getting a sense of how it feels to perform the action will help you to understand the order in which things move and settle.

1. Load in your setup scene, and save it back out as a working revision for Chapter 11, Section 6.

2. Giving yourself 20 frames (in 24 fps), recreate the animation from Figure 11.12.

3. After you're done, compare it with the animation from that figure, Scenes\chapters\ch11\Section_11-06_F.lws.

4. Make any refinements to your scene you might need to get your motion to express the same fluidity of overlapping action.

## 11.7 Entertainment Value (Presentation)

Entertainment! That's the business we're in, isn't it? Whether it be video games, television, or films, our job is to tell the story we've got to tell in the way that is going to be most interesting to the viewer. Even a "ready animation" (just some idle movement a character in a video game does while "waiting" for the player to decide what to do next) should be interesting to watch.

We must do what we do not only to the best of our technical ability, but also presented it in such a way that it leaves the viewer wanting more! This is entertainment value. The viewer must feel that they've gained something by sitting through and watching what we've done. (Or as Frank Thomas said, "Would anyone other than your mother like to see it?")

> **NOTE:**
>
> A good storyteller can make even the most hum-drum of stories riveting with the way he tells it.

When you get a scene to work on, go to a quiet place and think of all the unusual ways to get that story idea across that will be entertaining to watch. You, the animator, are the storyteller. You have to make sure that the characters continue to develop and show insights about themselves as your scenes progress. You have to make sure that the acting is believable and approachable. You have to make sure that the audience will want to know what happens next. You have to make sure that what you're doing is entertaining! And you have to do all of this and still make sure that your scene fits in as a seamless part of the unified whole, choreographed, cast, and orchestrated by the director.

In the exercise for this section, we're going to take a bit of ho-hum action (the character removing a bit of lint from his sleeve) and present it in three completely different ways. Give yourself as much screen time as you need to get the idea across. You may pose the character any way you like; I just want three of the most unusual, entertaining ways anyone might remove lint from his sleeve. These can be three completely different characterizations for each of the three takes, but I want this guy's being to show through every move in which he gets at that bit of lint!

For the first two passes, go as hog-wild as you'd like, but for the third pass, I want you to have his attention elsewhere, not on the lint, and still have the removal of said lint be unique and entertaining. This last foray will be an exploration into what is called secondary action. *Secondary action* is something a character does that doesn't really tell the story of what's going on in the scene. The scene could function perfectly well without it, but how the character does this action speaks volumes about the his personality. In live action or theater, it would be considered a "throwaway" line or action. If the audience catches it, great, but it should in no way overtake the primary storytelling intent of the scene. Subtlety is power! Your strength and confidence as an animator, and the character's life and energy will show through more clearly if your action reads with subtlety. Think easy power! Think, "Yeah, sure... if you get it, you get it. I know I'm good. I'm beyond having to prove myself."

It will help in this final take to have some sort of mental story or dialogue going on. Think of some reason for him to be focusing elsewhere, brushing at a bit of lint as he does so. You've got to get inside his head, get inside the scene itself. You've got to act it out in order to better understand the whys of his actions. You've got to understand his feelings about his actions—what he's trying to show, what he's trying to hide.

1. Load in your setup scene, and save it as a working revision for Chapter 11, Section 7.

2. Do two separate takes on our character removing that bit of lint from his sleeve, making them the most unique and entertaining ways for getting at a bit of lint you can think of.

3. Do one more take on the lint removal thing, but this time, let it be secondary action, something that isn't the primary storytelling point of the scene, but lends depth and detail to who this character is and how he feels.

How do your scenes hold up? Do they have entertainment value? Are they presented in ways that make their storytelling strong? How's your action? Is it good animation? Does the character feel like he's got an opinion on things, a reason for being, a soul? Can you read an inner dialogue through watching your character's actions? Do you care about seeing what happens next?

Rework your scenes if necessary, honing points and making them as strong as they can be.

## 11.8 Acting, Not Action

What we're working for is acting, not action. It is important for you to hone and finesse all the finer points that make animation great. But these things are learned, then forgotten so that the character lives and flows freely through you, not from you.

> **NOTE:**
>
> Good animation comes through you, not from you.

At first, you'll have all these things to remember—squash and stretch, drag, follow-through. You'll be asking yourself, "Is my character twinning?" Often, it's easy to lose that crystal of magic amid what really amounts to a lot of focused work. It's like learning a piece of music or a dance. You go through a period of time where you're just worried about not hitting a wrong note or making a misstep. Then, after you get all the bits and pieces of it down, you can go on "autopilot" and let the feelings the piece fills you with flow out through you as you do what you do. You become simply another observer to the beauty your hands or feet just happen to be creating.

**NOTE:**

This is actually the secret to all art, really (if art did have such things as "secrets"). You learn a piece of classical music. You hear it on the radio and you think, "Man...that doesn't sound anything like what I'm doing. I know I'm hitting all the right notes, but..." What you have to do is to pay attention to how the music you're hearing on the radio makes you feel as you're listening to it. Then, when you're back at the keys playing, replay those feelings you felt while listening to the concert pianist. Your music will suddenly sound a lot more like what you heard on the radio.

When you get done with a scene, take a break. Heave a sigh, and walk away for a bit. Get a latte or a cup of herbal tea. Do something that will take your mind off the long, tense time you just spent on this labor of love. When you feel like you've "walked it off" sufficiently, go back to your scene and look at it as if you're seeing it for the first time.

Ask yourself the all-important question, "Is this character alive for me?" Does he follow the direction of the scene and add to the story in ways that seem as believable as they are inevitable? When you acted this scene out, is the feeling you got inside the same feeling you're getting now as you watch it?

Remember, animation being the art of revision, if something isn't working, if the character isn't emoting, breathing, and living, break down what the issues are and revise. (Usually there's just a couple of things that when they do drop into place, the animation seems to do a 180; what was "just not coming together" suddenly is "totally spot-on!")

Animation is forever. The beings we're creating will live on long after we're gone. They'll continue to touch people with the dreams we dreamt while they were being brought into this world. Do everything you can to make their lives worthy of living.

# 11.9 The Importance of Thumbnails (Planning Your Scene)

When you get a scene, whether it has been storyboarded or not, before you start animating you need to take the time to do small thumbnail drawings of all the poses that will tell the story of your scene. This series of quick, loose drawings don't have to mean anything to anyone but you. They only need to show you what's going on over the course of the scene, how the character feels about what's going on, and his outlook on making it through (hopefully) in one piece.

Try to think like a comic strip artist as you do these quick little drawings. You're trying to distill an expression or an attitude into a single drawing. These drawings will have a strong line of action running through them and their silhouettes (it is often a good idea to shade in the thumbnails) will read with the full impact of the idea being portrayed.

**Figure 11.15** Here are some thumbnails for a scene in which the character is running with a flashlight, slips on a banana peel (does anyone slip on banana peels anymore?), and lands flat on his back.

Yes, the drawings in Figure 11.15 are rough; they are just a loose collection of circles and lines that don't have to mean anything to anyone but me. Yes, this is how loosely I work when I'm doing my thumbnails for my scenes. It took less than two minutes for me to run through three different takes on this scene; there's so little time invested in the drawings that I have no qualms about scrapping the whole idea and starting over. In doing three (or more, if necessary) versions, I break through the "Man, I have no idea how I'm going to handle this" phase of ideation. The first set was a mark on the wall. The second was closer, and the third was what I wanted; it feels like I felt when I acted it out. (Ow...just kidding!)

**NOTE:**

*Thumbnails* (storytelling drawings) aren't the most extreme drawings; they're the ones most comfortable for the eye to settle on.

**Figure 11.16** These are the thumbnails I'd show to a client. (I redrew what I had done for myself, tightening up in the process. Like I say, thumbnails don't usually mean anything to anyone but you; this set should clarify what's going on in the previous set.)

---

**NOTE:**

No matter how "artistic" a client may think he is, never show him anything he would have to use his creativity to figure out. This goes for thumbnails, animations-in-progress, whatever. Most often, they just won't get it and start complaining about how it just doesn't seem to be working the way they'd hoped. Never mind that you told them that this is just a rough draft. Or, on the other side of things, they could get grandiose ideas that there's no way you would have time to implement. It's a good idea to only show the client things that leave as little room for interpretation as possible.

---

These thumbnails help make sure you have the best presentation possible and the most entertainment value to your scene. (It's so much easier to erase a quickly scribbled line than it is to rekey a pose.) You're thinking out loud, throwing ideas out to see what sticks. Do a couple of quick versions and see which one reads best. (For some reason, I find it's either the first set or the third set that works best.)

Make sure your character's attitude reads through every thumbnail. Even if he's only walking across the room to get the door, his attitude and his opinions about getting the door, should remain front and center. Act your scene out. Sit. Ponder. Doodle. Let yourself open up to the flow of good ideas that come through you.

Thumbnails will also vastly reduce the time it takes to get a good pose in 3D. When you do sit down with the software, there'll be very little guesswork as to how this guy should be posed out. You'll probably find ways of pushing that loose, little drawing farther, making it read better, stronger, and more on character. In that quick little scribble, you have a signpost that tells you how to quickly get to where you want to be. When your character reads with the same vibrancy as in that loose collection of circles and lines, you'll know you're there and you can move on!

# 11.10 **Pacing**

As the list of things you can do as an animator increases and as you add "riffs" to your repertoire, it is only natural to want to show as many of these awesome little things as you can in a scene. Remember…easy power. If you give to the scene what <u>it</u> needs, and you do this with ability that looks effortless and natural, people will just assume that you could do anything you wanted to. You just (wisely) chose to show only what you needed to and you left your audience wanting more.

You don't want to rush the scene. You want to give the acting poses (the story-telling poses you thumbnailed, the poses that are comfortable for the eye to settle on) enough screen time for the audience to read them. You want the audience to be able to see the expressions change. You want to give the character time to think, and the audience time to digest.

You want to have the flow of action in a scene be strong enough that you keep your audience's attention too. (If you will eventually have music scored to your work, music can extend an audience's attention, as can waiting for the music to return—the "silence between the notes"). Achieving this balance between keeping the scene moving and giving the acting time to connect with the audience takes practice. Doing the work and revising until it fits within the scene length requirements and still carries this power is what will help to hone your own internal sense of pacing.

Watch animation from the great masters of the art. See what kinds of rhythms they use, and what kinds of emotions those rhythms create. Fill the well. Practice and make it yours. You are working in a medium where rhythm drives everything. Know beforehand the kind of rhythmic feel you want for the piece, and then stay true to your vision. Let that vision read clear and strong to the audience.

## Chapter 12

# Taking a Scene from Start to Finish

OK, so now you've got a scene assigned to you; what do you do? We're going to work here as if it came through the channels of a large production, where you've got departments, PAs (production assistants), PMs (production managers), APMs (assistant production managers), and the whole nine yards. But you can make these steps work whatever the size of your production, even if it's just you and your trusty computer at your side. It's all about breaking what can be a formidable task into small, manageable, "bite-sized" bits.

## 12.1 Do Your Homework…

Whether this is your first scene in this production or your one-hundred-and-first, you need to make sure you do your homework before jumping in with both feet. There are few things worse than doing some beautiful, brilliant work and having the director come by and tell you that, yes, it is beautiful but it doesn't fit with what the story needs, or that it doesn't link up with the previous and/or following scenes.

By "doing your homework," I mean "research." Go back through and re-read the part of the script that contains this scene. Walk around and look at the storyboards. Find out what got the character(s) into this place to begin with. Find out how they <u>feel</u> and <u>think</u> about being in the situation they are in. Find out how they <u>plan</u> to move onward, out of your scene.

Look at animations that have been completed and approved that go around your scene, watch the *Leica reel* (the timed storyboards made into a movie, also known as an *animatic*). Get a feel for the timings and pacings of scenes that have already been finalized. Understand your character's timing, pacing, posing, and acting so you can begin to feel the same things he does.

Get a clear picture of things <u>before</u> going to the director. If you have any questions about the scene, curiosities, comments, whatever, write them down! A meeting with a director can be a whirlwind. Make sure <u>all</u> the questions you can think of pertaining to your character's development through this particular scene are asked. You don't want to get back to your desk and remember those one or two (or ten) vitally important questions that just happened to slip your mind during the conversation.

# 12.2 **Talk with the Director**

After you've got a clear vision and feel for the scene, sign up for time to talk with the director. Have your list of questions handy, and check the items off as they get talked about. Make notes! Do everything you can to retain what you learn about the director's vision for the scene. The director is counting on your abilities as an actor and an artist, but in order for the show to succeed, it has to have one, clear (good, confident, worthy, etc.) point of focus from which the entire story radiates, and that is the director.

Listen to what he has to say. If you don't understand something, ask him to explain it another way. (Did I already mention taking notes? Unfortunately, you may need to *ahem* "remind" a director of an agreement on characterization or planning the two of you made earlier.) A good director will always listen to what you have to say, too. Talk through your feelings about timing, pacing, and acting. Make sure the two of you are seeing the same vision for the scene and its place within the film.

## 12.3 **Scene Planning**

If there is a background already built for you, or if your character is going to be interacting within pre-shot footage, talk with the scene planning guys about how your character will interact with and within it. Get a clear vision of how you see your character moving within the background. Make sure that the elements that are there permit his freedom to interact and emote in character and to fulfill the requirements of the scene. If it looks like your acting and the background may clash, talk to the scene planning people about it

If you're the one who has to build the background yourself, sketch out a floor plan and notate your character's blocking. Find out where the camera will stand and where you're going to have to hang lights to get the desired shot and lighting. Look to see if there are going to be any elements of the background conflicting with the character's movements, or drawing attention away from his acting.

> **NOTE:**
>
> The rule of thumb I use for nearly everything—animation, character design, set design, lighting design, you name it—came from a character in the film *L.A. Story*. Trudi (Marilee Henner) was telling another woman how she coordinates her fashion accessories. (Bear with me now.) She said that when she thinks she's ready to go, she turns away from the mirror, then turns back quickly. The first thing that catches her eye, she removes. (I would suggest doing this several times.) What she ends up with is a complete, contiguous ensemble with everything working together. As weird as it may sound, this is the very best technique I've found for analyzing nearly anything artistic. If it jumps out at you, if it stands out abruptly, it is like a jitter in an otherwise smooth curve. Everything should work as a unit; even the things that are meant to draw your attention!

If you are setting up your own background, there's one key bit of advice I'd like to give you on lighting and setting up your camera. Pretend you're on a practical (real) set. Pretend you've got to light it with real lights; pretend you're bound by the same physical limitations with which to shoot. We, the audience, have grown accustomed to certain conventions established by both still photography and motion pictures. Working within these conventions, we more easily form a connection with the viewers because they are preconditioned to understand the "language" you're using. This can be said for "steadycam" shots, too—save the flying camera for the high-dollar, mega-impact shots! (Hitchcock shot most of his suspense films from medium and long setups. When he hits you with the one or two close-ups in the film, those shots make you jump out of your skin because you haven't been numbed to close-ups!)

> **NOTE:**
>
> If you can tell a story with the camera left, unmoving, on its tripod, you really understand storytelling, and the story you're telling.

> **NOTE:**
>
> I use mostly shadow-mapped, klieg lights (spotlights) to light my scene; they're what I'd have if I were on a practical set. I use spotlights and distant lights (set to not cast shadows) as if they were *shinyboards* (also known as *skimboards*), bouncing diffused lighting where I need it. I'll use the occasional light with a negative intensity to tone down an area, as if I'm using a flag to block light from hitting an area. I use intensity falloff for lights and an almost imperceptible bit of black, nonlinear fog to enhance drama and "realism."

**NOTE:**

There's only one real trick to understanding good lighting: Watch what works, and figure out what makes it do what it does. I love *chiaroscuro* (a method of painting with strong lighting and shadows) and film noir, and my lighting styles reflect this. In beginning photographic portraiture, you learn that in order to make any object look three-dimensional, you hit the subject with a warm light on one side and a cool light on the other. (Subtle variations of "white" will do; you don't have to punch the saturation unless you're going for a specific effect.) One light should be brighter than the other. That's it! That's all you <u>need</u> to do, but there is more you <u>can</u> do. You should hit your subject with a light that makes one part of his outline brighter than the background he'll be in front of (a "rim" or "kick" light). Keep in mind the color of the "ambient" light, and use a shadowless klieg to fill in any overly dark areas. (I turn ambient lighting off unless I'm using radiosity.) We expect ambient light from above to be blue, reflected from the sky. We expect ambient light from below to be golden or green, reflected from ground or grass.

Now that LightWave has radiosity and caustics, we can think a lot more like a traditional director of photography when constructing our sets and lighting them. Make sure that the final imagery (colors, tonality, "pools of light," sharpness or softness of design elements, curves, angles, shapes, and compositional balance) works as a whole to convey the mood and direction of the scene. Pay attention to silhouette and design elements, just as you will with your character when he starts interacting within this environment. Areas of highest contrast (value, color, and saturation) should be where the character will move, drawing the audience's eye to these areas instantly. The composition of the BG alone should give you an instant feel as to what is going to happen in the scene.

When you're satisfied with how your background will work with your character to facilitate the best, most riveting presentation of your scene, it's time to move on!

## 12.4 **Visualize**

OK, now's the time to go to that quiet place and let yourself slip into the world of your character…into his thoughts…into his life. Turn off the phone. Put out a big "Do Not Disturb, Under <u>Any</u> Circumstance…. THIS MEANS YOU!" sign and let the rest of the world go on without you for just a little bit.

This is where you get in touch with the character as he exists <u>inside</u> of you. Yours is a unique viewpoint on his existence, his thoughts, his feelings, his actions, his dreams, his desires, his plans for the future, and his laments about the past. Within the quiet space of your own mind/heart, you can let go of your own past, and take up his. Let your mind wander…

Imagine what was the first thing he did when he got up that morning. How long has it been since he's eaten? Has he ever been in love? How does it feel to have those hands, that face? Why do you dress as you do? Does it make you feel safe? Does it remind you of someone you looked up to in your life? These may seem like esoteric questions, but questions like these are the keys to opening the doors inside yourself and letting you live as your character for the length of time you are working on this scene. And that is <u>exactly</u> what you must do! You have to live his scene. Every subtlety you feel, every nuance that would touch your own actions having lived a life like that, being in the surroundings he is, every minute detail breathes volumes of life into this character and this scene. It is through these details that the audience will share their own private selves; it is through these private details that the character gains his own life.

Wander back in time, back in his time. Live the days of his youth, his explorations, his sorrows, his joys. Experience the entirety of his being as a cloak that you wrap around yourself and get lost in. Know the decisions in his life that have brought him to the point where your scene begins.

Now, allow the scene you will work with play out before you. As you let the scene unfold before you, remember how you feel about what is going on. Remember how it feels to move as you do. Remember your ideas, your thoughts—both those open to others and those only open to yourself. Remember how the whole experience feels to live, continuing out the end of this scene and slightly into the next.

> **NOTE:**
>
> There's a thing about actors, especially good stage actors. I'm not talking about the grandiose ones who fill an auditorium with their overblown presence. I'm talking about the ones who make you believe they're really there in that moment. There are many, <u>many</u> things you can learn from studying these actors (and studying acting itself), but what I'd like to make note of is that no matter how many times a day they may have already gone through the same material, you feel as if it is only just now happening to them. You feel as if this set of events is only now coming into being, and that their responses to these events are natural and inevitable. They are merely continuing to make the same kinds of decisions (on a moment-by-moment basis) that they've made all their lives, the same kinds of decisions that have brought them to this point right now. The "actor" may know what happens at the end of the line, or at the beginning of Act 3, but the character lives in this one moment as we all do.

The reason I'm asking you to remember how it <u>feels</u> to experience his life is that for most people, it is hard to remember every nuance of things that happen as they happen. But feelings, kinesthetics, and empathy carry much more than just positional or temporal information. They are the doorways through which we can live again, in all the detail, the experiences in our past. When you're looking at your thumbnails, your action line on your X-sheet, and at your animation as it takes shape before you, you know if what you're looking at gives you the same feeling as what you experienced in your visualization. All the myriad of subtle cues, the volumes that would fill shelves upon shelves with information, all boil down to a single thing: They boil down to a feeling.

There's not enough room in this book to cover all the different techniques for letting yourself live as the character with which you work, and still cover all the other information that needs covering. I can, however, recommend two books to you that have helped me more than words can ever say. They are: *To the Actor* by Michael Chekhov, and *Audition* by Michael Shurtleff. (They'll be listed again in Chapter 17.) I cannot recommend these books enough. If you are serious about becoming the best actor/animator you can be, get them, study them, and practice them.

"...they are two sides of the same coin... or, being as there are so many of us... the same side of two coins."—The Player, *Rosencrantz and Guildenstern Are Dead*

## 12.5 Thumbnail

While your "Do Not Disturb!" sign is still out, sketch down your ideas. Do this as quickly as you can, still preserving as much of the echoes of your visualization as you can. When you get done with one set, do another and another. In this process of doing this just-being-in-the-moment drawing, not trying to "get it right" or "perfect," you again link with the feelings you felt as you lived that character.

All you're trying to do is to put into a kind of shorthand the things you'll need for your mind to travel back to that place where you walked with his feet, touched with his hands.

> **NOTE:**
> Small, fluid, strong, these drawings are your pitons; they'll keep you from falling.

## 12.6 **Exposure Sheet**

Before you go take down that "Get lost, Punk!" sign, reach for your exposure sheet. Use the action line to make a visual notation of the timing of the actions you've just been living. (If your project doesn't use X-sheets, I've included a 24 fps sheet in Extras/X-Sheet.jpg.)

Jot down this four-dimensional shorthand for the character and any other items that may be moving or interacting with him. Notate any camera motions you envisioned (clear them with the director, and the scene planning and editorial departments before putting them into play though). When you run your eyes down the sheet at a presumed 24 fps, you should get a feeling that rings true to what you felt in your visualization.

> **NOTE:**
>
> The action line of your exposure sheet is your four-dimensional thumbnail.

## 12.7 **Animate**

Using all you've learned, all your skills, and all your easy power, hold the feelings you felt when you lived this scene close to you as you work. With your thumbnails and your action line, you've got a lot of the work of animation done already. You can let your mind wander back to that visualization, and let the feelings you remember help you to fit the hands into just the right shapes, sculpt the spine into just the right arc, and swing the knees into just the right angle. When what you see before you resonates with what you feel inside you, you know you're there.

> **NOTE:**
>
> You are an actor. You are the character. Enjoy the luxury of being him for as long as you're working on this scene!

## 12.8 Examine

Look at your animation from all angles, not just the camera angle. Make sure that each part reads plausibly and that the feelings you get when you watch it are the feelings you felt when you visualized how it would be to live that situation.

Let the animation play at speed, looping again and again. Let your eyes focus on one part of his body as the scene repeats itself. If there's something in the motion of that part that catches your eye, slow it down and examine it. Track its movement with dry erase markers; is the motion exactly as it should be from all angles? (Sometimes a "pop" is caused by a part of your character moving improperly in Z, with respect to the camera, when the other two axes are fine.)

Focus on each part of your character in turn, and then watch your character as a whole. Are all the parts adding up to a sum that radiates life and believability? Walk away from your scene for a while; take a break. When you come back, look at it with fresh eyes. Does anything jump out that didn't before?

Examine, revise, repeat. Do this until the scene fits the criteria both you and the director agreed upon. Do this until the feelings you get from looking at the scene ring true with what you felt when you, yourself, lived the same experience.

## 12.9 Critique

So, now you're at a point where you want to get comments on your work, comments from a fresh point of view. Make sure that you seek comments from someone who knows what they're talking about, and that this someone knows how to look at partially completed animation (if your work is still a work-in-progress). Hopefully, these are all the same person, and hopefully, this person is the director.

**NOTE:**

Learning how to accept criticism is important. It is an acquired skill, but it is one that everyone can learn. Remember that animation is a team effort; what matters is the piece as a whole. But also remember to consider the source. If you just asked your cube-mate for a critique, and he mercilessly shredded all your hard work, ask yourself if your animation, which you thought was pretty darn good, threatens him or his position within the company. (Unfortunately, the more you stick your head out, the harder some people try to lop it off.) Seek criticism only from those people qualified to understand what they're looking at. Seek critiques only from those who genuinely have your and the production's best interests at heart.

Have your notes ready for when the director (and his entourage of yes-men and yes-women) comes to call. Refer back to your notes if something doesn't quite jive with what you thought he said the last time you spoke. Be prepared to talk about where you are with the scene, where you see it going, how you feel about where it is. Talk with him about how it makes him feel. Jot down any notes, and make sure you understand what he's saying. If you feel you nailed this scene spot-on, and the director isn't quite happy with it yet, talk about his vision for this scene and how it fits in with his plan for the sequence. (Compromise is not capitulation, but it is he, the director, who must be accountable for the vision of this production after all is said and done.)

If your studio doesn't incorporate *dailies* (where they call together all the animation staff or the entire company to watch what was completed the previous day or week), see what you can do to encourage the powers that be to implement them. This is the best way I know of to boost the quality of a production. Not only is everyone more inclined to do their absolute best on the work they did that day because everyone they work with is going to be seeing it, but everyone shares ideas on how to solve problems from watching each others' works-in-progress! If you do have dailies every single day, you really get to see how a scene evolves, you get to see how the other animators think and solve problems, you see how they develop their ideas. (I've also found that things I might not have noticed to be wrong just make my skin crawl when I have others watch my work in dailies. This is a great flag for problem areas!) The morale boost, the camaraderie, the learning that goes on in the showing of dailies is something worth looking into.

## 12.10 Revise

Make it as perfect as you can. Don't let anything that isn't your absolute best effort leave your desk. (Now and then, everyone does something they aren't completely happy with, but make sure you put every effort into making it the best you can.) Compile the comments you've gotten, put them through the "Do they know what they're talking about" filter, and revise.

They say a painting is never finished, that it only stops in interesting places. The same can be said for an animation. Even so, scenes must move on, production must continue. Learn to work your piece as a whole, exploring finer and finer details as the entire scene reaches contiguous levels of quality; don't fixate on the minutia of a single slice of time. Allow the entirety of your scene to carry the emotional read you felt in those quiet moments of touching another's soul.

> **NOTE:**
> The animation you do will outlast all of us. Make it something to remember.

## Chapter 13

# Important Points for Every Scene

What do you look for when you're evaluating a scene you've done? Almost every animator who's been around the block a few times will have something to say on the matter. And almost all that is to be said revolves around the points developed by the great masters of animation.

Use this list as a guideline to evaluate your work. (These points are signposts to aim you back to Chapters 10 and 11 if you need more detail on certain issues.) Scrutinize every detail to the best of your ability. When everything falls together and all the points are properly addressed, your work will begin to take on the same sheen of craftsmanship and skill as those in feature-quality animation.

## 13.1 Composition/Design

When you sit back and look at what you've done, really sit back and look at what you've done. Move your chair across your cubicle or office and watch it play out at a different size than what you've grown accustomed to. Disassociate yourself from the "groove" you've been working in, and try to see it as if for the first time. Break it down into its basic compositional elements.

Watch your work play out through eyelids closed just enough so your eye-lashes meet. This gets rid of a lot of the detail information and reduces what you're seeing to the basic compositional elements. This is how many painters break down the complexities of painting *alla prima* (all at once, usually on location) into design shapes they can more easily understand and make use of.

> **NOTE:**
>
> Another great thing you can do to help see what's "hiding in plain sight," if you have access to post-processing software, is to mirror the image horizontally. This is what you do when you flip a drawing over and examine it on a light table. When you reverse the image like this, every minute error that you might have been content to live with leaps out at you. This stops the rationalization of inaccurate balance, weight, and proportion.

Watch your animation play out as a constantly transforming composition. Its final presentation will most likely be on the 2D plane of a screen of one kind of another. Evaluate your work with the same criteria any other 2D artwork would have to adhere to. (Your 2D piece just happens to evolve through time, that's all.)

> **NOTE:**
>
> Use the flow of silhouettes and design elements to lead the viewer's eye just as in a still image!

Watch the balance of positive (character) and negative (background) shapes. Watch how wedges and other design elements lead your eye around the piece as it plays out before you. Is your eye being led to where you want it to go? Is your focus in the right places to catch the important cues? Does your eye end up in a good place to link with the following scene? Does your eye start in a place that fits well with the preceding scene?

> **NOTE:**
>
> If *head* and *tail scenes* (the scenes that sandwich yours) are available to you as either *animatics* (timed storyboards with camera motion) or final renders, compile a movie of all three together. Watch the flow of your scene as it leaves the previous one and enters the next.

Before you even begin to delve into the finer points of an animation, its broad strokes must be strong, solid, and powerful enough to carry your attention, powerful enough to carry the audience's attention. The audience may never know your usage of design and composition to manipulate their perceptions; all they'll know is that your work feels powerful, and that they want to see more!

## 13.2 **Appealing Poses**

Your characters must first and foremost read clearly with the action that is taking place. Second, and second only by a hair's breadth, is the need for them to appeal to the audience. Remember, appeal does not mean cutesy! It means your audience must find some way to relate to and empathize with the character and what he's doing, how he's feeling, and what he's thinking.

Your characters must read clearly as two-dimensional representations of thoughts, ideas, and actions! Your primary tool in this area is, what else, silhouette.

Squinting your eyes, as mentioned in the previous section, will help you to lose the surface details of your character and see him more as a silhouette. You can also render your animation in Quickshade mode, saving out only the alpha channel and compiling the frames into an animation to see how your silhouettes are moving.

Examine your silhouettes for clarity of action, strength of design (the balance of broad and fine details, curved and straight lines, and clear shapes orchestrating the viewer's focus), and appeal. Your audience needs to understand your posing, find it interesting, and be able to empathize.

# 13.3 Anticipation, Drag, Follow-Through

Do your character's actions need to express the concepts of drawing through time?

Do your characters anticipate their actions (in accordance with who they are)? Do these anticipations help lead the viewer into the action? Do the anticipations help build, accent, and punctuate the rhythm of the scene?

Do your character's body parts exhibit their own mass as their individual momentums carry them along? Do they drag, unfurl, and follow-through, each in its own time? Do your overlapping actions add to the overall, believable fluidity of the piece?

# 13.4 Weight/Timing

Does your character, and everything you're animating in the scene, have the appearance of the weight and mass the audience would imagine it to have?

Do your timings imply the extra "oomph" needed to get those massive objects moving, and then stopped again? Do your heavy objects (and body parts) accelerate much more quickly toward the ground than they do away from it?

Are your characters balanced, taking into account the perceived mass and motion of the character, his action, and anything he may be holding?

Have you used squash and stretch to give the audience that subliminal shorthand of sensation, implying the forces impacting your character?

## 13.5 Entertainment Value

Imagine looking at your scene from the eyes of someone who's never seen this production before. This someone may be considering an extra tub of popcorn or another soda. Does your scene have the riveting pull to keep him in his seat?

Are you presenting this scene in the most unique and entertaining way that is accurate for the character's personality?

> **NOTE:**
>
> Would anyone other than your mother want to see this scene twice?

## 13.6 Characterization

Do you feel the character's motivations, thoughts, dreams, and non-verbal comments through watching him move in the scene? Does he feel like the same guy you saw in the scene before?

Are his secondary actions serving to support his character? Are the secondary actions letting the primary idea of the scene shine through uncluttered?

> **NOTE:**
>
> Acting, not action, and always in character!

## 13.7 **Character Evolution**

Has your character progressed along his story arc from the time your scene began to the time your scene ends? Have the situations evolved him subtly, almost imperceptibly?

> **NOTE:**
>
> This can be a tricky one to nail. Subtlety is the key. As the saying goes, "It's easier to show the transition of five hours than five minutes." Still, your character has to be in a continual state of evolution in order to remain believable. Change is the only constant. Your character must continually grow emotionally, spiritually, and intellectually with everything he encounters in order to possess that elusive spark of life. Developing an inner dialogue that no one else need know about can help. But being attuned to the script and to the overall arc of his character as you work is key to get these subtle changes to read, almost unnoticed, as your scenes play out.

## 13.8 **Storytelling/The Distillation of One Main Idea**

Scenes in filmmaking serve one of three purposes: to develop the mood, to develop the character(s), or to tell the story. Everything else is distraction and should be done away with (hopefully before it ever touches an animator's hands). Your scene has one main purpose in this film. Make sure you understand what that purpose is before starting work on the scene. And make sure that that one main idea reads clearly through your scene; everything else is support.

> **NOTE:**
>
> Is the reason for this scene being in the film clear?

# 13.9 **What's Best for the Production (Don't Grandstand)**

I hate to say it, but nobody likes a show-off. Nobody likes to be intentionally "upstaged." Yes, you may be capable of doing some wonderful, flashy bit of action, but ask yourself, "Is this in character? Is this developing and defining the story? Would anyone else in their 'right mind' do this scene this way?" (You know if the real motivation behind your work is to say, "Hey, look at me!" And others will know it too.)

Animation is heady business. And when you're first cuttin' your teeth, it is so hard to hold back! You want the whole world to know all the great things you can do! It's not about you, it's about the production; you can handle those juicy acting scenes better than those stuck-on-themselves "stars." Someone just has to notice, right?

Sit back, chill. Take some deep breaths. You <u>will</u> eventually get noticed. The work reveals the craftsman. It may be tough to sit tight when you get long shots or crowd scenes while others get the ones rich with pathos. Let your work speak for itself. People <u>will</u> notice, and they'll notice you for all the right reasons. They'll notice that you always do what's best for the scene; that your work, no matter how small on screen, always reads with integrity, subtlety, and character. They'll notice that your work gets done on time and with a minimum of corrections. Nothing goes unnoticed in a production—the good or the bad. Remember that.

Animation is teamwork. Together, everyone from the janitorial staff to the director makes the film. The director orchestrates your visions; your visions sculpt your character; your character creates your scenes; all the scenes together craft the movie; the movie will be there forever. Make it something you are proud to have helped bring into this world. Do so with strength, honor, and integrity.

## Chapter 14

# Additional Practice Scenes

Now you know everything it takes to make good animation. But knowing and doing are two entirely different things. Animation must flow naturally and inevitably, like good acting. Thinking about the different parts of it too much usually gets you into trouble. What you need to do is practice the concepts so that they become as much a part of you as your own breathing. You need to learn them so well that you can forget them. You need to free your conscious mind from thinking about which controls produce specific results. You need to allow your unconscious mind to "feel" what is right, what needs to be done.

This is something you will attain with focused practice. You will need to take at least one step toward that goal every day. You don't have to sit and practice for hours and hours every single day; just make sure that you do at least one small thing toward being a feature-quality animator every single day. By doing this, you <u>will</u> get there.

> **NOTE:**
>
> I like to think of it this way: You've got a certain number of so-so animations in you. The breathtaking animations are sprinkled in this pack of so-so scenes, but you've got to get all those mediocre animations out of the way to make room for the good ones. So you'd best get moving!

The steps you take have to be good steps. Practice makes permanent, not perfect! Make sure you're practicing something worth ingraining within you!

This is where I wanted this book to stand out above all others, even the rare, good ones that cover both the basic and the advanced material, the ones that make things understandable. But how can I help you learn to judge for yourself what is good animation and what needs work when I can't stand over your shoulder and encourage your best work? I can do this by giving you good quality animations you can explore as 3D scenes to compare with your work, scenes you can pose-copy move-for-move in your earliest stages of learning the craft. With pose-copying (as we did in Chapter 10), you'll know immediately when your work is exactly as it should be. It will be like having me right there with you, showing you all the mechanics it takes to make a scene flow with life and entertainment. By balancing between pose-copying and creating your own scenes you will quickly wean yourself from needing my help. This is the quickest and surest path to becoming the animator you've dreamed of becoming.

> **NOTE:**
>
> An important thing to remember is that good animation takes time. The feature studios worth their salt will often give an animator two weeks to work on a three-foot (2-second) scene. Don't rush yourself! If it takes a guy who's been doing feature-quality animation since 1976 two weeks to get a three-foot scene out, don't beat yourself up if you can't get a feature-quality scene out in a day!

## 14.1 The Technique

This is the technique I begin with when teaching students in person, whether they are potential animators working for me, students, or friends. Through the balance of pose-copying and creating original scenes, you learn what to do, fast. And you begin internalizing good habits right from the start. Using derivations of this technique, you will be able to find the next logical steps in nearly anything you wish to learn. (You can use a variation on this technique to learn how to draw or paint in a particular style.) If you're being dropped into a production where you have to match a predeveloped style, you can use this technique with movies of approved scenes. You can also assimilate much more quickly the sensibilities of the great masters by working from clips of their traditional animation in this fashion.

For your first scene, choose a scene from the Scenes to Copy section (Section 14.3). These scenes are all ready for you to load in and have you move the character to exactly match pre-existing animation on the life drawing model. Work with your first scene for a week (or more) if you need it; make sure everything is an exact match—timing, posing, everything. Don't let your character deviate one iota from the life drawing model. (Yes, this can be tedious.) Give yourself as much time as you need, there's no rush! Just kick your feet back and enjoy the ride!

Next, pull a scene from the Scenes to Create section (Section 14.4), where you're only given direction. Look through them and find something that sounds fun. Go through all the applicable steps outlined in Chapter 12 in preparation for settling in to work. (If you fail to plan, you plan to fail.) Give yourself half a day to a day to get your bearings on how you're going to handle the scene (I do). Then settle in to working on that scene for one to two weeks—however long you might need to make sure everything is as spot-on as you can make it.

> **NEWBIE NOTE:**
>
> It's fairly common for this second scene to give you fits. Don't worry about it too much. Just do your best. Enjoy the process of exploring! "Run and find out!" (*Rikki-Tikki-Tavi*)

When you feel you've spent as much time with this second scene as you can without losing your mind, take another scene (or another two, if you feel really wobbly about things) from the Scenes to Copy section. Give the scene(s) a week or so (each), enough time to get everything absolutely perfect. Then go back to doing another scene where you're taking it from scratch. You should notice things getting significantly better this time around.

Go back and forth between copied scenes and original scenes until you feel you've got your "chops" down. Then, instead of pose-copying something from the Scenes to Copy section, make a movie of it from a stationary viewpoint and work entirely from this movie. Compare your work either by feel or by loading items from the scene you're copying. Use Loading Items From Scene only to compare; revert to using the movie alone when making adjustments.

Again, alternate original scenes and scenes copied from a single-view movie. Keep at this until you feel really sharp, able to understand what visual cues translate into 3D coordinates. Then, take a foray into what's outlined in Section 14.5; I think you'll like it.

You can come back to this technique, or your own modification of it, whenever you feel like you need a little "boost" in your skills. It is the quickest, surest way to sharpen, to learn, and to train your internal senses of what works. You're building muscle memory, good habits that you don't have to think about to employ. You'll just get a feel for what's right and what a scene needs.

Continue to study the basic and advanced animation mechanics as you do this. Make sure your mind knows what your body is learning. "Gut feelings" can take you fairly far, and with your mind attuned to the conscious, logical understanding of the principals of animation, there will be nothing you can't handle.

> **NEWBIE NOTE:**
>
> After you begin to feel pretty good about what you're doing, you'll probably find yourself going through a short period where you feel like you're just starting out again. You may feel like you can't quite seem to remember how to get things into place or the controls suddenly feel awkward, when everything was feeling almost natural only a few days before. This is normal!!! This is considered to be the "mammalian learning curve," when what we hold in short-term memory gets transferred to long-term memory. The information is temporarily inaccessible while the synaptic structures are being constructed in long-term memory. Just keep at it! Once those long-term memory synapses get physically shifted around to hold that info, you'll be on top of the world again!

## 14.2 Life Drawing

You'll find a collection of images to practice life drawing from in Extras\Life_Drawing\Images\ and scenes to pose-copy in Extras\Life_Drawing\Scenes\.

Life drawing is a great way to unwind. You don't have to worry about the same issues you do when your character is in motion; you just kick back and get that one pose you see in front of you. It's a great way to relax and get centered before staring your workday, and it's a good way to get loose and get past those "stiff" first poses.

Take your life drawing further than what you see in this book. If you have a laptop that can run LightWave, take it with you to a life drawing class. Take it with you at lunch and capture quick gesturals of the people you see around you. Life draw from the TV or a movie. Life draw from poses you find in paintings, sculptures, cells. Expose yourself to as much as you can. And have fun!

> **NOTE:**
>
> All that you truly examine adds to what you are capable of seeing!

> **NOTE:**
>
> Draw with verbs, not nouns!

## 14.3 Scenes to Copy

You will find scenes to copy in Extras\ScenesToCopy\. Use these in conjunction with "the technique," or to compare your take on a situation with mine. Each scene's title will let you know a little of what the scene is about, and the .txt file associated with it will give you direction as to the scenes to create. Work both with scene ideas that sound interesting, and scenes that you have zero interest in.

> **NOTE:**
> Usually, being turned off by a subject is a good sign that there is something you need to learn there.

## 14.4 Scenes to Create

Here is a list of directorial comments on scenes. With some, you may have to create your own simple props. Have fun with the process! These ideas are for you to springboard from. Take them, push them, make them entertaining; make them your own! The only directorial edict I'm going to issue is that you have to be able to imagine your finished scenes fitting in flawlessly amid a collection of the best animation you've ever seen. Take your time; do the best work you are capable of doing.

There are no deadlines here. There are no PAs rushing about, desperately trying to make quota. Dive into the scenes, and forget about (real-life) time for a while. Lose yourself in the process of simply doing. Play! Have fun! Let your fun shine right through the screen to your audience!

## Actions

These are just bits of action you should get under your belt. Each of these actions incorporates many of the basic and advanced animation mechanics. I'd like you to go through each of these actions twice; one time, perform the action as straightlaced and realistically as you can, then do it as cornball and cartoony as you can. With the realistic pass, make it as true-to-life as you can, make it feel like it has been motion-captured. With the cartoony pass, really push it to the extremes; give Tex Avery and Chuck Jones a run for their money! Whichever you do first is up to you, but you may find your realistic scenes benefiting from the looseness you work into your cartoony scenes.

Make the action read well in silhouette. Give the characters a reason for (and an opinion on) doing whatever they're doing. Make your work entertaining, both in the doing and in the watching!

▶ Swing a baseball bat

▶ Do a golf swing using a driver (the golf club used to really belt that ball out there)

▶ Do a golf swing using a pitching wedge to get the ball out of a sand trap and onto a nearby green

▶ Throw a javelin

▶ Do an Olympic-style hammer throw

▶ Throw a shot put

▶ Shoot a basket

▶ Throw a football

▶ Pitch a baseball

▶ Dive from a diving board

▶ Yo a yo-yo

▶ Swing on a swing

▶ Use your hands to "walk" across a set of monkey bars

▶ Skip rope

▶ Juggle (a real juggle and then a "cartoon, cascade" juggle)

# Walk Cycles

Cycles need to loop seamlessly, so that someone watching them wouldn't know which keyframe marks the loop's start/end. (If Frame 0 is the same as Frame 28, I make a preview or movie from Frames 1 to 28.) Watch for "pops" and problems with acceleration as the cycle nears its head and tail. I generally don't use the motion graph's "pre" and "post" behavior to repeat the cycle. When I want to integrate the cycle into a scene, I copy the keys manually for as many times as I need the motion to repeat itself. This way I can have unique action happen before and after the cycle if need be.

> **NOTE:**
>
> A cycle will amplify any problems an animation may have. Your audience will catch the third time what they missed the first (and begin to rant and rave about it after the tenth). Make sure that everything is as polished to perfection as you can get it.

DIRECTION: Walk cycle: You're a businessman late for an important meeting, but trying very much not to show it.

DIRECTION: Walk cycle: Do an exaggerated sneak-walk.

DIRECTION: Walk cycle: Do a "cool walk." (Think: Fat Albert and the Gang kind of thing.)

DIRECTION: Walk cycle: Do the absolute weirdest walk you can think of (something that would fit in with the Monty Python "School of Silly Walks" skit).

DIRECTION: Walk cycle: Do a light jog.

DIRECTION: Walk cycle: Do an all-out run.

DIRECTION: Walk cycle: Do a walk showing your character as light-hearted and happy as a character can be.

DIRECTION: Walk cycle: Do a walk showing your character in the depths of misery.

DIRECTION: Take the "all-out run" you did, and copy your keys to extend it. End with your character stumbling and falling, coming to a rolling, skidding stop.

DIRECTION: Using your "light jog," animate your character blithely running along, not paying attention to where he's going. Life is good until he runs smack into a brick wall.

DIRECTION: Take your character from standing into any of the cycles you've done and then back to standing again.

DIRECTION: Using your "light jog," have your character running along when he spies someone <u>gorgeous</u> and comes to a screeching halt. As gallantly as possible, have him do an about-face and strut sexily past the object of his attention.

DIRECTION: Using one of your run cycles, blend this in a cartoony fashion with a stealthy sneak and then go back to the run. (Think of cartoons where the character is going full-tilt, then has to sneak by an open doorway, then goes back to his full-tilt run.)

## Scenes

Use your creative license to handle these scenes in the most entertaining way you can think of. Create your own histories for the characters, devise reasons for them being there, opinions on what it is they're doing, and thoughts about where they are going next.

Play with multiple camera angles. First, establish the scene with a longer shot, let the audience know what is going on and where the character fits into his surroundings. Use medium shots and close-ups to showcase the action and to create strong, storytelling, design-oriented silhouettes. Allow your timing to sculpt the feelings of the audience; lead them down the emotional paths you want them to follow, and at the pace you decide!

Craft these scenes so that your audience will find something within them to connect with as they watch them. Let your scenes remind them of similar situations they've experienced. Choreograph them so those watching it will want to see it play through again, so that they want to see what happens next!

DIRECTION: You're walking down the street and stop because you find a coin lying there. You pick it up, and give it a quick flip into the air; heads you'll keep it, tails you'll leave it for someone else. The coin comes up tails. Get rid of the coin in an entertaining way.

DIRECTION: You're sitting in a chair, lost in thought and a little bit bored. The phone rings. You leap up to answer it and trip over another chair in your rush and tumble haphazardly to the ground.

DIRECTION: Using the ChromeFox setup in conjunction with your character, animate him trying to coax a timid, wild animal to him.

DIRECTION: Opening a letter: The contents are beyond your wildest hopes. You leap for joy!

DIRECTION: Opening a letter: The contents are depressing beyond measure. You collapse into the chair behind you, or down the wall and onto the floor. The key here is drama (perhaps even angst)!

DIRECTION: It is "high noon." Two chaps face off in a duel of "finger-pistols" (just pretending their fingers are guns). They draw! One "hits" his opponent who fakes a dramatic death. (Really play with camera angles with this one! Try to get that Old Western kind of feel!)

DIRECTION: You take a sip of coffee and jump because it is too hot, fumbling the cup. You spastically juggle the cup, trying to save it, finally having to leap out of the way as it crashes to the floor.

DIRECTION: You're putting up a fence. You lay another board up, pull a nail from behind your ear, and absently hammer until . . . you bash your thumb with the hammer!

DIRECTION: You are breaking into an old "dial" safe. With your ear to the mechanism, you eloquently turn the combination. You hear the click of success, then rubbing your hands together in anticipation, you open the door!

DIRECTION: You sidle up to a locked door. First, making sure no one is looking, you kneel and begin to pick the lock. The tumblers fall into place and you stand, peering about to see if the coast is still clear. You quietly turn the knob and back inside, softly shutting the door after you.

DIRECTION: Like a musketeer of old, you draw your sword and gallantly salute!

DIRECTION: Animate your character pulling an arrow from a quiver on his back, knocking it, pullin' it back, and lettin' it fly!

DIRECTION: Do the ol' '50s sitcom bit with the character screeching on a chair because of a mouse.

DIRECTION: You are the coolest hepcat in town. You've got your back turned to the audience at a poetry reading. You're snapping your fingers and tapping your foot to the beat of the jazz band. You motion for the band to stop. You turn, pose, and bow.

DIRECTION: It is freezing and you're improperly dressed, waiting for the bus. Rub your arms, stomp your feet, blow into your hands to try to warm yourself up. Amid this action, look at your watch, and listen to it to see if it is still running.

DIRECTION: You are shoveling snow. You stop to rest for a moment, wiping your nose on your sleeve, then start back to work.

DIRECTION: You're swinging a pickax at a spot on the floor. Hearing a "thunk," you stop digging, kneel, and carefully brush away the dust to find a handle of sorts. Using all your might, you lift a heavy case from the ground.

DIRECTION: Like the hags in *Macbeth*, you eerily stir a cauldron.

DIRECTION: Like in the old TV shows, do a sliding leap over a car hood.

DIRECTION: Two characters: One character kneels before the other, slipping a ring on the standing character's finger in a proposal of marriage.

DIRECTION: Two characters: The two characters run into each other's arms, one swinging the other around in a loving embrace.

DIRECTION: Two characters: One character hikes the unconscious other character over his shoulder and carries him.

DIRECTION: Two characters: Animate a round of "rock, scissors, paper."

DIRECTION: Two characters: One character slaps the other in the face (as in a soap opera).

DIRECTION: Two characters: Animate a "tug-of-war" where someone lets go of the rope, sending the other flying.

These scenes aren't just for practice. <u>These are the kinds of things that will get you a job</u>. Set aside movies of your absolute best work. (Don't expect anyone to see "potential," period!) Blend these best-of-the-best together to make a demo reel no longer than three minutes. (You lose your audience after three minutes, no matter how good your work is.) Put a nice, strongly graphic plate at the beginning, letting the art director know who you are and how to contact you, repeating it at the end. Burn it to a CD, put it on the Web, and/or render it to VHS. (Just as a side note: Most "art folks" and management tend to be on Macintoshes. Saving your reel as a QuickTime means they're not going to have to work to see your work.)

Leave your audience wanting more! Don't show everything you've ever done! If you have brilliant work and really poor work on the same reel, the person reviewing it will probably wonder if you have the sense to know what is good and what isn't. Only put your best work on the reel! If this means your reel is thirty seconds, fine! It is far better to have thirty seconds of feature-quality work than it is to have three (or ten) minutes of forgettable work.

Easy power! Leave them wanting more! Have them so enticed about what your work <u>shows</u> you can do for them that they'll fly you across the country just to talk with you!

Do not put anything but your absolute best on your reel!

And don't worry if you didn't make the models or IK the setup yourself. (I included these high-level models and setups so you wouldn't be stuck with great ideas and no way to execute them if setup just isn't your thing. Use them!) In most larger studios, animators only animate. In the smaller ones, you generally do have to be a jack-of-all-trades. So use this information to target your job search. Do you want to do everything, or just focus on only one thing? Do you enjoy setup as much as you do animation? Don't settle for the first job opportunity that comes along, even though it will be tempting. (Don't rationalize yourself into a job you will come to hate.) Target what you do for a living to what you love to do!

> **NEWBIE NOTE:**
>
> Please don't feel like you've got to rush through this whole training thing. You've got your entire life ahead of you to perfect this art. Make every step the best, absolute best you can make it. Remember that you will only achieve feature-quality animation if, and only if, you give yourself the time you need to achieve it!

## 14.5 **Where to Go Next**

So, what's next? Learning from the masters what you wish to be taught. You've reached a plateau where you can see the path before you. You can understand what you need to learn. You know what kind of animator you wish to be. In the distance, you can see the next logical steps that will take you there. This is where you branch from the teachings in this book and take your own path to where you wish to be.

You know what kind of animation just sets your world spinning. For you, maybe it's the beautiful work of Hayao Miyazaki. Maybe it's the way-out shorts of Tex Avery, or the brilliance of Chuck Jones. Perhaps early Disney makes your heart pound, or the later works of that studio line your shelves. I want you to dive into that work that you love. I want you to immerse yourself in it, live it, breathe it, and sleep it. I want you to use the pieces that make the blood rush in your ears to complete your training.

I want you to take your laserdisc, DVD, or VHS version of whatever is your favorite animated film of all time, and using what you've learned of character setup, craft a character of similar proportions to the one you either wish you were, or wish you were with. Then, I want you find your absolute favorite scene with him in it, and recreate his every motion with your own character. Your job is to make your character hit you with the same emotional wallop that this movie character does. You and you alone will know when you're there. And when you are, you'll know you are on the path on which you were meant to be!

Continue working like this for as long as feels right. Craft your own stories; build your own dreams into a reality you can share with others. Use everything you can to help you get to where your dreams are as tangible as the clothes you wear. And may your journey be one of wonder, excitement, and joy beyond measure!

## Chapter 15

# Digitigrade Characters

**NOTE:**

This is an advanced chapter. It assumes that you understand the details of character setup. (It does not hold your hand.) If there are parts where you are lost or confused, return to the earlier chapters on character setup for a refresher, and/or load in and examine one of the pre-built setups from the companion CD.

So what do you do when you have a character who walks on his toes? How do you get your *plantigrade* (flat-footed) character to walk heel-to-toe without having the animation be an exploration of counterrotation? *Digitigrade* characters (those who walk on their toes) need a bit of a change to the foot/leg IK in order to make things work smoothly. These changes (and their derivations) can help any character who needs special handling with their feet.

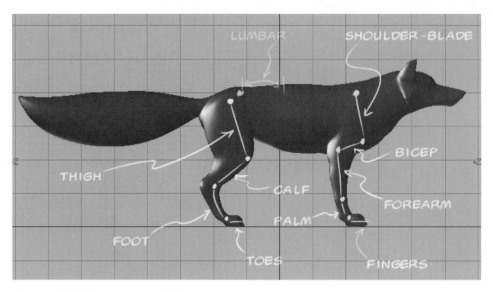

**Figure 15.1** The structure of a fox.

It is important that you understand the underlying structures of whatever being you're working with, whether "real" or imagined. As mammals, we all have basically the same parts. Understanding how the parts are used in different "chassis" is key to building successful setups that allow for intuitive posing!

---

**NOTE:**

Even delving into the subtleties that few people will ever consciously notice can increase the power of your work. For example, the front paws of a canid (a member of the canine family) are larger than the back; this helps to absorb the impact of their leaping gait. Cheetahs have no clavicle; only muscle and ligament hold their upper arms in place. This evolution is an adaptation for speed; the shoulder "joint" will slide back three to six inches during the compression stroke of their run. Knowledge like this is essential if you are attempting to recreate reality. And your fanciful beings will become all the more real when they are grounded in an understanding of physiology that would actually work!

---

**NOTE:**

There is more to quadrupedal motion than can be covered in this book and still get to all the things I feel are important as a strong foundation for animation. I'm including the ChromeFox model for those who wish to "leap ahead." If you choose to work with this or another quadrupedal character, take the time to deeply explore how they, or similar creatures, really move. There is almost no wasted motion in a quadruped's motions. Every movement flows perfectly into the next, like a wave flowing through their bodies. Contra-posto plays a key role in everything they do. Watch for reversals of the pelvis and shoulders on heading, bank, and pitch! The lumbar section of their back gives power to their gallop; knowing where the rigid pelvis attaches and how much this section actually flexes during the compression phase is key! There is so much more than just knowing which "foot" comes first in a walk cycle.

**NEWBIE NOTE:**

If you have an anatomy class somewhere in your future, try renaming the bones to their scientific names: metatarsals, metacarpals, scapula, femur, radius, ulna, etc. When you're working with the "proper" names every day, they sink in faster than you might think possible!

# 15.1 **Bones**

These bones are the same bones as in your character's skeleton. However, they are angled differently and of different lengths, taking into account the different positions and pivot points of the various body parts. We still have a puller for the leg, and we still have a control to rotate the knee. It is the foot where the change comes into play.

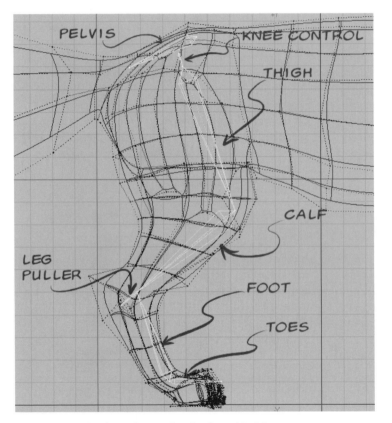

**Figure 15.2** The bone layout for the fox's hind leg.

The one major difference is that the foot control is reversed. In this new setup, the toes will be used to position and angle the foot; the foot bone will only be rotated. Rotating the foot bone will move the goal that will be attached to its tip, compressing and stretching the thigh/calf section of the leg.

The hierarchy for the leg is as follows: Pelvis => KneeControl => Thigh => Calf => LegPuller. And the hierarchy for the "foot" is: Toes => Foot => Goal (where Goal is a null object that will be added in layout).

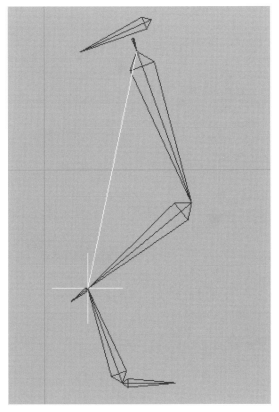

**Figure 15.3** The digitigrade leg setup with IK active in layout. (Thigh is set to solve for IK on two axes, while the calf only solves on one. LegPuller is using a goal strength of 80.)

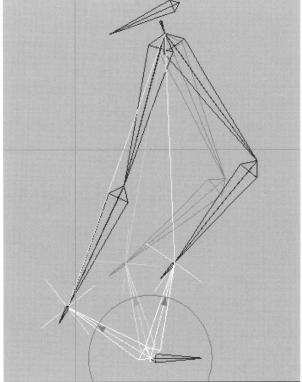

**Figure 15.4** This setup allows you to keep the character's toes firmly rooted on the ground while the "heel" of the foot causes the leg to flex.

**NOTE:**

Think! Imagine! Be!

**NOTE:**

As you work with characters that walk on their toes, whether they be quads or bis, always remember joint flexibility and proper distribution of weight! Feel the extra spring in the step that always walking with your heels off the ground gives you. You aren't restricted by platforms like high-heel shoes, and you have complete mobility through your entire range of movement; you have the strength in your calves to carry out whatever action you dream! And remember that even though your legs may be at a collection of angles (not the straight, rigid, locked form of a standing human), all your angles still must add up to a constant, structured balance!

## 15.2 **Plantigrade Modifications**

You can use modifications of this digitigrade setup to create enhanced setups for your plantigrade characters as well. It is wise to have a "stable" of these special-case setups so you can pull just the right one for the job at hand—or foot. (The proper tools make all the difference in the world.)

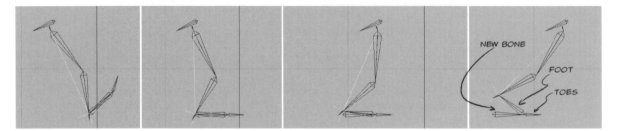

**Figure 15.5** This setup is made by adding one bone to the digitigrade setup. It makes it a lot easier to roll the character's weight from heel-to-toe as he walks. The new bone is the same length as the foot bone but heading in the opposite direction, with the toes set as a child of this new bone. The new bone doesn't control the character's points directly; it only controls the toes and foot which do.

> **NOTE:**
>
> "Enhanced" or special-purpose setups can save a lot of time in the long run, but they can also offer too much to think about for a novice. And while they may ease some tasks, they may complicate others. Only through playing and experimenting will you know what tools fit your style of working.

Explore! Experiment! The sky is the limit! And remember, if it works, it's got to be good!

## Chapter 16

# The Next Logical Step . . .

**ADVANCED NOTE:**

This chapter is more for those just starting out, finding their bearings, getting a handle on how to get to where they'd like to be. Still, you may find some interesting suggestions in Sections 16.3 and 16.4. These sections may give you some new ideas, or help to rejuvenate your career!

There is a wealth of knowledge out there from which you can learn. But you have to know where to look, and how to see what you watch. And though you know the films that inspired you to pick up the pencil or stylus, what about other animated works out there, the other worlds of symbolism and inspiration; how do you find them? (How do you weed through the mountains of mediocrity that line the video store shelves?)

## 16.1 Support

There's a lot of good out there, and there's a lot of not-so-good, too. Having friends also interested in animation gives you a wealth of viewpoints outside your own. They can direct you to what they like best, and past the things they've sat through and afterward wondered why they did. This group of friends can also be the momentum it takes to keep going during the rough spots. (Everyone has times when they feel like they're going nowhere. A good strong base of friends can help you look objectively at your work, and see your progress and your achievements!) Look to the Internet for camaraderie if your local base of fellows isn't what you would desire. With the resources available with just a quick trip to your favorite search engine, it shouldn't be that hard finding a crowd you can connect with!

With a group of friends also interested in learning 3D animation, there's almost nothing you can't do! If there's one who is farther along than the others, he can shine a light on the pitfalls. If you're all at the same level, all the better! With a group of close, dedicated friends, you'll be learning through a camaraderie that rarely exists in "The Industry" today!

Get together and draw out your own plans for making the short film you've always wanted to see. Find a particular style of animation you'd like to know how to do, something you'd like to have in your case-o'-riffs. Make your animation fit that style. Let the motions, characterizations, timings, character designs, and background designs all seem to be a 3D evolution of the films you've seen in that style!

> **NOTE:**
>
> A series of short films is a fantastic way to hone your skills. You see what you would like to be able to do, and you know what you are currently capable of. Use each short film as a stepping-stone for the next. Build on what you learn. Let each work showcase what you feel confident doing, while still pushing your skills to the next level. Easy power! Heavily stylized films are often easier to create than ones that recreate reality. Your first short may be heavily shadowed, like film noir, so you only see the parts of the characters you feel confident animating. Or you might make use of conventions that bypass the more challenging points of advanced animation mechanics. Work with your limitations; use them creatively! Build on them and let them lead you to where you want to be!

# 16.2 **Editing**

The problem with watching a film, any film, whether animated or live action, is that everything is intricately woven together to carry you deep into the story. It can be hard to figure out exactly what was done to tell such a compelling story. Using a jog shuttle on your DVD, VHS, or laserdisc player helps you to understand most motions, but how do you understand how the pieces fit together so well? How do these individual bits seamlessly recreate the "dream-time" patterns of events that allow us to completely accept the elements we are being shown as a contiguous, powerful story? How do you learn to piece your scenes together so that they also tell an accessible, lucid tale?

Learning to be a successful editor can take years upon years of schooling and practice. (A great editor can make horrible camera work and/or performances look stellar.) Even so, you can begin to grasp some of the concepts by watching movies with the sound off.

Music and effects key to our emotional centers as few other stimuli do. The score and *foley* (sound effects) of a movie are often considered "invisible actors," and are every bit as important as the other lead actors in sculpting the way we feel. When you watch a movie with the sound turned off, you are able to distance yourself from the events on the screen. You are able to see the positions of the characters as one scene cuts or dissolves to another. You are able to see the directions in which the characters and backgrounds are moving, and how this complements or contrasts with the previous scene. You are able to see the positions of multiple cameras as they intercut to tell the story of the conversation going on. You are able to see how the director choreographs establishers, longs and mids, close-ups and extremes. You get a peek at the gears and cogs of the movie, all working in harmony.

> **NOTE:**
>
> Watch. Learn. Copy if you need to. Do everything you can to understand why things do what they do. Apply this understanding to your own work and make it yours.

# 16.3 **Watching Movies**

The breathtaking animated films of today are so polished that you may have anticipations going back 24 frames or more before the actual action itself! There is so much subtlety woven into modern feature animation that unless you have the experience to (almost) do this level of work yourself, you can't see what's being done to create it. Go back to the early days of animation, and study and learn by watching the masters hone their skills!

In the early days of animation, most folks were at the same level of skill where you are right now. They were still working with understanding advanced animation mechanics, and figuring out how best to work them into the scenes they had. When you watch these early shorts and features, you get a chance to see beyond the polish. You get a chance to see how the animators were thinking, problem-solving, how they reasoned through their scenes. You can understand their processes because their work is around the same level of ability as yours is right now! You can clearly see their thoughts on squash and stretch, anticipation, drag, follow-through, timing, weight, balance, and all the other things that make good animation great! The art of a master makes what he does look effortless; that's what mastery is! You'll be there someday.

Luckily, you can, through their early works, watch them as they learned. You can study their solid logical steps toward their own mastery of the craft! Through an understanding of how they made their progress, you will be able to follow as well.

The old silent films are wonderful to watch too. There is the genius use of physical humor and pantomime storytelling in the works of Chaplin and Keaton. There are the incredible, graphic, painting-like visuals in films like *Metropolis* (1926, Director Fritz Lang). There is the groundbreaking editing and storytelling of *Bronenosets Potyomkin* (*Battleship Potemkin*) (1925, Director Grigori Aleksandrov).

> **NOTE:**
>
> Watch for the discoveries of lighting, camerawork, editing, and acting that have laid the foundations for the filmmaking of today!

Foreign films are replete with symbolism. It may take several viewings of a heavily symbolic film to begin to get the meanings that may be clear to a viewer from that culture. Symbolism deals in a kind of *archetypal imagery* (imagery that strikes a chord within the viewer regardless of experience or culture). You may not get the same messages or meanings as someone from that particular culture, but you will remember how the play of images made you feel. You can use similar metaphors in your own films, sculpting intricate patterns of emotion.

I've heard some "American" animators speak condescendingly about the works of Japanese animation, or anime. What these animators seem to miss is that often, the budget for an anime feature is less than what a single thirty-minute episode of a Saturday morning cartoon would cost to make. There is much to learn from these masters of a limited budget. They know when something has to move with the fluidity of "ones," and when a single, held frame will suffice. The master directors of anime know how to spend their budget wisely. And the delicate, finely crafted stills are so beautifully done, so full of symbolism, that often these are indeed the strongest ways to deliver the empathic vision of the scene.

> **NOTE:**
>
> Make an effort to learn as much as you can. "I do not like" often means "I do not understand."

As far as modern animation, I'm only going to name two that may have slipped by your radar. *The Iron Giant* (1999, Director Brad Bird) and *Cats Don't Dance* (1997, Director Mark Dindal) are two of the most brilliantly executed (on all levels of production) animated features of the "modern age of animation." Their story, storytelling, character designs, characterization, acting, animation, editing, scoring, and everything about them is absolutely heads and shoulders above most other modern animated features. (This is, of course, my opinion. And the reasons for their slipping through the theaters like greased lightning I'll leave to you to ferret out once you've entered the ranks of feature animation.)

# 16.4 **Other Studies**

An animator has to be the epitome of a "Renaissance man," (or woman). You have to be well-read, in both fiction and non. You have to have experience in many, many areas. (I like to think that this includes an understanding of all things rhythmic, from the earliest "early music" to the current beats pounding the dance floors on Sunset Boulevard.) You have to know how things work, and you have to understand how you would feel were you to be thrust into a myriad of different lifetimes. You are the ultimate method actor.

As an actor/animator, books that will help you immensely are *To the Actor* by Michael Chekhov and *Audition* by Michael Shurtleff. *To the Actor* will help you to get in touch with the energies that let you become different beings. There are exercises in that book that will astound you in terms of how much it will open up your perceptions of your worlds, both outer and inner. *Audition* will help you to quickly break down a scene into pieces you and the audience can relate with. It gets you to identify the motivating factor behind all interactions, as it exists within all scenes: love. Everything we do and everything we don't do is motivated ultimately through this single, unifying force. And through this single, unifying force, your audience will see themselves in what your characters do.

To help you plan your scenes, I recommend studying *Film Directing Shot By Shot: Visualizing from Concept to Screen* by Steven D. Katz. This book explains, better than any other, the rules and conventions used in filmmaking. It will help you to understand what you're seeing as you watch movies with the sound off. It shows you examples of how famous directors have storyboarded their scenes. It will help you more than any other resource I can think of on how to plan your production so that you get a finished product, and that this finished product is the one you had hoped for!

For another point of view on the principals of animation, my highest recommendation goes to *The Illusion of Life: Disney Animation* by Frank Thomas and Ollie Johnston. There is a lot of history in this book, and a lot of important information that is woven conversationally in the text. (Because of this, it is something that should be read cover to cover.) In it, you'll find many of the hows and whys of films and characters you've grown up with.

How do you find out what you "should" be doing? Read and do the exercises in *The Artist's Way: A Spiritual Path to Higher Creativity* by Julia Cameron. It is a great way to learn how to "enjoy the process of doing," and figure out where your dreams are leading.

How do you get an interview at the "big studios"? *What Color is Your Parachute?* by Richard Nelson Bolles is a fantastic resource for both people just starting out and those doing a 180 after already having had a successful career as something else.

Don't stop there. Explore your world; see where the hidden doorways lead! Take acting courses, take directing courses, find out how to do things in live action or on stage. Study physics, quantum mechanics, biology, mathematics, history, mythology, storytelling, and anything else you think might be exciting. Remember, your mind is a muscle, and if you keep exercising it, it'll just beg for you to give it more! Take a course on animal communication; how better to "become" your subject than "meeting them halfway" in understanding?

The key here is to light a fire under yourself to enjoy the process of learning! Animation is a life-long pursuit. You will never reach the point where there's nothing more. There is always something more! If you can train your mind/body/soul to enjoy the process, to regale in that which you do not know (. . . yet), you will have a life the likes of which most would never believe!

## Chapter 17

# Finding the Character

In the previous chapters, I've talked a lot about letting yourself live as your character. For some of you, this phrase instantly connects with experiences you've had where you have done this. You know what it means to imagine yourself so thoroughly as some other being that you know what it is to experience life through another set of eyes, for a while. Though it is similar to the "lands of make believe" we visited as children, this kind of focused visualization is much more.

This is similar to how the shamans of different cultures call to them the wisdom and knowledge of the different archetypal beings. By allowing themselves to so fully let the essence of another being flow through their entire focus, they have access to information they would not otherwise have. We as animators must do very much the same thing. We also work with archetypes, letting their essences flow through us and into our work. The characters we animate are much more than "everyday Joes," even if our project is grounded firmly in the "realistic" vein. Our characters are something more than real. They are, in essence, symbols of ways of being. Just as to a medicine person the falcon may represent sharp, clear seeing, quickness, and sureness, in our work, Perdita (*101 Dalmations*) represents the essence of maternal love and strength, feminine caring, and gentleness of soul.

Ours is with the place of storytellers within the global fire circle. We work in ideals and in symbols that evoke change within our audience. And just as the shaman draws through him the essences of the totems (the archetypal symbols as represented through the exemplification of an animal) of his traditions, so we draw through us archetypal symbols in the forms of the characters with which we work.

The shaman allows his senses to reach out, to touch and be enveloped by the essence of the totem spirit; everything about him becomes influenced by this connection. To look at him with your feelings, his essence would be that of the totem, not the man. As actors, we let the essence of our characters envelop us as we work; in the final animation, all you feel is the being of the character, not the artist.

Animation has the capability to crystallize, to transform, to completely winnow out all but that which needs to be there. We as animators have the ability to perfect a performance. We don't have to create it all at once, on stage or in front of a camera; we can work at it slowly, delving into it, making sure that each and every movement sculpts the feelings we intend. The characters we work with can be perfect in their conceptualization, in their encapsulation of ideas, essences, thoughts, gestures, and purposes. These characters are so much larger than life, they are archetypes representing core motivations within us all!

But how do you get into character? How do you explain the techniques, how it feels to don another's essence, to "shapeshift" as it were? How do you teach the techniques that facilitate these transformations to someone who has never been able to do this? Well, the truth is, at some point or another in our lives, we were all able to do this. Perhaps this was a long time ago, before those "looking out for our best interests" told us to stop daydreaming, or get our noses back into our books and our feet back on the ground. At some point in our lives, we were like Calvin from *Calvin and Hobbes*, living alternate lives battling incredible odds or receiving beauty and adulation. At some point in our lives, all of us knew how to live as another, for just a little while.

At this point in our lives, a lot of us have to shed this "stuff" (for lack of a better word) that has been heaped upon us as we tried to conform to what we thought was asked of us. In this area of visualization, of acting, of shapeshifting, we have to unlearn how to be responsible, respectable adults. We have to relearn how to be kids again. The great thing about relearning this now at this point in our lives is that now most of us are indeed adults (or on the verge of being there), and we can look at the disapproving and say, "Go take a hike, I'm working!" This is our job now! It is our privilege and our duty to daydream, to wear another's essence as our own for a little while. This is what we get paid "the big bucks" (well, hopefully) to do! And we are completely, unequivocally, and altogether within our rights.

You have reached a point in your life and career that by dedicating yourself to the pursuit and study of animation, you have given yourself all the credentials you need to do all the wishing, daydreaming, pretending, play acting, role playing, and everything you wanted to dream as a youth but never had the time to do or the vocabulary to defend! This is one of the many reasons why this job, above all others, is the best job in the world! Let the producers, critics, and hangers-ons—those who wish they had the guts to actually do what you're doing—let them all have their fun thinking they're getting the good part of the deal. You know that the magic is all within you. And it is your magic that touches the audiences, making them wish they were what you have dreamed. And it is this wish that keeps the cycle turning anew.

# 17.1 Radiating Focus

What we are doing, living moments as "another being," is actually method acting. *Method acting* is the art of becoming the character you are portraying. You aren't just putting yourself, as you are in day-to-day life, into a set of strange circumstances. This is actually becoming the character you are portraying, through and through, mind, body, and soul.

I don't think anyone out there would dispute that the single best source for studying on method acting is the book written by Michael Chekhov himself, *To the Actor*. There is no way I can come close to putting in text the kind of guidance, the kind of experience Mr. Chekhov has with teaching this kind of acting. I will, however, do my best to present for you the things I have learned over my career that have helped me the most. This chapter is in no way a replacement for *To the Actor*. I cannot recommend strongly enough that you read and study that text and its exercises. You will be surprised at how much it will help you as an actor, as an animator, and how much more enjoyment you may find in the simple, educated study of experiencing life.

An animated character radiates his essence to the audience with everything he does. We've explored how silhouette, gesture, and arc of motion are all used to create this experience on the two-dimensional plane of the screen. But how would you, personally, radiate? If you were to try to radiate your focus right now, how would you do it? Being louder? Being more forceful? No. There are many strong but gentle, shy characters who radiate their focus without ever raising their voice or "bossing" another around.

This "radiating focus" is a little like the focus in the martial arts. You project your mind, your being, and your essence into a point and let that projection guide your actions. With your mind leading, your body follows. And though your audience may not be able to "see" this focus, they will be able to read what it is doing; they will read it through every line of your body, with the very way you interact with the space around you.

The first step in being able to produce something is to be able to perceive it. These first exercises are designed to help you get comfortable with focusing your awareness and using your perceptions to experience, create, and control your radiating focus.

## Exercise 1

Sit in a relaxed position, either in a comfortable chair or cross-legged on the ground. Rest your arms on your thighs so your palms hang loosely, facing downward.

Start by listening to your breathing. Remember how it sounds to hear someone breathing while they're deeply asleep. Remember how this sounds, the pattern of intake, pause, outflow, pause. Remember how the breath sounds as it flows through the sleeper's trachea. In remembering the sounds, allow your own breathing to fall into this rhythm.

> **NOTE:**
>
> This pattern of breathing is the "deep breathing" people talk about in association with meditation. We've all heard this kind of breathing, and we all seem to know instinctively what it means. There is something in this manner of breathing that kicks our mind into producing the brainwave patterns that come with either being deeply asleep or in a deep meditative state. And I find that having people reproduce the sound/feeling of hearing someone else making this pattern of breathing (no, not snoring—that doesn't count) is the quickest way for the light bulbs of understanding to go on, as it were.

It may surprise you, even if you're familiar with meditation, as to how quickly this breathing technique lets you drop into the "hum" of a meditative state. Your stress levels lower, your heart rate slows, and you have access to a great deal more of yourself than you do when you're in "daily do mode."

After about two or three minutes of listening to yourself breathe as if asleep (without actually falling asleep), bring the attention of your mind to your hands. Allow your imagination to explore your hands. Visualize the focus of your mind running along every fold of every finger. Allow your imagination to touch the surface of your palms, exploring the areas between your fingers, between your forefinger and thumb, along the backs of your hands, and over your fingernails. Imagine every detail, every crease and fold. Imagine the temperature difference as your body warms the layer of air nearest your skin.

Now, think about the surface of your palms, the inside surfaces of your fingers again. With your eyes closed, you can imagine the exact angles each of your fingers has in relationship to each other and to your hand itself. This close, mental scrutiny draws your focus to what you are exploring. You are focusing on your hands, how it feels to have them, how it feels to be inside and around them.

Now I want you to concentrate on letting a bit of a light, gentle tingling build within your hands. This may not happen right at first; if not, imagine it to be there. Through your imagination and pretending, you will allow yourself to make it real. Believe in it; trust that it is there. It doesn't have to exist for anyone but you, and you are the only one who needs to know of its existence. By falling into this imagination, exploring it without rush or hurry, you allow yourself to believe in it; by allowing yourself to believe in it, it becomes real. Perception defines reality. Focus on it; wrap the imagining of it around you like a cloak. Allow yourself to drift into the sensation of this tingling in your hands.

Now allow there to be warmth along with the light, soft tingling. Let this warmth build slowly, but steadily. Allow it to radiate from your hands as if they were glowing. This glow builds softly, slowly. You can feel the warmth, the pressure of the warmth against your legs where your hands are nearest them. Your hands warm the layers of air around them. The soft, gentle tingling increases as does the glow of light from them, as does the warmth, building to a comfortable presence radiating from your hands.

Let the sensations of this stay with you, gently letting them be. Explore this radiating warmth, the soft, gentle tingling. When you're ready to come back to "normal awareness," take a deeper breath, holding it for just a moment, then letting it out. As you exhale let the warmth, the light, the soft, gentle tingling dissipate from your hands. Flex your fingers gently, reaching, stretching, and curling them slowly in a wave. When you feel comfortable, open your eyes.

You have explored a meditative state in which you focused your attention and your "energy" on your hands, and allowed this focus to radiate from them. You have felt the effects of this radiating focus as warmth, and perhaps even the light pressure of it against other parts of you. With a little practice, you will be able to achieve this point of radiating focus without having to go into a meditative state.

The radiating focus is the "clay" we will use to sculpt our dreams and visions into a (almost) tangible reality that will directly impact our work as actors/animators. This radiating focus shapes the way in which we perceive and interact with our world. It can also shape how others perceive us in person.

My first dramatic experience with someone using radiating focus in this manner (outside of theater) was in a life drawing class many years ago. We were drawing from a model who was absolutely gorgeous; she was absolutely-take-your-breath-away drop-dead gorgeous. The time came for her to take a break. Wrapped in a robe, she seemed somehow more plain. I thought perhaps I had imagined this incredible beauty. When she stepped onto the plinth again, I watched as she, over the course of two seconds, seemed to transform again into this goddess-like beauty. What had happened? When she began to strike her pose, she had allowed her focus to radiate with her visions of ideal form and beauty. Everyone in the class noticed these transformations. Now, there are those who might say that it was only how she used her body (her posture and carriage) that made us perceive her as beautiful. I say there was more going on than just the mechanics of how well she struck poses worthy of the great masters. I say it was her "energy," her radiating focus, her complete belief in herself becoming this ideal, and allowing this belief to so overflow the bounds of her physical vessel. In this outflowing of belief, we too believed.

## Exercise 2

Now we are going to work with exploring the physical presence of this radiating focus. Remember that though this may seem a lot like mysticism, this is simply exploring the worlds of imagination that we all knew and embraced when we were children. No one is watching to see if you're "doing it right." Success is measured only in how much you can let go and play! (And if you just don't feel like you're getting the results you think you should, pretend!)

Sit and relax again. Allow yourself to reach that strong, gentle "hum" of the meditative state.

When you're comfortable, bring your palms together in front of you, almost touching, about 1/3" apart. Hold your elbows out from your body; let your fingers form a flat extension of your palms.

Let your focus explore your hands again. Mentally, run your imagination down the length of each finger, into the closed spaces between them, along your palms, over the backs of your hands. Let your mind hover in the space between your hands. Let this space begin to build with the soft, gentle tingling you felt in the previous exercise. Let this soft, gentle tingling build into a warmth that fills the narrow space between your hands and fingers. Let this warmth build, forming an almost tangible presence of its own.

As you explore this focus, feel it as an almost magnetic cushion between your hands. This magnetic cushion not only keeps your hands from touching, but also draws them back together when you pull them apart. Explore the sensations, the pull as you separate your hands minutely, the push as you bring them minutely closer together. Explore this "surface tension" that exists between your hands and the radiating focus you've created. You can feel where the warm, soft surface of this essence exists—this place that draws your hands into perfect equilibrium.

Then, let this radiating focus expand, slowly, putting pressure on your hands to move apart. Let the focus grow, the warmth, the soft, gentle tingling press your hands farther apart, coming to another, comfortable space of equilibrium when they are about six inches apart. Feel the surface tension again, let your hands be drawn back together, pulled with a power that extends beyond their backs as you pull gently apart. Feel them pushed apart by this magnetic cushion that now radiates in the expanded space between your palms and fingertips.

Explore the sensations. Then let the space between your hands narrow again. Take back into you the energy/focus you've used to create the warmth, the soft, gentle tingling that exists between them. Allow the space to close once again to about 1/3". Feel the focus that once kept your hands in this cushioned equilibrium seeping back through the palms of your hands, up your arms and into your heart. Take the energy back into you, let its light fill you. And when you have let the space between your hands resolve to being about 1/3" again, explore the magnetic surface tension once more to know you're there. Gently push and pull your hands together and apart, feeling the radiating focus draw them again into balance.

Then, when you are ready to come back to "normal" awareness, open your fingers; let this field of softly tingling warmth envelop your hands like a cloud. Let your hands drift apart and your fingers bend slowly in a wave. Let the radiating focus dissolve softly back into you. Take a deeper breath, hold it for a moment, then let it out, and rest your hands at your sides. Feel your senses coming back to a more "normal" kind of awareness, and when you feel ready, open your eyes.

The focus we were exploring is something that need only exist for you, within the space of your own mind. Even so, you can see how it can have an almost physical effect on you. When you are working with an older character (Yar, for example, in Walt Disney's *Dinosaur*), you don't actually become old, you simply feel it, through and through, so that every action, every thought, and every belief you have is shaped by the radiating focus that exists within and around you as that character. Using this technique, you can turn around and jump onto a character who is as young as the other is old (Suri, also from *Dinosaur*), and with a few minutes of focused meditation, become the young girl as convincingly as you were the old man. You do this through the use of the radiating focus to permeate yourself with the character, inside and out.

## Exercise 3

Let's do one more exercise with this radiating focus. With this one, we'll be exploring creating a focus, then letting it stand on its own without our "physical" proximity.

Relax, and attain the deep, meditative state again. Focus on listening to your breathing, hearing it sound exactly like someone else, deeply asleep. When you are ready, cup your hands together in front of you as if holding a delicate moth: hands close but not actually touching.

Let the soft, gentle tingling fill your hands; let it fill the space between them. Feel the almost physical presence of the tingling, noticing when the tingling begins to build into a warmth that caresses the insides of the curves of your palms and fingers. Let this warmth continue to build, the soft, gentle tingling continue to build. Let the sensations build. And as they do, through the imagery of your mind, see a golden ball of light forming in the open space between your hands.

This light is gold, bright, and comforting to "look" at. Allow these sensations to push gently at the surfaces of your hands and fingers, pressing them slowly apart. Let your hands spread as the sphere of golden light presses them slowly, gently farther apart. When the sphere reaches about 4" in diameter, allow it to build in strength, maintaining its current size. Feel the sureness of its light, the soft, golden warmth, the gentle, warm tingling of its surface build definition and confidence.

Raise your hands slowly, keeping the golden sphere within them. Raise the sphere up to your eye-level. Hold it there for a little bit, continuing to visualize its presence within your hands. Then, slowly, let your hands drop away, keeping your focus on the radiating, golden ball before your eyes. Allow your hands to drop to your sides, your breathing to continue as if one deeply asleep, and the sphere of golden light to hover in your mind before your eyes.

What to work for in this exercise is to maintain this radiating focus for as long as you choose. It takes practice. At first, it may dissipate or dissolve when you let your hands drop from its proximity. Your mind may wander, or you may lose its focus. This is natural. Practice this until you can keep the small sphere hovering before you until you choose to dissipate it, or to take the energy back into you.

You are exercising the parts of your mind that allow you to maintain a radiating focus while your thoughts are elsewhere. With practice, you will be able to maintain your focus while drawing, moving controls, or doing any of the other myriad tasks that present themselves to the digital animator (waiting through computer crashes, autosaves, network hiccups, or whatever).

Other explorations you can do with this particular exercise are to work with other colored spheres: blue, green, silver, etc. You can have multiple foci existing before you at once, each with a different color, moving them with your hands and with your mind. Explore! Play!

# 17.2 **The Psychological Gesture**

The *psychological gesture* is like a living gesture drawing. It is a gesture drawing you assume with your body. It is one of the points in Chekhov's *To the Actor* that has the closest correlation to animation. And like a thumbnail sketch or gesture drawing, it is more important that it feels like the essence of your character than it looks like him. The psychological gesture takes the idea, the essence, the one main concept of our character, and distills that thought into a physical pose you take on with your own body.

Like with a drawn silhouette, this gesture must be strong, simple, and interesting. It has to have all the qualities of good silhouette, even though you read it primarily with the feedback your body gives you as to the relationship of its parts. Working with this gesture before you animate, as you animate, holding the kinesthetic, empathic understanding of it in your mind as you move controls will have an amazing effect on the integrity of your work. You will create stronger, more powerful, more convincing animations that radiate with this essence of the character.

The psychological gesture is the distillation of all the attitudes, plans, thoughts, experiences, wants, and wishes of this character, drawn up into one physical pose. Why is it important for you to put yourself into this pose? Because the logical, rational mind will only take you so far. You are tapping into the kinesthetic, archetypal associations of the mammalian experience. Just as you were able to attain a meditative state by breathing as if one deeply asleep, there are certain keys that unlock states within our bodies that even though we might not understand them, their power is there nonetheless.

They are like the fabled doors in the library at Alexandria: archetypal, symbolic, keying deeply to essences within the human experience.

## Exercise 4

Imagine you'll be working on someone like Maleficent, the evil fairy from Disney's *Sleeping Beauty*. What is she? Who is she? How do you define her as an essence? You don't need to, at this point, delve into all the experiences that made her how she is; all you need to explore right now is how her primary impact on her world is, right now, this moment, as you see/feel/experience her during her performance.

Maleficent is a strong character, very strong. Her will is powerful and unbending. She is consumed with a desire to control and dominate. She is filled with hatred and disgust; the world is unworthy of what she has to give. Part of her appeal is in the power that radiates from her elegance, how each movement is carefully sculpted; nothing is left to chance.

Work with this essence. Use your own body as the loose initial strokes of a gestural drawing. In every angle of your arms, head, hands, legs, the shift of your weight capture the essence, the single, defining crystallization of this character. Feel the strength, the desire to dominate rising in your own carriage. You look down at those around you; they are not worthy of your most worthless thought. You command with your every gesture, yet you do not need to exert physical strength for this to happen. The presence and force of your will bends those around you, kings and paupers, to your control. Through this, your poise, grace, elegance are seen, felt, and tasted. Shape these feelings with your mind, feel them in your heart, allow them to sculpt your body.

Your gesture needs to be strong and well-crafted. Engrossing, encompassing the space around you, it chisels out of the very air the essence of your desires, thoughts, and needs. You are a living shorthand for the essence of this character. Repeat the gesture again. Allow yourself to settle into it from a nondescript "idle" pose. Allow the sculpting of your space to play a part of the gesture, the "getting there," a part of the idea itself. Repeat it again. Let the strength of your will increase, the desire to rule, dominate, control, the hatred, the disgust roiling within you, etching the breaths you take with acidic malice. Hold your poise as a weapon, capable through it of unleashing the fury of a thousand hells. The feelings seep, permeate your entire body, radiating outward from your mind/body union.

**Figure 17.1** Perhaps your psychological gesture for Maleficent is something like this.

## Exercise 5

Now, if we took a look at Peter Pan, we'd see some things that conflict with the "traditional" image we have of him with his feet spread wide, hands on his hips, and head thrown back.

Peter embraces much of the youthful joy of living, but he also consciously, willfully turns away from things that are "adult." These scare him. Were he to even contemplate that "grown-up" things would one day be a part of him, he would lose his powers. His abilities come not so much from himself, but from others' belief in him, from Tinkerbell, from the Lost Boys. In this manner, it is also Hook's belief in their conflict that gives him strength. So, Peter's confidence comes not from himself, but from the beliefs of those around him. He needs to portray enough of a mystique to keep these beliefs going; he is actually very dependent upon them. Yet, at the same time, he must keep everyone at arm's length. They can't get too close, otherwise they might see him for

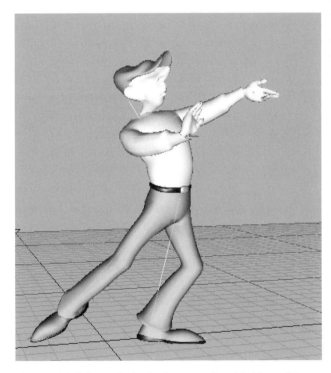

what he is, a scared little boy. To help effect this, he creates a personage that radiates a kind of unattainable perfection; he is the Pan, no one else can ever come close! He is dependent upon the energy of others, yet he can't look like he is; otherwise they would have power over him. This is a delicate balance.

**Figure 17.2** A psychological gesture for this idea of Peter Pan.

## Exercise 6

There is a young girl in the film *Angel's Egg* by Yoshitaka Amano. (This is one of those films so rich in hypnotic symbolism that it takes many viewings to gain an understanding of it. It is brilliant in the fact that there is barely one page of dialogue in the entire film!) The entire film could seem to stem from psychological adaptation to trauma; it could be entirely her vision of a schizophrenic fugue.

The young girl keeps all the bizarre occurrences, happenings, and visions that take place in the film distant from her. Memory seems unimportant, as does a vision of a future. She is withdrawn with no desire to come in contact with the world in which she lives. This isolationism isn't of weakness, but of strength. She forces her way through the film, protecting the treasure of this "angel's egg."

**Figure 17.3** The young girl's psychological gesture may be like this, shutting out everything but that which is within her and her scope.

## Exercise 7

Now, if we were to take someone gregarious, slightly hedonistic, with a kind and generous heart, but whose mind is easily side-tracked, say, someone like Baloo from *The Jungle Book*, what kind of psychological gesture would capture the essence of him?

Baloo lives in the moment. He is open to receiving all the pleasures this world has to give with abandon. He means well, but some times his lack of foresight gets him into trouble. For him, the world holds very few things to be wary of. He embraces every new experience that holds the potential of enjoyment with the same kind of rapture as those he already knows to be groovy.

He is firmly rooted in this world, strong with base Chakra energy. You might spread your feet wide, grounding yourself and your energy, strengthening your connection to the Earth and earthly things. He gives himself completely to the sensations of living, holding nothing back, knowing no fear. There is a beat, a rhythm to everything, and he can hear it. This beat moves everything he does in step with the rhythm of his world!

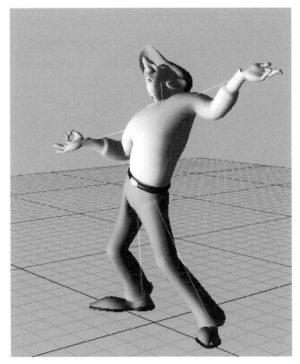

**Figure 17.4** *A psychological gesture representing Baloo might be something like this.*

## Exercise 8

Now we're going to look at a character with formidable power, but due to a lack of belief in herself, she allows herself to be swayed easily into fear. This character is Hitomi, from *Escaflowne*.

On Gaea, Hitomi finds that her "knack" for knowing the future is much more potent, so much so that she eventually finds herself shaping the reality around her with the force of her belief in what will happen. These are seldom conscious thoughts, and she often draws to herself "negative" experiences because she believes that this is what she is "supposed" to have.

She has physical strength and agility as a track and long-jump athlete, but she does not trust herself to be able to deal with what her worlds may throw at her. She doesn't exactly turn away from adverse experiences, but often wishes they weren't happening to her and doesn't confront them completely. She has a sense inside her of her own power, but she is afraid to trust it. She explores

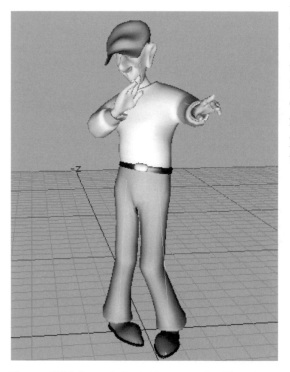

tentatively, touching but ready to draw her hand back at the slightest hint of being "burned." Her one exception to her trepidation is where matters of her heart are concerned, but this again is born from a desire to find someone to protect her, so she doesn't have to protect herself.

**Figure 17.5** A psychological gesture for Hitomi might encompass something like this.

By studying the gestures, by allowing yourself to slide into them, you strengthen your connection with these archetypes as they exist within you.

> **NOTE:**
>
> I like to think of each one of us as being like the shards of a hologram. The image each one of us represents is the universe, the ultimate all of everything there is. Goddess, God, Allah, universe, (etc.)—this is the image, this is the hologram. If you were to take a hologram and break it in two, each half of that photographic plate would have the entire original image but from its own unique viewpoint. Break it into a thousand pieces, and you have a thousand complete representations of the original whole, but a thousand slightly different points of view. Within each of us is the understanding of everything there is, but from our singular viewpoint. The wonderful thing about our minds being as they are is that we can extrapolate from our own solitary point of view and understand many, many others. These archetypes exist within us all, balanced and blended, particularized to become the us of everyday life. How we balance the archetypes as they represent facets of ourselves and how we allow these facets to impact our world(s) defines us as beings. The archetypes, what the psychological gestures represent and help us make tangible to ourselves, exist within us. Understanding them (both the positives and the "negatives") is important, as actors, animators, and positive additions to this world and the worlds we touch.

The psychological gestures I've illustrated here are by no means "correct," or even necessarily "on target" for anyone other than me. They are right, for me, for my own point of view on existence. Try them on, allow yourself to don them from a "neutral" position; see how the gesture affects your own psychology as you draw nearer and nearer to the pose. How does the pose itself make you feel when you reach it? How does it feel to hold the pose? What are the differences you feel between successive repetitions of the poses?

Explore what you know of these characters to hone this psychological gesture to what you know to be true for how you see them. If you're unfamiliar with a particular character, go on the description I've included to craft something that you feel is a kinesthetic representation of that idea—simple, strong, interesting, powerful. Let the focus of the character swirl around you in an almost tangible mist. Your confidence in the "rightness" of the pose is your power.

> **NOTE:**
>
> There's a wonderful thing about high-energy physics. And that is the acknowledgment that the act of observing an event alters it. This is why Heisenberg laid out his "uncertainty principle," which says that you cannot simultaneously know both an object's position and momentum. You can see this if, instead of using photons to measure the position of a hot-dog cart, you were to use a '67 Camero to figure out where the hot-dog cart had been. Because of this, one can extrapolate this to mean that we each measure things slightly differently; even two people standing side by side experience the same event slightly differently. Both are correct, but both are unique. This holds true with our perceptions of beings as well. To me, Simba (to pick "someone" most of us are familiar with) is quite different than the Simba that you know. We're both right, and both very different. (Just as no two of your friends have the same impression of who you are.)

> **NOTE:**
>
> "Perspective" is the illusion created when you see things from only a single point of view.

Now, how do you apply this "psychological gesture" stuff to actual, practical use in a production you may be working on?

The wonderful thing about animation is that chances are, you have more than just a collection of lexical symbols representing the idea of a character to work from (a script). You have character model sheets, pose sheets, storyboards, dialogue tracks, and probably video reference footage from the voice actor as he recorded the dialogue. This is a blessing that stage actors (and the folks whose job is to create these first passes at the characters' identities) don't have.

When you are analyzing anything creative—a script, a painting, a piece of animation—you have basically two separate directions you can take. Both directions start from the same point, the point of you interacting with this creative essence, and from there, they attempt to form an opinion on what it is that is being experienced. You have your logical, analytical, cerebral mind you can throw at the task, or you can use your empathic, intuitive, emotional side.

I'm not going to knock using your intellect to penetrate the layers of a creative experience. It can be a useful tool, but I am going to suggest saving "left brain" tasks for after your "right brain" has had its full shot at the matter. Someone's right brain, after all, had the directorial role in the manifestation of any creative experience. Using your empathic, intuitive, emotional right brain, you will be "speaking the same language" as the creator of the work, as he was deeply steeped in the process of creation. There are volumes of information which can be transferred in a moment through right brain centers. Allowing yourself to experience a piece as you would a psychological gesture, mentally wrapping the experience of the work around you, letting it penetrate through you, you are instantly and intuitively, kinesthetically, and empathically aware of everything from the pivotal to the trivial within the piece.

By using only your analytical mind (your left brain) you reduce emotion, sensation, and intuition to concepts. You blunt their edges so the impact is far less than it is with a more emotive experience. Using only the left brain to experience a creative work, you can far too easily drain it of warmth, feeling, and passion.

> **NOTE:**
>
> "The more your mind knows about a character, the less you are able to perform it."
> — Michael Chekhov

It is only through a blending, a balancing of both left and right brain functions, allowing each to do what it does best, taking turns at the proper time, that you can fully assimilate a creative work. After you are full of feelings, after the right brain has flooded you with the indescribable, your left brain must sift through the information, classifying it and aligning it with things you've already experienced, emotional states you already understand and can create with your own work. By letting the two halves of your mind work together, each doing what it does best and when it can do its best, you are beginning to unlock undreamed-of potential within the human mind.

> **NOTE:**
>
> The secret to life drawing isn't in drawing exactly what you see; it is in learning to draw your own imaginary model so well that you can instantly identify how the "real" model deviates from what you know.

This is why I have stressed throughout this book (when talking about the creative issues) to go by "feel." Does this or that have the "feel" it did when you imagined it, when you lived it, when you held the character's psychological gesture pose? Going by your "gut," you will be able to look at something and though you may not know why it doesn't quite "feel right," you know that you have to take another visitation at that part. You might not know exactly what it is you have to do to make it "right," but in trusting your intuition (right brain) and knowing how you achieved certain results before (left brain), you will almost always arrive at this point of "perfection" light-years ahead of trying to use only logic to solve the same problem.

Using every asset at your disposal, every technique you know, understand, and have internalized, approach your creative issues as first "gut feelings," then holding that feeling close, not letting it falter or disintegrate, turn your analytical mind loose on the task of using your tools to recreate that gut feeling within the medium at hand. Your right brain provides a road map, your left brain provides the means to get there. And this is why you need to internalize the tools and techniques so well that you can forget them. You need to trust your left brain implicitly to know how to take you there. You don't want to get in its way as it's doing its job—you'll just slow it down! Allow your left brain the luxury of using every trick, ability, and skill you can give it. You and your right brain will just be along for the ride, getting there with as much enjoyment and ease as you can.

So, with the materials given to you—the storyboards, the dialogue tracks, the script, the pose sheets, the test animations—allow yourself to craft a psychological gesture for the character. You don't need to be "right"; this is just a jumping-off point. (And besides, the only person who can say whether your psychological gesture is "right" is you—even the director can only make suggestions or improvements; he is also just another point of view on this tool you will use to create a final product.) Try the character on. Your right brain will know if the psychological gesture fits, or if it doesn't. Your intuition will tell you if one part of your gesture rings true, while the rest needs to be shifted.

Ask yourself what the main, focusing thread of the character is. Even if all you get is a vague inclination from this question, give it a go. You may only get a feeling for a part of the gesture, say for a hand or an arm, or the cant of your pelvis, the shifting of your weight. Let this lead you onward, let it help sculpt the rest of your body. For a character who seeks interaction with his environment, you feel that at least one arm needs to be thrust outward. Adjust it until it rings true. Palms open, facing upward to receive inspiration from the Divine, perhaps facing outward as if to ward off a blow. Cup your hands together as if asking for alms. Gnarl them to fearful, evil claws, grasping at power you cravenly desire.

Just getting one part of your body to resonate with the character's psychological gesture will continue to lead you onward, each part falling into place almost without thought. You will know when your gesture is there. The pose itself will lead you. You can build on a psychological gesture for another character you already know to have power. You can build the power within you by reaching a pose you know you can settle into with comfort and ease, building your focus, letting it radiate from you. Then you can use this energy to sculpt what you intuit of the character into an archetype of form and gesture.

Drop the pose, shake it off, then assume it again. Each time, make small adjustments as the feelings come to you, honing it, sharpening its focus closer and closer to the ideal represented by the character. By honing the psychological gesture, exploring, adjusting, perfecting, you are allowing the energies that focus within this character to move also through you. You are becoming the character yourself!

The psychological gesture, by the very nature of its archetypal symbolism, resonates with key parts of your own being, unlocking and opening pathways within you. You feel the character begin to stir and awaken within you as feelings and understandings that are not your "normal, day-to-day" self. You begin to know how this character would hold his hand, head, or torso, you begin to know what this character's timings and responses would be. You know this because you feel this essence moving within you. You can look at a keyframe you've done and know in an instant whether it fits with the essence that this psychological gesture holds.

There is such information within the psychological gesture, this single, intuited pose because your own body is moved, through and through, by the condensed energy of the character. His core, his most primal motivating goals and ideals, his experience is now yours. The information contained within a single, psychological gesture could take a thousand books to explain the hows and whys of a character. Yet, you know it, through and through. You know it because while you exist with the psychological character, you are one with the character's soul.

This is a key difference between the "left brain" and the "right brain." The left brain is the mind that likes to cubbyhole things into nice, orderly arrays. It is almost entirely responsible for us being able to encapsulate information and knowledge so that it doesn't need another living being there to propagate it; it is responsible for writing. Left brain information changes little from observer to observer. The left brain is the key to standing on the shoulders of giants when those giants are no longer there to help us.

Right brain is the mind of intuition, of "knowing," of "feeling," of "intuiting." Its realm is much more volatile. When right brain stimulus isn't there, right brain experience dissipates, like smoke in the wind, leaving (usually) only a left brain symbol of the memory of the experience. Music, with its ability to convey emotion and, at its best, information across language and cultural barriers, slips like a mist through the fingers of your mind after the last echoes have played themselves out (unless you have trained your mind to "replay" this kind of information—something anyone can do with practice). A painting, deep and visceral, moving you as no other work you've seen ever has; how does it look when you turn away from it? You may be able to remember bits and pieces of it, or remember symbols of it. (He was holding a bronze plate of smoldering herbs—I think there was a fan of raven-wing feathers in his other hand.) But the instant knowing, the emotional, empathic, perhaps even "tele-pathic" conduit of bidirectional informational flow is reduced to the memory of echoes when the experience of the right brain stimulus is gone.

A balance of both left and right brain is required as an animator. (And I think working to attain and maintain a balance of left and right brain functionality will serve you best as you move through life.) You can train yourself, you can hone the areas of your mind if you feel you are lacking in one or the other. Classes on symbolism and myth, the works of Joseph Campbell, and Eastern works of art can all help strengthen both your left and right brain, and the connection between them (the corpus colossum).

Your mind will give you what you ask of it. You can increase the aptitude of a lesser-used half of your brain. And you can increase the flow of information across the corpus colossum (and women, medically, seem to have a higher initial capacity for throughput). If you ask of your mind, it will be given. Our brains physically restructure themselves every single moment! Sound far-fetched? Consider that memory is stored physically, in the shape of synaptic connections!

If you feel you need help with right brain work, play short clips of a symphony or other musical work, and focus on replaying what you heard in your mind. Not just "remembering" but actually hearing it again in your mind, in its entirety. Practice hearing just the oboe or just the second violin, both as you replay it, and as you listen with your ears. Practicing with the radiating focus is another way to increase your powers of experiential cognition. Imagine seeing the room in which you sit from another point of view, another vantage point, with or without your eyes open. Imagine what it would look like to be flying around your room, your house, or your yard. These are wonderful, quiet ways of honing your right mind and helping to strengthen its bridge to your left. And of course, studying painting (*alla prima*, "all at once," painting seems to have the strongest impact on training the right mind), acting, dance, music, any other "art" you can find enjoyable to study is only going to help you on your journey.

Can you have individual psychological gestures for certain scenes, bits of dialogue, or action? Certainly! They must all be refinements, dissertations, or explorations of the primary, core psychological gesture. Even for Cruella DeVille (*101 Dalmatians*), as close to bordering on "split personality disorder" as she is, each of the psychological gestures that represent her mood swings are still parts of her core psychological gesture. Her personality turns on a dime when she finds Perdita's puppies to be without spots, then again when she finds out that they will eventually become spotted. In each section of this sequence, she is completely within a different psychological gesture, but each one is an aspect of the core of who she is.

The shifts between scene- or sentence-based psychological gestures need not be as drastic as with Cruella. Subtle shifts show the character as he evolves and changes. And in order for a character to live, we need to see him evolve and grow. The things he experiences must have an impact on him that shifts him from where he was to where he will be. As with ourselves, a character's "present" is an ever-shifting conduit from his future to his past. I believe this is why Shan-Yu from *Mulan* was such a two-dimensional character. He looked the part of a villain, often he moved as one, and his dialogue was executed with believability, but very little was done to show any evolution within his character. He remains much the same at the end of the film as he began. This is boring to an audience, and unbelievable in storytelling.

The best kind of progression for a character to make through a story can be seen as a "spiral." This is the *mythic mode* of storytelling. The *masculine mode* of storytelling can be illustrated as a straight line, forever marching forward, never looking back, never revisiting the same position as was once held. The *feminine mode* of storytelling can be seen more as a circle. This is the kind of evolution that leaves the character right back where he was where he began, following the same path. ("Masculine" and "feminine" are only classifications of different modes of storytelling structure; this is not mean to be derogatory to masculine or feminine energy in any way.)

A mythic type of storytelling (or character evolution) is one that combines both masculine and feminine modes. The character "comes full circle" (perhaps two or three times within a story), yet at each revolution, he has progressed along a path and is not quite where he was when he began.

A key to the old mystery schools (even within the foundations of Judaism and Christianity) is to use storytelling to effect change within the audience. This is done by connecting with and then altering the mental focus of the audience. This is done through symbolism that leads the audience along paths that connect with patterns of archetypal levels within them. Archetypal levels are emotional states that are common to all, hard-wired into the fabric of our psyche.

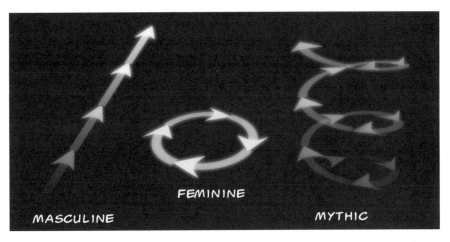

**Figure 17.6** A visual representation of the "masculine," "feminine," and "mythic" modes of storytelling.

> **NOTE:**
>
> Archetypal levels can be associated with the different Chakra points (energy centers) within certain aspects of Eastern philosophy (the Kundalini), from the "root" or Sacral Chakra representing grounded, earthly energies to the Crown Chakra representing the OverSoul, the connection with the Divine. A character's mythic evolution can be traced as his focus moves through each one of these archetypal foci: Crown, "Third Eye," Throat, Heart, Solar Plexus, Stomach, and Sacrum. Each of these represents an archetypal, psychological/emotional state of being.

Exposure to certain symbols actually causes chemical changes within the brain. (Though it may seem far-fetched, there are thoughts that are equivalent to a form; the reverse is also true.) The symbols that affect this kind of change upon us are *archetypical symbols*. This does not mean that these symbols are ancient, from times long ago and places long-forgotten. Archetypical symbols can be any symbol that has a strong and moving impact on the audience, an impact that is common regardless of the boundaries of language or culture.

In a mythic story, where the characters evolve along a spiral path, each "turn" finds them learning new things, not just remembering what they had once known but actually progressing forward, building new elements within their psyche. The symbology that incorporating Chakra centers represents is a wonderful overview to make sure that your characters are indeed evolving, and evolving archetypically (though any kind of association with archetypal traits will do, Eastern or Western). When you can see your characters moving from one focus to another, fitting more completely in a new archetypal state than the one they recently held, you know that the symbology the being of your character is exuding has evolved archetypically. Knowing this, you also know that you are making a deep and direct impact on your audience!

> **NOTE:**
>
> Symbols need not be a single, static image or shape. Symbols encompass ideas, essences, emotion, and experience; they are metaphor. Symbols can exist within any medium we can perceive!

The fact that symbols have actual chemical effects on the brain is why we spend so much time analyzing silhouettes (symbols) within our animation. It is why we work so hard to capture the essence of an idea or form in a series of drawings that combine to create motion. It is also why the best animators and actors are able to move us so deeply with the performances of their characters. They are not simply representing an occurrence, a happening; they are encompassing an archetype, carefully sculpted so the modern audience feels the subtle complexity of a living being, that is in essence himself, a subtly shifting, ever-flowing archetype.

This is the magic. This is why you and I have found such a pull toward animation that we have been drawn to becoming animators. This is why we must give this gift of experiencing a beautifully woven, powerfully moving story, with characters alive with archetypal ideals of mythic storytelling to others.

Acting, storytelling, animation—they are something more than "real life." Real-life gestures, actions, and thoughts don't have the power, the ability to stir us to our cores. They don't have the archetypal essences to move us into elemental states of being. "Real-life" gestures are too insubstantial, too weak, too splayed, or too specific. They do not fill our body and soul; our focus is elsewhere while we go through the motions of daily life. Archetypes and psychological gestures fill you entirely with their focus, body and soul.

The best acting is a subtle blending of archetype and everyday. Just as in every good drawing there is an element of caricature, within even the most "realistic" animation, there is archetype, there is mythic nature and structure, to move the audience, carry them along into "learning states," where they are receptive to the story you have to tell. Just as a mythic character would seem drastically out of place in the corner diner, a character who is only "real-life" gestures and motions is hopelessly lost within good acting, within good animation, and within good storytelling.

Back to creating and working with psychological gestures. Though the feeling from the psychological gesture should be strong, full of power, stirring the soul and honing the will, it should not encompass unnecessary tension. The crooked hands of a hag are clawlike from flexers and extensers battling with each other; a mother's embrace of her newborn is no less powerful, but done with the delicacy of a summer breeze. Power and strength come from focus, letting your focus radiate from within you, not from exertion of your muscles.

Just as in Exercise 6, the *Angel's Egg* girl's gesture and silhouette are not weak; they radiate with power and emotion. Concepts of softness, gentleness, laziness, or tiredness do nothing to reduce the strength of the psychological gesture; it is an aspect of it, but its power is still without question.

And just as the silhouettes we evaluate in animation are critiqued, so are the psychological gestures! They must be simple, as understandable as possible, able to be grasped in a split second, and without the need of the analytical mind kicking in for even a moment. There should be nothing vague whatsoever about the pose. Psychological gestures also have to be interesting; they have to hold your attention. (If you are bored, your audience will be bored as well!) Use large, broad strokes, with fine detail in which to delve, leading the eye, leading the heart of the holder. Layer upon layer, the information within is almost fractal in its simplicity. There must always be something more.

As you work with psychological gestures, experiment with timing and tempo. The tempos of animated characters are as varied as Droopy and Woody Woodpecker; the tempos of your psychological gestures should be just as varied.

The tempos of the gestures in Figures 17.2 and 17.3 vary greatly. Tempo can be achieved in many ways, from the speed with which you assume the pose to the carriage of the pose itself (as in Figures 17.2 and 17.3).

A character's evolution can sometimes be shown just through simple changes in tempo, preserving the same essence of the psychological gesture. A change in tempo can also completely redefine a psychological gesture. If you assume the pose of Figure 17.1, slowly, deliberately, with great care in the arcs that resolve themselves into the gesture, the pose feels very much like Maleficent; elegant, plotting, patient, brilliant, and self-controlled. If you were to assume that pose quickly, in a flash, the pose might feel more like the first encounters with Beast in Disney's *Beauty and the Beast*.

Changes in tempo can show the progression of thought, the interaction of external stimuli, and the evolution of the character. Understanding tempo through experimentation and feeling its effects on your own psyche as you take on and work with psychological gestures allows you to use this powerful acting tool with subtlety and strength.

Using a different tempo for the character's inner thoughts and his outward actions can be a powerful tool for creating depth within a character. The character's actions may be slow, well-thought out, planned, and carefully executed, leaving not a nuance to chance. But his thoughts may move at lightning speed, formulating, testing, calculating, reassessing. Mandible from *Antz* is one such character. Gene Hackman's voice work suggested many instances where a myriad of possible things to say flashed through Mandible's mind as he searched for the words that would best further his desires. The animators brilliantly took this dialogue and worked in subtle pauses showing this train of thought, the differences between his inward and outward tempos. All the while, they preserved Mandible's connection to his psychological gesture (which might be similar to Maleficent's in Figure 17.1).

A quick outer tempo and a slow inner tempo can do much more than imply a "fast talker," covering for his lack of inner "oomph." This contrast can imply the practiced skill of an outright master. And this mastery doesn't have to be over something like swordsmanship; it can be something as mundane as shipping parcels. Practice allows the body to go on "autopilot," running quickly through familiar tasks as the mind relaxes.

How can you show these combinations, these contrasts? Our physical bodies can reach limits of what they are technically capable of showing. How do you let these subtleties read through? You do this by bringing into play techniques of the radiating focus.

When you've "entered" a psychological gesture, and your body has given you all it can give in terms of rotations and translations, don't just let it drop. Hold it for another ten to fifteen seconds. And as you hold it, plus it with your mind! You've reached a point where moving a hand or an arm isn't going to increase the strength of the gesture, so let the force of your presence that fills you seep beyond the physical bounds of your body, enveloping and sculpting the space around you. Use the techniques we worked on in practicing the radiating focus to fill yourself with the essence, the energy, the archetypal focus of this gesture. Feel the essence of this pose within you, filling every corner of your mind's impression of your body; instead of a "sphere" of focus, your entire body is your focus, what your body represents is your focus, and it cannot be bounded by simple things like flesh. Allow it to radiate out from you, to fill the space around you with the very pressure of the gesture itself!

> **NOTE:**
>
> When you finish with an experience such as combining radiating focus and psychological gesture, remember to take a moment to let the focus dissipate, to "take the energy back into you," or to reconnect with the centers of your own essence. This is as important as the gesture itself. It helps to outline a path to return to the gesture, and to yourself. C.S. Lewis remarked that the writing of *The Screwtape Letters* was one of the most unnerving things he had ever done; he had to become this creature jockeying to tip one man's soul toward evil. You have to give yourself a path back to yourself, as it were. (Archetypal symbols will create changes within you, just as they do within your audience. Some of these you may be thankful for; others you may wish to shed.) Method acting is a potent tool for creating the most powerful of performances; used properly, it can also help you to know yourself, and it can help with your own personal, emotional, and spiritual evolution. We can experience "challenging" lives as if they were our own, and then come back to the "safety" of our own, quiet existences. And by learning to appreciate who you are, with respect to another spirit you've known as well as your own, you not only know the character more deeply, but yourself as well.

## Exercise 9

Subtle changes within the form of a psychological gesture can completely alter its emotional keys within you, even inverting them entirely.

Take on the pose in Figure 17.7. As you go from your "rest" position to the gesture, say, "I wish to be left alone." Allow the sensations of calmness, of a certainty that you know what you want and that it is within your rights to ask for it to permeate your essence. Allow this to radiate through both your voice and your gesture. Repeat this until you feel a union with the essence you are working toward, your voice and your body. Everything should be an extension of the primary core of calmness, a gentle but firm strength of will to close one's self off from one's current environment.

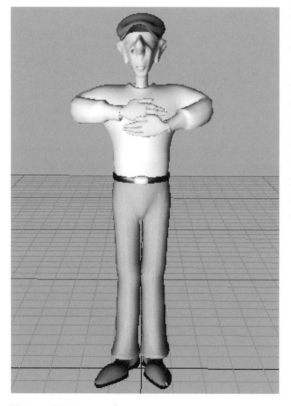

Now, repeat the gesture, but this time, resolve it with your head tilted downward. What affect does this small change have on your feelings? Did it make you feel more stubborn, more insisting? These feelings should be added to the base you've already achieved. Repeat the gesture a few more times until these new colorings fill your psyche, your voice, and your body.

**Figure 17.7** A simple gesture suggesting calmness and closing one's self off.

Now to alter the feeling entirely. Resolve the gesture with your palms turned to face outward, and your head thrown back, tilting it to one side, your eyes closed. Now the pose radiates pleading, vulnerability; the trauma of an attack. Tears may well up, your voice may falter as you beg your perpetrator to leave you alone.

Explore different, small changes to this gesture (any we have gone through already, or one of your own creation). What we are doing is building a sensitivity to the subtlety minute change can evoke. The more subtle the changes you explore, the greater depth of sensitivity you will find within yourself.

Subtlety and sensitivity are tools that will help you attain mastery. What you are working toward is to have a unity between your psyche, body, and speech. As you work with these and similar techniques, the definition between these elements of you will begin to blur. You will eventually be able to say with confidence that your body and speech, the <u>poses</u> that come through you are tangible representations of your soul.

The psychological gesture is a tool for yourself and your director only. It is not something to be shared with the "uninitiated" public. Like unfinished animation or rough thumbnail drawings, the psychological gesture requires an understanding of it in order to comprehend and appreciate it.

The psychological gesture is something that you "hold" with you as you draw, as you manipulate controls, as you examine your work for purity and truth to what you know to be the character. Your character will (most likely) never assume the psychological gesture on screen. The psychological gesture is an archetypal symbol, kinesthetically, empathically, and visually; and it is for you and you alone. It retains holographically all the information you know about the character. You can go to it mentally, emotionally, physically, verbally, any time you need to create, review, or revise. It is your tool through which you will do great works; keep it safe, and use it well.

## 17.3 **Characterization**

Character and characterizations are not the same thing. A *characterization* is a little thing you develop to personalize the character and help define him. This may be fumbling with his clothing, folding or hiding his hands, scratching an ear. These are little symbols that the audience comes to identify with your character.

Characterizations are "finishing touches," and can endear an audience to the character. The viewers can begin to expect, anticipate, and look for these personal features whenever your character is on-screen. They are symbols in and of themselves that serve to reinforce the character as a whole.

Someone being officious and trying to exert his presence within his surroundings could habitually rearrange the items around him, aligning them to right angles to the desks and shelves on which they sit. You could even build in a gag with this as the person with whom he must interact purposefully sets something askew again to assert his own dominance (especially if it is his space). If the pedantic character is subordinate, you can run a gag showing his resolve weakening as he fights with the desire to set the newly askew knick-knack straight.

Someone who doesn't like to be around others could push items within their reach away from them. A dominant, intimidating person may have developed an unconscious habit of shaking his head "No" as if to interrupt the speaker. Someone who is shy may continuously glance away from someone interacting with him, at the ceiling or floor or at objects just beyond the other character.

Imagine and play! Rewatch old favorite films and try to catch the characterizations the great actors and animators bestowed upon their characters. But as you watch, build within yourself the intuition of what you yourself would do as that character.

> **NOTE:**
> "The ability to observe becomes more acute when you know exactly what you are looking for."
> — Michael Chekhov

# 17.4 **Character**

One of the most enjoyable and creative techniques for developing your character is something I was taught long ago in a college course on directing. It is a technique that blends everything in this chapter into a single powerful tool.

What is this tool? It is a technique Chekhov calls "the Imaginary Body."

The wonderful thing about learning this tool in a collegiate setting was that it lent validity to "flights of fancy" I had enjoyed since I was very young! No longer was I guilty of "daydreaming," "wasting time," "lollygagging," or being generally irresponsible. No, this was work! This was dedication to my craft, to my Art (with a capital "A"). This was my responsibility, what I needed to do in order to become the best animator/actor/director/writer I could be!

What using the technique of the Imaginary Body does for an actor is that it alters what you perceive through your body, and what others perceive of your body. Your physical body radiates with the essence of another, and its senses are filtered through this Imaginary Body. It can alter the way a thin actor carries himself to convince the audience beyond all doubt that he is indeed corpulent, and without the addition of prosthetic make-up! It is how a young actor can convincingly play someone aged, a male can convincingly play someone female, and how someone wise can play an imbecile, or vice versa!

What this means for an animator is that we begin to know and understand the character to a degree not possible any other way. We have lived as the character. We understand the intricacies of his being, his littlest habits and his grandest dreams, because we have become them, walked miles not just in their shoes but with their entire body! With this technique, there is no grasping as to what a character will do when you're handed a sequence to work on; you know, because you have been them, and when the need arises, you are them again.

Allow your mind and body to relax. Then, letting the creative powers of your mind radiate outward from your body, using the techniques of the radiating focus, and helped by an understanding of the psychological gesture, "clothe" yourself in an Imaginary Body that is the character. (You know what this character looks like; you have model sheets, pose sheets, CG models, and pre-production art.)

Within the same space as your own "physical" body occupies, you use your radiating focus to create the body you know to be your character. This body exists between your real body and your spirit. It touches your soul, as it moves your body. You begin to think as he does, to experience the world as he does, to move, to speak, and to evolve as he does. It changes your whole being, both psychically and psychologically. It transforms you entirely into this other being.

As you build this Imaginary Body, don't rush into moving around in it too quickly. Sit or stand quietly, becoming comfortable with the sensations of feeling with another's hands, of seeing through another's eyes, of breathing through another's nose. Let it become comfortable and natural to you. When you do begin to get up and move around, trust this Invisible Body to guide your movements. Trust it implicitly; don't try to sculpt it into the performance you might be expecting. Allow it to reveal bits and pieces of the character you may be as yet unaware of.

Let the character be your guide. Don't force things, or try to overexaggerate things. Just let the experiences flow naturally around and through you. Only when you feel completely comfortable in this Imaginary Body should you rehearse the lines of your sequence.

To rehearse in this manner, as an animator, you can imagine the lines your character says, or you can let your dialogue track loop as you act out the scene. (Be sure to have the loop padded with silence at the head and tail so you can reposition yourself and analyze what you just did as the character!)

> **NOTE:**
>
> Some people have suggested venturing into public with this Imaginary Body as means of exploring the character. I would tend to caution against this. You have to look out for your own physical safety (say, if you're riding a public bus as a loud and boisterous character, and you are not naturally loud or boisterous), and the safety of the character himself. Any "emotional wounds" he may receive that aren't congruent with the story he must live may leave "emotional scar tissue" that could make it difficult for you to effectively play certain scenes.

In addition to the Imaginary Body, you can use the tools of radiating focus to help hone the character.

You can place (and maintain) your glowing, radiating focus in any of the archetypal centers (Chakras) to heighten the aspect of your character that they represent.

As your character evolves from one archetypal level to another, visualizing the radiating focus moving from one archetypal center to another will help lead you to experiencing that change yourself! And in experiencing it, you are more capable of portraying it through your art!

Moving your radiating focus from your heart to your head moves you from emotional to cognitive centers. Moving it to your crown enhances the connection with the divine.

You can also play with foci outside the body as well. If you were to be animating a meddlesome, prying character, you could envision a tiny, hard focus just beyond the tip of your nose. Moving a focus to a few feet out in front of your eyes can enhance a sense of a keen, penetrating character.

If you have to play an absent-minded character, moving the focus quickly, just beyond his "mental reach," can effect a feeling of dishevelment. If you are asked to animate someone who is drunk, letting the focus wander aimlessly through his body will give you a convincing performance.

As the focus works through your own bodies (physical and imaginary), so it should work through your character's model as you animate. No one else need ever know where his focus is, or of what kind, but you should know. You should know and feel this, beyond any doubt, as you watch your poses take shape before you, and as you watch the final scene play before you. You should feel your own memories of how the focus felt within you resonating in sympathetic vibration with what you see in your character's performance.

## 17.5 **The Animator's Trust**

These are only a few of the tools open and available to you. Perhaps I may be placing too much weight on what we do, but I feel that there is a huge trust placed within animators, and other dreamers of this world. We have been given the responsibility to shape the visions and dreams of those out there, young and old. It is a place of honor. It is a position of responsibility.

I've always felt that we as animators should do everything within our power to create the best, most moving, thought-provoking, memorable, evolutionary, and powerful experiences for those who seek to be enveloped by the worlds we create, again and again. Not only does every new step to becoming a better animator make what you do more enjoyable and fulfilling, it makes your work more alive, more real (to both you and the audience). Study as much as you can, study everything you think might be interesting; it can only add to your well of experience. Do everything you can to fall head-over-heels in love with this beautiful, wonderful honor and gift we are given, this gift which we in turn give back to the world!

**Chapter 18**

# In Conclusion

So how do you feel?

You've learned how to set up a character and how you can modify that setup to create anything you desire. You've learned the controls, and probably surprised yourself with how easily you took to life drawing in 3D. You've followed me in animation, and you've begun to create your own. And now you realize that this dream of yours, this dream that you might never have told anyone about, this dream of becoming an animator may indeed be possible!

I'll let you in on a little secret... You <u>are</u> an animator! You've followed me through the exercises, you've made your own artistic decisions, you've learned all the tools you will need to become a feature-quality animator. The rest is up to you. If you don't believe me, go take a look at one of your old scenes. I imagine it looks like it was done by a completely different person. You've got confidence in your abilities now. Even though the road to mastery stretches out over the farthest horizon, you know you can get there under your own power! You've seen the logical steps that have brought you this far, and you can look down the path and see where the next ones are. And you know that whatever the path brings, the sights you'll see will make the journey worthwhile!

Congratulations! I'm really proud of you! You've proved to yourself that you <u>can</u> do this; you can fulfill this dream that you've had perhaps for as long as you can remember! It is a wonderful path that lay open before you; where you go now is entirely up to you.

> **NOTE:**
>
> Realize though, that with power comes responsibility. "We are such stuff as dreams are made on." (Prospero, *The Tempest*) And although you may see all the ways in which you can (and must) improve, others will begin to hang their dreams from the high points of your craft. Make your dreams that others see be the best and brightest they can be! And when those who have shaped their lives to your work ask for your help, be kind. Lend them a hand, for they are the ones who allow you to be who you are.

Remember as you journey this path that we are storytellers. No matter how interesting the technology we may use to create our visions, our magic exists only in how we connect with the audience. It is in characters you want to be or to be with. It is in situations you wish you had lived. It is in scenery you wished you had touched. We are creating dreams for others to hold. Tell the stories you wish you had been told, and in them, let us dream with you.

I wish you well on this wondrous journey. I look forward to seeing your work, whether it be television, feature film, video game, Internet, or some completely new medium as yet undreamed of in the minds of common men. May the beauty of your vision shine far into the future!

Be well, my fellow animator!

Timothy Albee

# Index

# www.GameInstitute.com
## A Superior Way to Learn Computer Game Development

The Game Institute provides a convenient, high-quality game development curriculum at a very affordable tuition. Our expert faculty has developed a series of courses designed to teach you fundamental and advanced game programming techniques so that you can design and develop your own computer games. Best of all, in our unique virtual classrooms you can interact with instructors and fellow students in ways that will ensure you get a firm grasp of the material. Whether you are a beginner or a game development professional, the Game Institute is the superior choice for your game development education.

## Quality Courses at a Great Price

○ **Weekly Online Voice Lectures** delivered by your instructor with accompanying slides and other visuals.

○ **Downloadable Electronic Textbook** provides in-depth coverage of the entire curriculum with additional voice-overs from instructors.

○ **Student-Teacher Interaction** both live in weekly chat sessions and via message boards where you can post your questions and solutions to exercises.

○ **Downloadable Certificates** suitable for printing and framing indicate successful completion of your coursework.

○ **Source Code** and sample applications for study and integration into your own gaming projects.

*"The leap in required knowledge from competent general-purpose coder to games coder has grown significantly. The Game Institute provides an enormous advantage with a focused curriculum and attention to detail."*

–Tom Forsyth
Lead Developer
Muckyfoot Productions, Ltd.

### 3D Graphics Programming With Direct3D

Examines the premier 3D graphics programming API on the Microsoft Windows platform. Create a complete 3D game engine with animated characters, light maps, special effects, and more.

### 3D Graphics Programming With OpenGL

An excellent course for newcomers to 3D graphics programming. Also includes advanced topics like shadows, curved surfaces, environment mapping, particle systems, and more.

### Advanced BSP/PVS/CSG Techniques

A strong understanding of spatial partitioning algorithms is important for 3D graphics programmers. Learn how to leverage the BSP tree data structure for fast visibility processing and collision detection as well as powerful CSG algorithms.

### Real-Time 3D Terrain Rendering

Take your 3D engine into the great outdoors. This course takes a serious look at popular terrain generation and rendering algorithms including ROAM, Rottger, and Lindstrom.

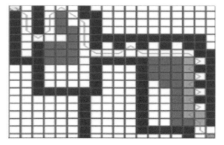

### Path Finding Algorithms

Study the fundamental art of maneuver in 2D and 3D environments. Course covers the most popular academic algorithms in use today. Also includes an in-depth look at the venerable A*.

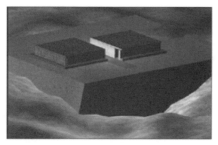

### Network Game Programming With DirectPlay

Microsoft DirectPlay takes your games online quickly. Course includes coverage of basic networking, lobbies, matchmaking and session management.

MORE COURSES AVAILABLE AT

# www.GameInstitute.com

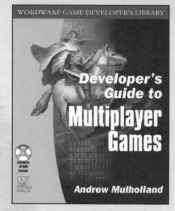

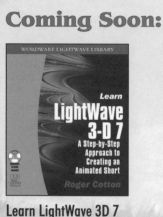

# About the CD

The companion CD contains:

▶ Models and setups for the characters shown on the cover

▶ All the illustrations for the book in color .jpg form

▶ Exercises and practice scenes

▶ An animation timer/time-base converter

▶ 3D life drawing models

▶ 3D scenes to study and learn from

▶ Additional artwork by Timothy Albee (animation drawings, paintings, and 3D renderings)

These files are all accessed through Windows Explorer.

## Warning:

By opening the CD package, you accept the terms and conditions of the CD/Source Code Usage License Agreement on the following page.

Additionally, opening the CD package makes this book non-returnable.

# CD/Source Code Usage License Agreement

Please read the following CD/Source Code usage license agreement before opening the CD and using the contents therein:

1. By opening the accompanying software package, you are indicating that you have read and agree to be bound by all terms and conditions of this CD/Source Code usage license agreement.

2. The compilation of code and utilities contained on the CD and in the book are copyrighted and protected by both U.S. copyright law and international copyright treaties, and is owned by Wordware Publishing, Inc. Individual source code, example programs, help files, freeware, shareware, utilities, and evaluation packages, including their copyrights, are owned by the respective authors.

3. No part of the enclosed CD or this book, including all source code, help files, shareware, freeware, utilities, example programs, or evaluation programs, may be made available on a public forum (such as a World Wide Web page, FTP site, bulletin board, or Internet news group) without the express written permission of Wordware Publishing, Inc. or the author of the respective source code, help files, shareware, freeware, utilities, example programs, or evaluation programs.

4. You may not decompile, reverse engineer, disassemble, create a derivative work, or otherwise use the enclosed programs, help files, freeware, shareware, utilities, or evaluation programs except as stated in this agreement.

5. The software, contained on the CD and/or as source code in this book, is sold without warranty of any kind. Wordware Publishing, Inc. and the authors specifically disclaim all other warranties, express or implied, including but not limited to implied warranties of merchantability and fitness for a particular purpose with respect to defects in the disk, the program, source code, sample files, help files, freeware, shareware, utilities, and evaluation programs contained therein, and/or the techniques described in the book and implemented in the example programs. In no event shall Wordware Publishing, Inc., its dealers, its distributors, or the authors be liable or held responsible for any loss of profit or any other alleged or actual private or commercial damage, including but not limited to special, incidental, consequential, or other damages.

6. One (1) copy of the CD or any source code therein may be created for backup purposes. The CD and all accompanying source code, sample files, help files, freeware, shareware, utilities, and evaluation programs may be copied to your hard drive. With the exception of freeware and shareware programs, at no time can any part of the contents of this CD reside on more than one computer at one time. The contents of the CD can be copied to another computer, as long as the contents of the CD contained on the original computer are deleted.

7. You may not include any part of the CD contents, including all source code, example programs, shareware, freeware, help files, utilities, or evaluation programs in any compilation of source code, utilities, help files, example programs, freeware, shareware, or evaluation programs on any media, including but not limited to CD, disk, or Internet distribution, without the express written permission of Wordware Publishing, Inc. or the owner of the individual source code, utilities, help files, example programs, freeware, shareware, or evaluation programs.

8. You may use the source code, techniques, and example programs in your own commercial or private applications unless otherwise noted by additional usage agreements as found on the CD.

## Warning:

By opening the CD package, you accept the terms and conditions of the CD/Source Code Usage License Agreement.

Additionally, opening the CD package makes this book non-returnable.